Nelson's Duchy

A Sicilian Anomaly

NELSON'S DUCHY

A SICILIAN ANOMALY

by

Michael Pratt

Photographs by Philip Boucas

SPELLMOUNT
Staplehurst

British Library Cataloguing in Publication Data:

A catalogue record for this book is available
from the British Library

Copyright © Michael Pratt 2005
Photographs © copyright Michael Pratt 2005

ISBN 1-86227-326-X

Published in the UK in 2005 by
Spellmount Limited
The Village Centre
Staplehurst
Kent TN12 0BJ

Tel: 01580 893730
Fax: 01580 893731
E-mail: enquiries@spellmount.com
Website: www.spellmount.com

1 3 5 7 9 8 6 4 2

The right of Michael Pratt to be identified
as the author of this work has been asserted by him
in accordance with the Copyright, Designs
and Patents Act 1988

Printed in Italy

Contents

List of Maps — ix

Acknowledgements — xi

Foreword — xv

Introduction — xvii

THE GREAT MONASTERY — 1

I The Coming of Maniakes and the Normans — 3

II The foundation of the Abbey — 9

III Disobedience and disorder — 17

IV Decline and disintegration — 25

V The rule of the Hospital — 35

NELSON'S DUCHY — 53

VI The hero's reward — 55

VII Duke of Bronte — 77

VIII The Reverend Doctor — 95

A TROUBLED INHERITANCE — 107

IX Illusion and disillusion — 109

X In search of a solution — 127

XI The compromise with reality — 139

THE HOODS AND MANIACE   147

XII   A naval family   149

XIII   The absentee proprietor   157

XIV   Riot and revolution   167

XV   The consolidation of the Duchy   175

SIR ALEC NELSON HOOD   193

XVI   'A little bandbox duke'   195

XVII   An uncertain succession   211

XVIII   Life in the Duchy between the Wars   225

THE MODERN ERA   233

XIX   War and expropriation   235

XX   Land reform and modernisation   245

XXI   The sale of the Duchy and afterwards   259

Bibliography   265

Index   269

For Janet, with love

List of Maps

1 Sicily in 1420   30–31

2 Sicily in 1860   164–165

Acknowledgements

This book was, in fact, almost finished twenty years ago. I am very grateful to the following friends from those days who helped me in my researches:

Peter, Viscount Bridport & Duca di Bronte
Sheila, Viscountess Bridport
Frank King
George Woods
Philip and Maria Boucas, to whom I am extremely indebted for most
    of the beautiful photographs in this book
Col. Wingate Charlton
Manfred Pedicini Whitaker
Fulco, Duca di Verdura
Barone Riccardo Winspeare Guicciardi and Baronessa Winspeare
    Guicciardi
Principe Ferdinando di Ledorano Acton
Barone Francesco Acton
Principessa di Paternò
Prince Peppino Biscari
Donna Arabella Salviati
Signor Pietro Labisi, then owner of La Falconara
Sir Joseph Cheyne Bt
Prince Cyrille Toumanoff
Professore Salvatore Agnello of Syracuse University
Viscount Hood
The Hon. Mrs. J. Acland Hood
Mr. Taylor, then owner of Cricket St. Thomas
Raleigh Tevelyan
The Hon. Alexander Hood

Tertius Murray-Threipland
Robin Mackworth-Young, Royal Librarian
Robin Wiseman of the Crown Estates
The Most Revd. John, Bishop of Fulham & Gibraltar
Rag. Pippo Carastro of Maniace
Bastiano, Salvatore, Salvino & Greco, staff at the Castello di Maniace
Culver Sherrill
Daphne Phelps
Arthur Garbutt
Jane & Dickie Manley
Gwendoline Trewhella Manley
Gaetano, Duca di Carcaci, and his brother Franz

Sir Harold Acton, who had kindly agreed to write the Foreword to this book but sadly died before it was published

More recent thanks go to:
Alexander, Viscount Bridport & Duca di Bronte
Linda, Countess of Suffolk
H.E. GianCarlo Aragona, Italian Ambassador to the Court of St. James's
Viscount Walpole & the Nelson Society
Dr. Colin White, Colin van der Merwe and Anna Wallis of the National Maritime Museum
The Staff at the photographic libraries of the National Maritime Museum and the Royal Naval Museum, Portsmouth
Michael Wade, present owner of Trafalgar Park
Anna Tribe
Dott. Aldo Bevacqua, without whom this book would certainly not have been possible
Dickie and Jane Manley, again, the direct begetters of the present edition
Helen Spence, my resourceful editor
Jamie Wilson, my intrepid publisher
Fiona Campbell, my patient lawyer

In Sicily I must thank:
Onorevole Gaetano Lombardo, President of the Province of Catania
Dott. Antonino Scimemi, Director of the Province, and his daughter Maria Concetta
Prof. Elio Rossito & Dott. Aurelio Bruno

ACKNOWLEDGEMENTS

S.E. Barone Manuel Scammacca
Dott. Mario Ciancio
Dott. Arnaldo Lombardi
N.D. Giovanna Moncada Paternò Castello
Mayor Salvatore Leanza of Bronte and the Comune di Bronte

Foreword

'A turbulent crossroads of history, a pawn of conquest and empire, and a melting pot for a dozen or more ethnic groups, whose warriors or merchants have sought its shores virtually since the dawn of recorded history' – that is how Sicily is described in *Encyclopaedia Britannica*. With its strategic location at the centre of the Mediterranean, the island has seen a multitude of foreign rulers and invaders come and go, leaving behind them a variety of memorials. Of these perhaps none presents a more curious historical anomaly than the Duchy of Bronte, the estate given to Nelson by the Bourbons in 1799 and, until twenty-five years ago, still owned by his heirs.

The story told in this book encompasses a vast span of history, for its setting is on the slopes of Mount Etna in eastern Sicily, where myth and reality have been entwined for centuries. Thus both the mythological and classical past are described, for Etna was the domain of the legendary Cyclops, as well as of the historical poet Theocritus, while on the coast nearby the Greeks made their first landfall in Sicily at Naxos. Just beneath the mountain, the Byzantine general, Maniakes, defeated the Saracens, and it was to him that the Norman Queen Margaret dedicated the great Abbey she founded nearby. For some six centuries this book chronicles one of the island's major monastic foundations, which endured many vicissitudes of fortune and eventually sank from an apogee of power and wealth to a state of almost total ruin and neglect.

As Maniace formed the centre of the large estate that Nelson was given, its story is followed right through the book, though after 1800 it is interwoven with the career of England's greatest naval hero. I have not attempted to write a biography of the admiral, so only his time at Naples and Palermo, which is directly relevant to my subject, is described in detail. After Nelson's death the Duchy passed to his brother, then to his brother's daughter who, suitably enough, married into another of England's most distinguished naval families. And since the Hoods remained in possession of Maniace until its recent sale, I have also included an account of their exploits in the wars against France.

When I started this book I had certainly not intended to write an epitaph for Maniace, although this is in fact what has happened, because during the course of my work Alexander Bridport decided to sell the property. It had been, until then, the most tangible remaining memorial to Nelson – for Trafalgar had been sold by his distant cousins, the Nelsons, in the 1940s, after the Labour government had abolished the family's 'state pension in perpetuity'. The house is now a museum and the land has been split up, so I am describing a world that has vanished for ever. Indeed I have done so in a wider sense, for the English community in eastern Sicily, so active in the 19th century, has now virtually disappeared. Even Taormina, still an international resort fifty years ago – albeit a fairly bizarre one – has lost most of its foreign residents, whose foibles provide an amusing footnote to this story. Thus in a similar way to Raleigh Trevelyan in *Princes Under the Volcano*, (an account of the English merchant families of Marsala), I have tried to shed light on some neglected facets of Sicilian history.

The background has always interested me. An historian ever since school and university days, I was fortunate that my first book on the Ionian islands and Corfu shared many historical links with this subject. Moreover having first-hand knowledge of Maniace, as well as of Taormina and of Sicily in general stretching back over thirty-five years, I feel I am well qualified to write it. It is in my opinion a story well worth telling, looking at an aspect of Sicily's past that also involves an important part of England's national heritage.

Introduction

'One of the great landowners of England boasts that he has possessions which were once in the fee of Harold, the last of the Anglo-Saxon kings. What is that to the boast of a Duke of Bronte, who can say that Theocritus may have wandered thus far up the Symaithos; that down from yonder hills came Demeter looking for her daughter Persephone; that, according to a local legend, Persephone herself disappeared in the high shallow lake between Maniace and Randazzo; and that Empedocles climbed this stupendous northern flank of Etna which towers over the region of inland Sicily with vast and menacing supremacy.' (William Sharp, journalist, 1903)

The purple prose is accurate enough for Maniace lies in an area rich in myth and legend. The landscape is dominated by Etna, at over 10,700 feet the highest mountain in Sicily, estimated to cover one thousand square kilometres, while the circumference of its base is around one hundred kilometres. Variously known as Monte Gibel or Mongibello to the Arabs, its present name derives from a Greek word *aitha*, meaning to 'burn'. Etna has erupted on a large scale more than 130 times since records were first kept in the 5th century BC. Diodorus Siculus reported that the streams of lava made the Sicans, Sicily's prehistoric inhabitants, move from their original settlements on its slopes to safer countryside. 'At a later time, Etna sent up volcanic eruptions in an increasing number of places, and a great torrent of lava poured forth over the land . . . And since the fire kept on consuming ever larger areas for a number of years, in fear they left the eastern parts of Sicily and removed to the western. Last of all, many generations later, the people of the Sicels crossed over in a body from Italy to Sicily and made their home in the land which had been abandoned by the Sicans.'

Many of the myths stem from the imagination of these people, who explained natural phenomena by anthropomorphising them. Hence the legend that Etna was Vulcan's forge, where the god of fire fashioned Jupiter's thunderbolts. The Cyclops, savage lawless giants, the sons of Neptune and Amphitrite according to Homer, worked for him and kept flocks of sheep and goats. One of them was Polyphemus, the giant whom Ulysses and his men tricked and blinded, and who pursued his escaping prisoners down to the shore, throwing the rocks after their departing vessel which can still be seen in the sea near Acitrezza. Hesiod however claimed that the Cyclops were really three Titans, called Bronte, Sterope and Arge, the sons of Uranus and Hygea (Heaven and Earth), people of fire and tempest, who were imprisoned under the mountain. In the Theogony he describes the battles of the Titans as symbolic of Etna's eruptions. The one eye in the middle of their foreheads derived from the belief that they needed a kind of Davey lamp for their subterranean labours, although these can also be explained as the craters of the volcano. The historical evidence for the Cyclops or the cannibal Laestrygonians whom Ulysses also met, is of course non-existent.

On the slopes of the mountain innumerable temples and shrines were built, dedicated in Roman times to Jupiter, Ceres, Pluto, Vesta, Vulcan, Proserpine and Aesculapius. The indigenous people were primarily concerned with fire-worship, and the great temple dedicated to Hadranon, their god of fire, stood in its eponymous town (the modern Aderno). It was reputedly surrounded by a sacred wood, guarded by 1,000 dogs, consecrated to the god and fed by the priests. A perennial flame burned in the temple, and the dogs welcomed all pilgrims, who came to worship there provided they were free of sin. But, the tradition went, if they approached with blood on their hands or lust in their hearts, they were bitten and driven away, while the dogs escorted any drunken pilgrims home.

Obviously the smoking craters might be seen as the entrance to the underworld. Local legend therefore claimed that Pluto emerged from Etna to carry off Persephone, and the two vanished into the under-world at Lake Gurrida, now so shallow that the waterbed is completely dry in summer. Likewise, to prove his divinity, Empedocles of Agrigento – musician, poet, philosopher, astrologer and legislator – who had performed the miracle of raising from the dead Pantea, a woman dead for thirty days (a parallel perhaps with Christ and Lazarus), is supposed to have leaped into the crater, which spewed out one of his iron sandals. 'Etna's pillar-peak that pierces air with ice bestrown, the yearlong nurse of nipping snow. From whose recesses jets the awesome flood of fire that none may near.' (Pindar's *First Pythian Ode*, 5th century BC) The ruins of the Tower of the Philosopher, a Roman building, can be seen near the summit.

The difficulties of separating fact from fiction are well illustrated by the story of Empedocles, who was a real historical figure. Similarly modern research has failed to draw a clear line between the Sicans and the Sicels, and whether the latter, arriving from the mainland, drove the earlier inhabitants westwards back into the mountains. What is undoubtedly true is that in 734BC, Ionian colonists from Chalcis in Euboea landed at Cape Schiso near the modern Taormina. On the headland there, under the direction of their *Oikist* Theokles I they founded the first Greek settlement in Sicily, which they named Naxos. Situated on a narrow coastal strip, and lacking enough cultivable land for its people, Naxos was never important or powerful, being more of a resting-place for the further expansion which soon followed. By founding almost simultaneously Katane (Catania) and Leontinoi (Lentini) in 729–28, the Ionians controlled the fertile plain to the south of Mt Etna, while their settlements at Rhegium (Reggio) and Zancle (Messina) commanded the narrow straits. At exactly the same time Dorian colonists led by Archias from Corinth chose the marvellous site of the island of Ortygia with its twin harbours for their settlement of Syracuse. Rivalry between these two Greek factions would determine the history of eastern Sicily for centuries to come.

Then too, it seems likely that the Sicels, pushed back into the mountains by the new arrivals, settled the area around Bronte. Along the banks of the Simeto and Saraceno rivers many caves were hollowed out. Some of the larger ones were used for living quarters, as grave finds have shown. The Sicels seem to have enjoyed friendly relations with their Ionian, although not with their Dorian neighbours. Trade developed between the two communities and some fine clay vases suggest a period of prosperity.

Before long, however, the Greeks, realising the strategic importance of this river route from Taormina to Catania, began to penetrate the interior. They settled at Tissa, where the remains of buildings, sarcophagi and coins of various ages suggest that a small town existed not far from modern Bronte. Certainly a Greek word, Βροντη (meaning volcanic thunder) was the name given by settlers near Etna. As inscriptions in the Sicel language show, the races did intermingle and the Ionian settlements, both pastoral and maritime, encouraged the development of pottery, bronze objects and coinage which have come down to posterity.

Colonisation, unfortunately, did not bring peace. Hiero, the tyrant of Syracuse, captured Katane and Naxos in 476, forcibly transplanting their populations to Leontinoi. Katane was resettled by 10,000 Dorian colonists, half of whom came from the Peloponnese and was rechristened Etna, while the tyrant's son, Deinomenes was proclaimed as its King. Pindar dedicated the first Pythian Ode to him and Aeschylus wrote a tragedy, *The Women of Etna*. A powerful leader, Ducetius, led a native uprising to regain their territory and freedom; Etna was captured and its inhabitants dispersed, but this Sicel revival did not last. Syracuse recovered its hegemony in the area, and although the Naxians had been allowed to return and refound their old settlement, it was sacked again by Dionysius in 403, and the population sold into slavery.

The Hellenisation of the interior continued. At the castle of Bola, a site which commands the broad river valley between Maniace and Bronte, Syracusan, Greek and Roman vases and coins of have been found. Further down towards the plain at Hybla Geleatis (the modern Paterno), a great shrine was built to a goddess identified with the Greek Aphrodite. The region remained important to Syracuse, and in 271BC, Hiero II led a campaign against the Mamertines, capturing Alesa Mediterranea, a major town believed by some Sicilian historians to lie between Bronte and Maletto. The Mamertines were mercenary soldiers from the mainland who had established military posts along the river route north and west of Etna, and controlled the mountain passes.

By the mid 3rd century BC the Greek city states in Sicily as elsewhere were in decline, and the island was fought over in the epic struggle between Rome and Carthage. Cultural life no longer flourished, and Theocritus, whose Idylls depict the Sicilian landscape as no other poet has ever done, departed for Cos and Alexandria after Hiero II had refused him his patronage. His 9th idyll extols the pastoral beauties of the area: 'Oh, Etna mother mine: A grotto fair, scooped in the rocks have I: and there I keep all that in dreams men picture! Treasured there are multitudes of she-goats and of sheep swathed in whose wool from top to toe I sleep.' However the island was still rich; on Etna's slopes grew enormous trees, used to build Syracusan naval vessels, and from which Hiero had constructed the famous galley with 100 banks of oars and 30 rooms, which he presented to Ptolemy of Egypt.

The island was the first Roman province, but there is little information about the area round Bronte under the Republic or the Empire. Coins dating from the 2nd century BC are of the type sent by the Senate to troops in distant outposts, suggesting that military colonies were maintained along the consular routes, which followed the rivers. It has also been claimed that Alesa Mediterranea was re-established as a major settlement, only to be destroyed by one of the Triumvirs, Marcus Emilius Lepidus. Sicily was certainly fertile, indeed the main granary for Rome; yet corruption was rife as the extortions of Verres show. As Cicero said in his great *Philippic*: '. . . the countryside is a lonely wilderness where the farmers have fled from their farms and the whole land become a neglected desert.' This may have been a little overdone, for Virgil and Ovid could still praise the lovely countryside watered by the Simeto. The Emperor Augustus levied a cash indemnity of 1600 talents on the Sicilians for supporting his enemies, and deported the entire population of Tauromenium (the town on the site of the modern Taormina, which had grown up since the destruction of Naxos). But, although Roman rule may have been financially exacting, it did provide security and prosperity for the island. Tauromenium for example was not only resettled and expanded; it rebuilt its Hellenistic theatre, the second largest in Sicily after Syracuse, with a spectacular view over Etna and the beaches and headlands beneath. Roman Catana, as Katane had now become, was an especially privileged city for it had supported Augustus from the outset.

Archaeological evidence suggests a largely well-populated country-side, with little of the abandonment of the land and deforestation which was later to take place. Under the later Roman Empire the great Villa Imperiale at Piazza Armerina was built, while the foundations of a building with a bath conduit and two fine mosaics of the same period have been discovered near Bronte. On that same site corpses were found buried with sea-shells arranged as pillows under their heads, a symbolic arrangement believed by the early Christians to ensure resurrection. The Etna area was of course subject to the whims of the volcano. Half the recorded eruptions took place before AD1100, several of which attracted widespread attention. Pindar and Aeschylus des-cribed that of 475BC; the 396BC eruption was said to have interposed a stream of lava between Syracuse and an advancing Carthaginian army; while that of 122BC destroyed part of Catana, not for the last time alas, causing a temporary remission of that city's taxes. Pliny the younger describes: 'Mount Etna, with its wonderful display of fire at night – the circuit of its crater measures twenty stadia (ie 2½ miles). The hot ashes reach as far as Catana or Taormenium and the noise yet further.' Seneca's opinion that the volcano was gradually sinking into itself was to prove decidedly wishful thinking.

The decay of the later Roman Empire allowed first the Vandals, then the Goths to gain military control of Sicily in the 5th century AD, although how far they penetrated into the interior is unknown. In 535 Belisarius, the great general of the Eastern Emperor Justinian, easily recaptured the island, which was to remain a Byzantine province for three centuries; indeed for five brief years under the Emperor Constans, Syracuse was made the capital of a revived Roman Empire. Meanwhile Christianity had slowly percolated into the countryside; there were twelve Sicilian bishoprics by the time of Pope Gregory the Great, although the fundamental Greek heritage, especially in the eastern part of the island, led the people to look to Byzantium rather than to Rome for cultural and religious inspiration.

It was the Arabs, the new dynamic force in the Mediterranean world, who were to change this equilibrium for ever. Already in possession of North Africa, they launched a full-scale invasion of Sicily in 827. Palermo fell four years later, and within two decades they had subdued most of the rest of the island. Along the eastern seaboard however, where Christianity had struck its deepest roots, resistance continued. Syracuse was taken and sacked in 878 when the booty removed was fabulous – perhaps a symbolic end to Sicily's classical glories. Tauromenium eventually fell in 902, and the fortress was razed by the vengeful Arabs. The last pockets of resistance remained in the mountains, and the Val Demone, along the valley of the Alcantara river which flows inland from near Taormina, sheltered many fugitive Christians. Only with the capture of Rometta in 965 was the Arab conquest finally complete.

Once established the new regime was reasonably tolerant. Active proselytisation did not take place, although there was some discrimination against Christians and Jews, while during the next two centuries much of the population converted to Islam. Taxation was lighter and economic policies more progressive than under Byzantine rule, so Sicily flourished. Even in the countryside some intermingling of the races took place. Arab settlement in the area around Bronte is evidenced by the name of the river Saraceno (a tributary of the Simeto which flows past Maniace); the Caves of the Saracens along the river (although Caves of the Sicans might be more appropriate, as prehistoric remains have been found there), and many words of local dialect.

Some of the records cannot be verified. Centuries later the Brontesi, anxious to prove that their town predated the foundation of the Monastery of Maniace, instructed a lawyer, Vella, who 'discovered' two documents. The first recorded that in 830 the Emir, resident in Catania, despatched a governor to Bronte with 600 men to rebuild the ruined castle, and shortly thereafter 160 cripples and their families were sent to live there. The second was a letter written by the governor at Bronte to the Emir in Catania in 998 with a population census of the village showing 994 Moslems and 664 Christians, a total of 1,658 people. But as the Arabs only subdued this region around 950, it seems scarcely credible they could have established a colony there some 120 years earlier. The authenticity of the second document is thus undermined by the falsity of the first. Nevertheless a flourishing settlement unquestionably existed by about 1000, when it appeared that Sicily was set for a long era of Arab rule.

The Great Monastery

CHAPTER I

The Coming of Maniakes and the Normans

'Since the conquest of Sicily by the Arabs, the Greek emperors had been anxious to regain that valuable possession, but their efforts, however strenuous, had been opposed by the distance and the sea. Their costly armaments after a gleam of success added new pages of calamity and disgrace to the Byzantine annals; 20,000 of their best troops were lost in a single expedition; and the victorious Moslems derided the policy of a nation which entrusted eunuchs not only with the custody of their women, but with the command of their men.' (Edward Gibbon, Volume VI, *Decline and Fall of the Roman Empire*)

Indeed so far all the efforts of the Eastern Emperors to reconquer their lost province had failed. By the 1030s however circumstances seemed more propitious. As Gibbon writes: 'After a reign of 200 years the Saracens were ruined by their divisions. The Emir disclaimed the authority of the King of Tunis; the people rose against the Emir; the cities were usurped by their chiefs; each meaner rebel was independent in his town or castle, and the weaker of the two rival brothers implored the friendship of the Christians.'

Thus it was that the Emir Al Akhal appealed to Byzantium for help against the Sicilian rebels led by his brother, Abu Hafa. Emperor Michael the Paphlagonian, who had recently come to the throne, was only too glad of a pretext to intervene. He assembled a large expeditionary force under the *protospatarios*, a gigantic general called George Maniakes, who had distinguished himself campaigning in Syria a few years before. The army was composed of Greeks, levies from the principalities of Southern Italy, part of the Emperor's personal Varangian guard (inaccurate tradition claimed it was commanded by Harold Hardrada, later king of Norway who was to die at the Battle of Stamford Bridge when invading England in 1066),

3

and 300 Norman knights. These latter were mercenaries recruited by the Lombard Arduin, and under the command of the redoubtable William de Hauteville. Although the Normans had only arrived in Italy a few years before, they were already feared and respected throughout the peninsula as peerless soldiers, whose services the various powers on the mainland were all eager to acquire.

Unfortunately their ally, the Emir Al Akhal had already been assassinated in Palermo by his own men, and the Arabs had reunited in the face of a common foe. Undaunted by this news, Maniakes crossed the straits in 1038. Messina was promptly captured, but Rometta, the fortress commanding the mountain route to Palermo only fell after heavy fighting. By the first months of 1040 the Byzantine army had subdued most of the eastern seaboard of Sicily and was besieging Syracuse. Arab reinforcements were however on the way. Stiffened by troops from North Africa, the Emir Abd' Allah marched across Sicily with a force 60,000 strong by some accounts, to take Maniakes' besieging army in the rear. He encamped somewhere near Troina, not far from where the fortress of Ghiran-ed-Dequq is supposed to have been, which commanded the valleys of both the Alcantara and Simeto. Maniakes quickly turned his army round full circle to engage the enemy.

The ensuing battle probably took place in the spring or early summer of 1040, near the Byzantine camp on the plateau of Gollia, although the chronicler Malaterra argued it was fought much nearer Troina. The account of it contained in the life of St Philareto tells how Abd' Allah had iron missiles fired at the enemy cavalry, not realising they wore armour. Maniakes divided his army into three divisions, and helped by a wind which blew hard in the Arabs' faces plus a decisive charge by his Norman mercenaries gained a complete victory. The enemy dead by some estimates amounted to 50,000. The Normans had fought magnificently; William de Hauteville earning his nickname of 'Bras De Fer' by unhorsing the Emir of Syracuse with a blow from his fist and leaving him dead upon the ground. While they pursued the fleeing foe, the Greeks proceeded to a division of the spoils.

It was then that the first disaster occurred. Arduin as their spokesman ('a man of great heart and intellect', as Amari, historian of 'I Mussulmani di Sicilia' described him), protested that the Normans were not being allocated a fair share of the booty. Maniakes' reply was to have him stripped and flogged for his presumption. Not surprisingly, Arduin then demanded to leave the expedition and return to the mainland, which, carrying a safe conduct from the general, he duly

4

did, taking the Norman contingent with him. Smarting from his humiliation, he immediately set about raising a revolt against Byzantine rule, which within a few months was to shake the position of the Eastern Empire in Italy to its foundations.

Maniakes had gained a complete triumph on the so called 'Piano Della Sconfitta' (the plain of defeat). But the fatal flaws in his temperament were soon to cause his downfall. The Emperor Michael's all-powerful minister, the eunuch John, had persuaded him to appoint their brother-in-law Stephanos, an ex-ships' caulker with no previous experience of warfare, to the naval command of the expedition. The folly of this was soon exposed when the Byzantine ships under his incompetent command allowed the fleeing Emir Abd' Allah to embark at Cefalu and to slip through their blockade to Palermo and North Africa. Maniakes, deprived of his prey, flew into a towering rage and calling his colleague a coward, villain and traitor beat him over the head with his staff. The outraged Stephanos wrote forthwith to Constantinople, demanding the recall of one who had insulted the Emperor's relations. As the family were anyway regarded as bourgeois upstarts by the military aristocracy, they bore no love for Maniakes, who was recalled in disgrace. He had restored thirteen cities and much of the island to the Empire, but after his recall the Sicilian expedition soon collapsed in chaos, and the Byzantine troops were withdrawn to combat the spreading revolt on the mainland.

A contemporary historian, Michael Psellus gave this vivid description of Maniakes in his *Chronographia*. 'I have seen this man myself, and I wondered at him, for nature had bestowed on him all the attributes of a man destined to command. He stood ten feet high, and men who saw him had to look up as if at a hill or the summit of a mountain. There was nothing soft or agreeable about the appearance of Maniakes. As a matter of fact he was more like a fiery whirlwind with a voice of thunder, with hands strong enough to make walls totter and shake gates of brass. He had the quick movements of a lion and the scowl on his face was terrible to behold.' Such was the formidable general, who according to tradition built a chapel near the battlefield, and as a thank-offering for his victory presented an icon of the Virgin and Child, reputedly painted by St Luke, which still hangs above the altar in the abbey church of Maniace.

The subsequent career of Maniakes provides an interesting postscript to the story. Emperor Michael died in 1042, but his successor did little to make amends. Having again appointed the general to lead the Byzantine forces in Italy and retrieve their fortunes, the Emperor sent him a delegation shortly thereafter which insulted rather than flattered his pride and relieved him of command. In a fury Maniakes had the envoys killed and, deciding to seize the Eastern Empire for himself, crossed the Adriatic. The Constantinople government raised a large army under his old enemy, Stephanos to crush him. But Maniakes was not overawed. In Psellus' words: 'thundering out words of command, riding up and down his ranks he struck terror at once into the hearts of everyone who saw him. Nevertheless he met his downfall. It was one of those acts of God, the reasons for which are beyond our ken.' Cheering on his soldiers, who were scattering the foe, Maniakes received a deep wound on the right side from a lance. Trying too late to stop the bleeding, he could not turn his horse and fell off between the two armies stone dead. Emboldened, the imperial troops cut off his head, and the rebels made haste to submit. This battle took place near Ostrovo in Bulgaria in 1043. Psellus notes: 'That at all events was the manner of his death. Maniakes had undoubtedly suffered injustice during his life, although one cannot commend all that he did.'

After the short-lived Byzantine triumph, Sicily had reverted to Arab rule. This was not however destined to last. In the next twenty years the Normans, playing off the Eastern against the Western Empires and both against the Papacy, rose to be the foremost power in Southern Italy. William de Hauteville's nephew Robert (nicknamed *Guiscard*, or 'the cunning'), became Duke of Apulia, Calabria and, in due course, Duke of Sicily. The Normans had cast covetous eyes on the rich island, particularly after the capture of Reggio from the Byzantines in 1060 had given them control of the narrow straits. In February 1061 Robert despatched a small force under his younger brother, Roger, which landed near Messina and besieged the town. Vastly outnumbered by the Arabs, they soon had to reembark; but in May they returned and quickly captured Messina. From this stronghold, and in alliance with one of the rival Emirs, they began a slow advance into the interior. Roger, now joined by his brother with reinforcements, encamped near Bronte, and the Christians of the Val Demone flocked to offer them gifts and homage. The Norman advance continued and the Simeto was crossed. Although checked under the walls of the fortress of Centuripe, the fighting again showed the superiority of Norman tactics and discipline.

For the next several years, Roger gradually extended his sway. Based at Troina, he controlled the north-eastern quarter of Sicily, until his decisive victory at Misilmeri in 1068 and the fall of Palermo three years later effectively broke Arab power. Taormina held out until 1079, and the last pockets of Arab resistance in the south of the island were only subdued after Noto was taken in 1091. But the Norman conquest was assured, and Roger, Great Count of Sicily and tenant-in-chief of his brother, who was preoccupied with larger political struggles on the mainland, was the undisputed ruler.

It is a measure of Roger's greatness that he set himself to win the hearts of his new subjects. The Greek population, suspicious of their Latin overlords, were wooed by the foundation of fourteen orthodox Basilian monasteries, of which one, San Filippo di Fragala on the north coast near Frazzano, was to play a large part in the history of Maniace. Similarly the Arabs were mollified by the retention of their law courts, most of their officials, their language and the right to keep their mosques and practise their faith. After Robert's death, while his sons squabbled over his inheritance, Roger became the most powerful Norman ruler, courted by everyone. The Papacy in exchange for his support, left him a relatively free hand in governing the Sicilian Church, formally investing him and his heirs with legatine powers. Roger had the largest army in Italy, although he sensibly refused to join the First Crusade since it would alienate so many loyal Moslem subjects. At his death in 1101, he ranked as one of the foremost princes of Europe.

During these momentous times, the population around Bronte did not suffer too badly, for the area remained rich and fertile, enjoying a strategic position on the routes around Etna and across the island. In 1089 its people probably saw Pope Urban II pass on his way to Troina to request Count Roger's help. After the foundation of San Filippo di Fragala, Gregory, one of its monks, built a Basilian hospice and may have enlarged the small adjacent chapel, dedicated to Santa Maria di Maniace, in honour of the heroic general. The exact date of foundation of the settlement of Maniace beside the Saraceno river and near the modern village, is uncertain. It had probably existed since Byzantine times, and was now augmented by a colony of Lombards, of whom no traces remain. The lands of Maniace and Randazzo were also raised to a county, and granted by Robert Guiscard to his companion-in-arms, Giovanni Calafato. According to one Sicilian scholar, Casagrandi: 'The Calafati were sprung from the highest Byzantine nobility. They had come to Sicily with the Normans, who by way of recognition of their services and of their exalted origins had invested them with titles and fiefs of the first importance.' Exactly how much territory the Calafati actually held is uncertain, particularly as their fief must be reconciled with the huge feudal landholding, which formed part of the dowry of successive Norman queens and included the monastic estates of San Filippo di Fragala.

Roger II, at first a minor under the Regency of his mother, Adelaide, succeeded his father and proved a great ruler in his turn. With a prosperous and vigorous state, he longed to expand and reunite Sicily and Southern Italy. In exchange for his help he extracted the title of King from the Papacy, and was crowned with oriental splendour at Palermo. More of an administrator than a soldier he brought order and security to the island. In 1121 he built a bridge across the Simeto in honour of his dead mother, and a Brontese myth held that a giant Arab stood with his legs on the opposite banks of the river to provide a model; indeed it was called by an Arabic name – Cantara. The same year was also ascribed to the nearby church of San Giorgio, which King Roger was meant to have founded on his way from Bronte, and which was destroyed in the last century to make way for the new cemetery. That the area was well-known is shown by the description written by the royal geographer, Al-Edrisi. 'This Maniace is a village in a well-populated plain, which has a busy market and many traders, with fertile soil and abundance of everything . . . The land is watered by a river, which rises about three miles away and drives several mills.'

CHAPTER II

The foundation of the Abbey

'Had it lasted, had it succeeded in preserving those principles of toleration and understanding to which it owed its existence, had it continued to serve as a focus of intellectual enlightenment in a blinkered and bigoted age and as the cultural and scientific clearing-house of three continents, then Sicily at least might have been spared much of the suffering that awaited it in the centuries to come, and it might have been the happiest, rather than the most ill-starred of Mediterranean islands.' (John Julius Norwich in *Kingdom in the Sun*, lamenting the passing of Norman Sicily.)

Its glory can however still be appreciated in its monuments, and among these the Abbey Church of Santa Maria di Maniace, albeit much restored, is one of the most charming. The Abbey was founded when Norman Sicily was already in decline. After Roger's death in 1154, his surviving son, William 'The Bad' succeeded him. Possessing cultured oriental tastes like his father, he lacked Roger's application and skill in government. Married in his early youth to Margaret, daughter of King Garcia IV Ramirez of Navarre, he took scant notice of her or their four sons. William's bursts of energy were followed by long periods of lethargy when the direction of all affairs was left to his Emir of Emirs, Maio of Bari, with whom the Queen was allegedly infatuated. After the dictatorial and unpopular minister had been assassinated in 1160 and the royal family kidnapped by discontented nobles, William managed to overthrow the conspirators and brutally reasserted his authority. He died, an exhausted voluptuary aged a mere 46 in 1156, leaving Margaret as Regent for their thirteen year old son.

The Queen proved quite incapable of holding the realm together. Disliking the advisers she had inherited, she welcomed the arrival of her young French cousin, Stephen du Perche. Although just ordained and in his early twenties, he was appointed Archbishop of Palermo and Chancellor of the Kingdom. Rumours abounded that the cousins were lovers, and plots against the regime multiplied. In 1169 the citizens of Messina killed the Chancellor's envoys and rose in rebellion. The communities round Etna, such as Maniace, pledged their loyalty to the regime and offered to put 20,000 men in the field against the rebels. But Stephen had too many troubles nearer home. A conspiracy in Palermo almost cost him his life, and he was lucky to be allowed to leave the island. Of the thirty-seven Frenchmen who had originally formed his entourage, only two survived to depart with him. Peter of Blois, an eminent scholar and former tutor to the boy King, summarised their feelings: 'I would not be persuaded by gifts or promises or rewards to stay.'

Not surprisingly, although Margaret remained as Regent until the young William attained his majority in 1171, she had lost all power. A council of nobles, clerics and palace bureaucrats ran the country, and Margaret was unable to prevent her enemy, the Englishman Walter of the Mill, from being installed as Archbishop of Palermo, despite her appeals to the Pope and to Thomas à Becket. Thereafter she retired into virtual obscurity, living until 1183, devoting her life to acts of piety and good works. Among these one of the most notable was the foundation and endowment of the Abbey of Santa Maria di Maniace in 1173.

Passing the little chapel on her way from the coast to Troina, she was presumably enchanted, as generations of visitors have been since, by the beauty and sanctity of the spot. She therefore decided to found a monastery there incorporating the existing small hospice with an Abbey church, providing a fitting setting for the precious icon. This was a century of major church building in Sicily: the Cathedral at Cefalu, the churches of La Martorana and San Giovanni degli Eremiti in Palermo, and greatest of all the Cathedral at Monreale; so the Queen was following established tradition. She also possessed the means to endow it. She owned much of the surrounding land; (the fact that in 1171 she had reconfirmed to Abbot Pancrazio of San Filippo di Fragala the original grant made by Roger provides evidence of this). She also decided that the Benedictines, not the Basilians, were the monastic order she wished to occupy it, an unsurprising choice in view of her own Latin antecedents and the gradual supersession of the Greek Orthodox element in the Sicilian church. She therefore arranged that the monks should come from the French Benedictine community of St. Agatha in Catania.

At Margaret's request, Nicholas, Archbishop of Messina in whose diocese Maniace lay, ceded his rights over the new community, which on March 1st, 1174 was placed directly under the authority of Monreale. This concession was confirmed by Pope Alexander III and later by his successors. The first abbot she appointed was a Frenchman, William of Blois, brother of Peter, her son's ex-tutor. He had come to Sicily in the retinue of Stephen du Perche, and had been nominated as Bishop of Catania. The canons of the Cathedral however refused to accept him and the Queen then suggested him as the head of her new monastery, asking the Pope and the Archbishop to grant him all the symbols of episcopal dignity: the mitre, the crozier, the ring and the sandals, all of which pomp as his brother tartly remarked ill became a mere abbot.

The exact length of his tenure of office goes unrecorded. But it seems that he suddenly resigned about 1176, to the delight of Peter, who unabashedly rejoiced that William could now return to France and drink the good Loire vintages in place of the acid Sicilian wine. As he wrote: 'Who, I ask, can live in safety in a place where, leaving aside all other afflictions, the very mountains continually vomit infernal flame and foetid sulphur? There beyond any doubt is the gate of hell ... where men are taken from the earth and descend living into the regions of Satan.' William had obviously been only too glad to escape from Maniace; indeed his sole motive in becoming Abbot seems to have been to gain the right to sit in Parliament and occupy the fifteenth seat in the ecclesiastical branch.

Concerned for the future of her new monastery, the Queen turned to Bishop Theobald of Monreale. At her request he granted the privilege of March 5th 1177, permitting the monks of Maniace to elect an abbot from among their own number, or in case of discord to elect an outsider, provided he belonged to the same order. They must receive the chrism and the holy oil, build a baptistery and a cemetery, while all monks must swear an oath of allegiance to their abbot. Every inmate of the monastery had also to be ordained by a bishop. In return, the monks had to pay an annual levy of two pounds of wax and two of incense to Monreale, and provide everything necessary for the Bishop's visit: provender for thirty men and enough barley for their horses.

The monks willingly elected one of their brethren, Timothy, who dutifully filled his office for eleven years until his death in 1188. It was during his abbecy that the church and other monastic buildings at Maniace were completed and dedicated. His position was further defined by the Bishop in that the Abbot must be present in his church for the feasts of Christmas, Easter and Pentecost, in return for which episcopal jurisdiction was limited to confirmation and ordination, which would prove a bone of contention for the future. Even more so was the proviso that the Abbey, like all fiefs, should contribute periodically to the state treasury. Further concessions were also made by Archbishop Nicholas of Messina in 1178. At the Queen's renewed request, he ceded to the Abbey his jurisdiction and the tithes from the five churches of Maniace village and the neighbouring communities. As a sign of this concession he only retained an annual tribute of two loaves and two measures of wine from the monks, although twice in the ensuing sixty years the latter had to be ordered by the Pope himself to fulfil their obligations. Even as late as 1346 the Abbot was being cited to appear before the diocesan court for nonpayment of his tribute.

The extent of the Abbey's estates at this time remains unspecified, although in his grant of 1178 the Archbishop mentioned 'the farms which the monks already possessed.' The exact nature of feudal relationships under the Normans cannot be reconstructed but it is a fact that the feudal lord conceded the rights of pasturage, of sowing and reaping, the taking of water and wood to their villeins, who in turn provided free labour to cultivate the lord's demesne. Count Roger had always distinguished between feudal and allodial lands – those free of all feudal ties – though not from service owed to the Crown. But with the growing violence and lawlessness in the later 12th century such allodial lands were being gradually annexed by the baronial class in defiance of King and people. In such conditions people often voluntarily offered their lands to a powerful protector, such as a monastery, to whom they swore fealty. In return they could cultivate their holdings as tenants, free from taxes and feudal obligations to the Crown. Maniace, with a fortified tower that could easily be defended against armed attack, was just such a protector. Thus its original property was augmented by the piety and prudence of the local population. As the Brontese historian, Benedetto Radice sourly noted: 'The devout ignorance of the people was transformed by the shrewdness of the monks into obligations.'

In 1169 a major eruption of Etna had been followed by a tidal wave, which overwhelmed Messina, and by an earthquake which killed 15,000 people in Catania. Lava largely destroyed the village of Bronte as well. Hence at the time of the foundation of the Abbey, the Brontesi like the other neighbouring communities were enfeoffed to the monks without protest. Yet even at this early stage trouble between the local people and their new overlord was not unknown. In 1183 the King had to order the villagers of Maniace to relinquish various lands, in particular the wood of San Giorgio di Agrappida, which they had usurped at the Abbey's expense. Three prominent local figures, two of them priests, protested at this decision. The opportunities offered by the prevalent insecurity to acquire dubious titles of property which the monks were evidently exploiting, in return for affording protection, were certainly not likely to make them loved by their neighbours.

The early years of the Abbey's existence saw the final demise of Norman Sicily. Maniace lost its patroness with the death of Queen Margaret in 1183. She remained interested in the fortunes of her foundation to the end. Popular legend claimed that her jewels were buried within an arrow's flight from the church, and conceivably the marble figure of a woman, which still stands beside the altar, represents her. Unfortunately her son's nickname of 'The Good', by way of contrast to his father, did not prove particularly apposite. The chief monument to William's reign is the building of the great Cathedral and monastery at Monreale, which symbolised the power and wealth of the Sicilian Church, as well as its independence from the Papacy. His elevation of the see to an archbishopric meant that the ecclesiastical overlord of Maniace now ranked as first cleric in the kingdom.

William II died childless in 1189 aged only thirty-six. By agreeing to his aunt Constance's marriage to Henry of Hohenstauffen he had sealed the doom of his dynasty. The German marriage proved so unpopular that many Sicilians supported the nomination of Count Tancred of Lecce, the late King's illegitimate nephew, to the throne. His military career was distinguished, and until his premature death in 1194 he showed himself to be an able ruler. His was however a reign beset with problems. The Kings of England and France both stopped in Sicily en route to Palestine for the Third Crusade and proved equally obnoxious. Richard Coeur de Lion seized and sacked Messina, and it took all Tancred's tact to persuade him to depart peacefully. It was also his ill fortune that tensions between the Moslem and Christian portions of the population threatened the kingdom at this crucial time. Throughout the island, in settlements such as Bronte or Maniace, the Arabs were driven out by their neighbours; many fled into the hills and became bandits.

Maniace, in common with most other communities in the region, had rallied to the cause of Tancred. So, after his death the people naturally supported the claims of his infant son, William III, and a force of 3,000 men was raised in the area, although the monks appear to have held aloof. However the Emperor Henry was at last ready to claim his wife's inheritance. His army crossed the Straits unopposed (indeed Messina welcomed the Germans enthusiastically) and advanced into the interior. The rabble soldiery, led by Boniface, Marquis of Montferrat, plundered all the hostile villages, including Maniace, along the way. Meanwhile the Emperor himself had landed, and stopped at the Abbey on his triumphant progress to Palermo. On Christmas Day 1194, Henry crowned himself King of Sicily. All opposition had collapsed.

The new regime was harsh and tyrannical, and rebellion soon broke out again. Life in the countryside must have been hazardous, as rival armed bands marched and counter-marched across Sicily. Nevertheless the new Abbot of Maniace, Brother Scoto, chosen from among the monks after Timothy had died in 1188, managed to keep his little domain from being plundered, for Henry stayed there again on his way to besiege Castrogiovanni in July 1197; indeed several of his charters are issued from there. It was probably in the marshes along the Simeto that while out hunting the emperor caught malaria, from which he died aged a mere thirty-two. Once more the future of Sicily looked uncertain, and the Abbey, which had seen so many changes in its first quarter-century was shortly to face further challenges to its survival.

Apart from its other features, Maniace was situated in an area still widely believed to be the haunt of supernatural forces. Christianity had adopted the old pagan superstition that Etna was the very gate of Hell, and indeed many of the early Fathers of the Church had taught that from amidst the flames of the volcano could be heard the cries of the damned. A tale dating from the 8th century recounts how in midwinter a female beggar, repulsed by the villagers, sought refuge in a cave on the mountain. At midnight subterranean rumblings were heard accompanied by a terrible cry. Some days later three shepherds found the woman's corpse lying outside the cave. The skull was an awful sight, for the eyes had been burned out, the mouth blackened and the nostrils flattened. The local people pronounced the place, where the Devil had apparently celebrated his midnight marriage, accursed.

Fresh myths about the mountain had arrived with the Normans. Etna became the domain of King Arthur, of his sister, Morgan, and of a numerous retinue. One day the Bishop of Catania's favourite charger disappeared. The groom sent out to track it down followed a narrow path around the mountain, which wound on and on between high rocks. Suddenly it opened out on to a beautiful and verdant landscape, where rose a wonderful palace. Here the horse was peacefully grazing, and as the groom advanced to catch its bridle, he noticed a bright light in front of the palace. In the middle of this radiance King Arthur lay on a couch unable to move, for every time he did so, the wounds he had sustained in battle against his nephew Mordred, reopened. It is surprising to find this legend recorded by Brontese historians, for it belongs to Celtic and Northern rather than to Sicilian mythology.

In fact there seem to have been fewer serious eruptions of Etna during the Middle Ages than either before or since. After the explosion of 1169, the volcano remained relatively quiescent until 1329, when it again caused widespread damage. So for a century-and-a-half after its foundation the Abbey was to enjoy the produce of a fertile countryside, unharmed by the hand of nature, although not as time progressed by the hand of man. Maniace's geographical importance was not lessened by the lack of communications. The coastal route from Messina to Palermo would remain almost impassable by land for centuries to come because of the difficult terrain, while the huge bulk of Etna made even the direct road from Taormina to Catania frequently hazardous. It is sad to note that the Abbey did not benefit from the many advantages it enjoyed from a rich endowment and a useful location to become one of the great religious houses of mediaeval Sicily, which could have done much for the well-being of the surrounding people and immeasurably enriched the cultural life of the whole island as well.

CHAPTER III

Disobedience and disorder

'If we go back through the centuries we can discern neither piety nor honour in their lives during the turbulent events of the 13th and 14th centuries. The plots and corruption lent little lustre not only to the Benedictines but to various other monastic orders as well.' (Benedetto Radice, historian of Brontte). As a good Brontese, Radice understandably has little to say for the monks, whom he believed had ruthlessly exploited his ancestors. But when the history of the Abbey during these centuries is examined, his strictures do not seem far off the mark.

Certainly the monks were as ready to pick quarrels as to pray and serve the Lord. For all their wealth they had apparently an irresistible attraction to their neighbours' possessions. Near Maniace was the granary of Santa Maria di Gollia, owned by the Basilian monks of San Filippo di Fragala. Their Benedictine brethren diverted the water course, illegally pastured their flocks on the adjoining lands, and when the Basilian in charge of the granary protested, they tied his hands behind his back and held him prisoner for three days. The Abbot of San Filippo took proceedings, and in 1217 the Maniace monks were summoned before the Imperial Justiciar. Despite repeated injunctions, they failed to appear before the Court, although they were eventually made to pay compensation.

The lawless behaviour of the Abbey merely reflected the general lawlessness of the age. Henry's death in 1197 had left a three-year-old infant, Frederick, as King. His mother, Constance, died the following year, so the boy was brought up in the royal palace at Palermo by tutors, while his nominal guardian, Pope Innocent III, undermined the throne by a series of intrigues. During his childhood, anarchy reigned throughout the island. Gangs of Arab freebooters terrorised the countryside, while the royal troops were more interested in accumulating plunder than maintaining order. Soldiers under the Royal Seneschal pillaged Randazzo and the surrounding area in 1200, although they were scattered by a sortie of the inhabitants on a plain just outside the town. So when the young King, a precocious and brilliant boy, took over the government at the age of only 14 in 1208, his first priority was to reassert his authority. A royal progress through North-Eastern Sicily in 1209, which probably stopped at Maniace, temporarily restored order, but when, three years later, Frederick was called away to the mainland by wider political issues, anarchy resumed its sway.

Not until 1220, when he returned again to Sicily as Emperor, did the island enjoy firm government. Frederick was determined to restore peace and prosperity to what he still regarded as his home. Traditionally Kings had been treated as divinities by the Sicilians, so it was the perfect place for him to try to recreate the mystique of monarchy. The island remained his ideal country; indeed when on Crusade he blasphemously remarked that God could never have seen Sicily, otherwise he would not have so greatly overrated Palestine, by choosing it as the home for the Jews. To a contemporary chronicler, Sicily was 'the apple of his eye', 'a haven amidst the floods', and 'a pleasure-garden amidst a waste of thorns to which he turned full of longing when he sailed to and fro upon the Empire's seas.'

In the ensuing years Frederick's benevolent despotism promised a return to the golden age of Roger II. The laws were codified into a more unified system, a systematic means of raising revenue, the 'collecta' or property tax, was introduced, and agriculture encouraged. Feudal abuses had to be checked, so it was necessary to reconfirm the titles to most fiefs. Thus, in 1221, Giovanni Calafato of Messina was regranted the fief first given to his ancestor a century-and-a-half before.

The overmighty towns were brought to heel too. Messina rose in revolt in 1232 after some of its privileges had been revoked, but the Emperor brought over an army from Italy and burned or hanged the ringleaders, while he utterly destroyed Centuripe which resisted him, deporting the population to a new town he named Augusta. Fortifications were constructed to improve security, and the square castle he built to command Syracuse harbour was named Maniace after the Byzantine general. As his relations with the Church were far from harmonious, Frederick endowed no new monasteries or bishoprics; indeed he was repeatedly excommunicated and verbally deposed by the Papacy. This perhaps explains why there is no Abbot recorded at Maniace after Scoto, whose length of tenure is unknown. Presumably a delegate was appointed to run the Abbey ad interim, while Brother Giacomo's election in 1254 had to be confirmed by a Bull of Pope Innocent IV as Sicily still lay under an Interdict.

By the time of the Emperor's death in 1250, the island again knew the blessings of good government. Although he visited it less as the centre of his interests shifted to the mainland, Frederick loved to hunt the wolves, which infested the wooded slopes of Etna, so it is likely that he visited Maniace. Nearby Randazzo was a favourite residence of his, where he first came with his wife in 1210 to escape the plague then raging in Palermo. The fresh mountain air and the excellent sport proved so appealing that the Emperor decided to make it one of his residences, choosing as his castle the strongest of the eight towers in the town walls, which was duly enlarged and embellished. Many local landholders were granted titles of nobility and built houses in Randazzo, some of which survive today, while royal patronage brought added prosperity to the area.

Frederick's reign was followed by fifteen years of vendettas and civil war, in which rival claimants struggled for the kingdom. Central authority dwindled once more, agriculture suffered, and according to some estimates the population fell by half in the next two centuries of misrule. Frederick's son, Manfred was crowned at Palermo in 1258, and promptly deposed by the Pope, who loathed the Hohenstaufen. An ambitious new candidate for the throne was found in Charles of Anjou, brother of the King of France. Manfred was defeated and killed in 1266, and two years later, his nephew and heir, Conradin, was beheaded on the field of battle. The Angevin cause had triumphed and Sicily was subdued by degrees. But the regime, religiously and racially intolerant as well as uninterested in the island, was widely hated. Needless to add in true Sicilian fashion an explosion was not slow in coming.

Both the Abbey and the village of Maniace were to play a part in the ensuing drama. By the late 13th century the village was a flourishing community, which ranked as a university (i.e. a separate administrative entity), and had a bailie to dispense justice and collect taxes. Bronte, still a small village, was entirely tied to Maniace. In a mixed population, with Greek, Lombard and Arab elements, everyone was judged according to their own laws and customs. The villagers were as quarrelsome as their monastic brethren, and continually feuded with the inhabitants of Rapiti, a village perched on a high rock above the banks of the Simeto, of which no trace remains. The latter were feudatories of the Monastery of San Filippo di Fragala, and irreconcilably hostile. In fact a Brontese proverb for describing two bitter enemies says: 'They are like Maniace and Rapiti.'

The heavy taxation levied by the Angevins combined with the depredations inflicted by their foreign troops, made the people only too ready to revolt. On Easter Monday 1282, the citizens of Palermo rose and massacred their French garrison. After the so-called Sicilian Vespers, Angevin forces were expelled from the island within a few weeks, and the barons invited Peter of Aragon, who had married Manfred's daughter and thus embodied the Hohenstaufen claims, to assume the vacant throne. That September he landed in Sicily and was acclaimed King. The Maniacesi eagerly adopted his cause and supplied their quota of fifteen bowmen, some of whose names have been recorded: Manescalco, Budo, Nicolo Pipirello and Roger the German. Under the command of Giovanni Celamida of Troina they were to guard part of the road from Taormina to Messina. The Aragonese army made Randazzo one of its principal assembly points before moving to challenge King Charles' forces across the Straits of Messina.

The monks had not followed the villagers in supporting the Aragonese cause, for they were now under the direction of a remarkable man, who would never have allowed them to defy the Papal excommunication of the opponents of Anjou. After Abbot Giacomo had died, on June 15th 1269, the monks had unanimously elected an outsider, William, Prior of Santa Maria di Latina, as his successor. Then aged forty, he was an intelligent and moral man whose origins are unknown. Some sources assert that he came from the noble Catanese family, di Scamacca, others that he was a French refugee. In any case he was a man of strong personality, respected by the local people for his profound religious faith and for his loyalty to the Church.

When by the autumn of 1285, the struggle between Anjou and Aragon remained unresolved, many Sicilians had grown sick of both parties. The Aragonese had enraged the Abbot by repeatedly asking for men and provisions, although Maniace was specifically exempted from such feudal dues. They had just bloodily suppressed one rebellion and while King Peter had returned to Spain, his lieutenant, Roger di Lauria continued to campaign against the remaining pockets of resistance and to devastate the countryside. The time for a Papal counter-stroke seemed ripe, so when two emissaries arrived from Rome, they found a receptive audience in the Abbot. The letters they had brought from Pope Honorius IV exhorted him to raise Sicily against the Aragonese and claim it for the Church. The Abbot was assured of help in money and men, and was promised a variety of favours in return.

Abbot William needed little encouragement, and immediately set about recruiting some fellow-conspirators. His two nephews, Nicholas and Francis, several petty nobles like Bonamico da Randazzo and Simone Bongiovanni, the same Giovanni Celamida from Troina who had been appointed to guard the Taormina road, and some other townsfolk are all mentioned as accomplices. Maniace, with its strategic position on the roads to the south, north and west was ideally placed as the plotters' headquarters. But before any definite plans had been formulated, two Franciscan friars betrayed the whole conspiracy to the Grand Justiciar. Both Papal envoys were captured in a mendicant house in Messina, where they had gone to enlist recruits. Most of the other plotters were also caught, and the Abbot's two nephews with Celamida were beheaded. Bonamico however escaped to the woods on the slopes of Etna; some time later he gave himself up and eventually obtained a pardon. The Abbey was surrounded by troops, although William, the prime mover in the whole affair, eluded his pursuers and fled to Palermo, where he too was captured.

Careful not to irritate the Pope any further, the Aragonese treated their clerical captives leniently. The two envoys were released without trial and sent back to Rome. Abbot William was deported as a prisoner to Malta, but a few years later was freed to live in exile in Rome. Accounts differ as to his fate. He is recorded as having died on November 30th 1315, when he would have been 86, although documentation of this is lacking. Perhaps he was permitted instead to spend the end of his life at the Abbey, for it seems much more likely that it is he, not William of Blois, who is the 'Beato Guglielmo' buried in the church. The bones were originally interred under the high altar, but were reburied in the 17th century in a new and splendid tomb. The Abbot's holy life and quasi-martyrdom made him revered by the local people, several miracles were attributed to his relics and he is usually entitled 'Beato', although no formal canonisation ever took place. Indeed stories of this cult figure still abound. One day he was said to have confronted a band of marauding Arabs, and finding his words falling on deaf ears, he seized a passer-by's luckless donkey and wrenched off its hind-leg. Thus armed, like a mediaeval Samson substituting a living limb for a dead jaw-bone, he set about the ungodly and routed them. When he stuck the donkey's leg back on

21

again, he did so the wrong way round; a pity for the animal but an attestation of his miraculous powers.

The confusion in the Kingdom of Sicily, where four sovereigns from the House of Aragon succeeded one another in eleven years, was equalled or even exceeded in the annals of the Abbey. Because of the conspiracy the King had given Maniace with all its property to the Bishop of Neocastro. When the latter nominated one Francesco as the new Abbot, the indignant Pope Honorius promptly deposed him. Therefore for ten years the monks lived with no control and in increasing debauchery, scandalising the faithful. On December 16th 1295, Pope Boniface VIII, in an attempt to reestablish discipline, united Maniace to the Cistercian monastery of Marmossolio, which was situated near Velletri and not far from Rome. The Papal envoys threatened the Bishop's procurator for the Abbey with excommunation if he opposed them. It was however the monks who took violent exception to this measure, and refused to be cowed into submission by any threats of hellfire.

When on September 13th 1302, Anthony, Abbot of Marmossolio and Maniace appointed Brother Rainieri as his procurator to administer the community in Sicily, the Bishop of Neocastro with the monks' support forthwith reelected Francesco as the rival Abbot. So when Rainieri arrived to take up his duties, he found obstacles strewn in his path, and he had to get the civil authorities to remove Francesco and his henchmen. The latter protested vigorously that he had been slandered to the Pope, claiming that since his election he had always lived at Maniace, supervising the monks and celebrating divine service. Only at the most dangerous moments in the recent disturbances had he temporarily retreated to Randazzo.

He had furthermore gained a powerful ally in Arnaldo, Archbishop of Monreale, who saw himself deprived of his traditional rights. By 1306 the Archbishop had persuaded Roffredo da Baucco, the Cistercian Prior representing the Abbot of Marmossolio, to renounce his claims. In the presence of the monks and the magistrates from Randazzo, Roffredo confessed that his possession of Maniace made him uncomfortable, that his superiors had lied to Pope Boniface to arrange the union, and that none of them had any rights over the Abbey, in recognition of which he surrendered the keys of the main gate to the Archbishop's envoy.

Naturally the Abbot of Marmossolio proved less tractable, and a fierce lawsuit began. At the height of it, the Abbot's procurator at Maniace was summoned home to give an account of his stewardship.

Instead he fled, carrying the treasure with him, to the protection of the Archbishop of Monreale. Hearing of his flight, some of his colleagues set off in pursuit. However the tables were neatly turned on them, for Brother Biagio had found a detachment of the Archbishop's guards, who locked up the entire party. A gang of cutthroats, under the orders of the Monreale faction then laid siege to the Abbey. The doors were battered down and all the monks tied up and imprisoned irrespective of which side they supported. Each of them was then forced to renounce his rights in favour of the Archbishop, who reemphasised his role as overlord of the Abbey since its foundation.

News of these outrages took some time to reach Rome. Hearing of them the new Pope, Clement V, acted swiftly to avoid further disgrace being brought upon the Church. He gave the case to Cardinal Pietro Colonna for judgement, summoned all the parties concerned to appear before him, although only after the fourth summons did the Archbishop send a procurator to represent his interests. Colonna eventually determined that the union of the two monasteries was valid in Canon law. The Archbishop was told to compensate the Abbey for any damage, and to refrain from further lawsuits. Brother Biagio was ordered to give back to Maniace everything he had stolen and to return to Marmossolio to receive condign punishment. Pope Clement published this judgement in a Bull of November 18th 1310. This was not however the end of the matter. All the parties continued to litigate and on March 28th 1318, further arbitration decided that after an annual payment of 1,000 gold crowns for three years to Marmossolio, Maniace would regain its freedom. Alas, neither propriety nor discipline was to return with it, for the Abbey had begun a long period of decline.

CHAPTER IV

Decline and disintegration

'We live only for the war,' wrote one chronicler in 1330, and when peace at last arrived in 1372, after ninety years of intermittent warfare between the Aragonese Kingdom of Sicily and the Angevin Kingdom of Naples, it was impossible to count the cost. The strength and cohesion of the system of government inherited from the Normans and Frederick II had been permanently sapped. A decline in the power of the Crown had fostered the growing pretensions of the baronage, and feudal abuses increased apace. Independent jurisdictions flourished, fiefs became virtually inalienable in practice, while the obligations to King or tenants regarded as theoretical. Agriculture was in ruins, particularly in the East of the island, where Angevin forces retained control of some of the coastal areas, until the advent of the Black Death in the 1340s decimated a population already reduced and impoverished.

It is against this gloomy background that the fortunes of the Abbey and village of Maniace in the 14th century must be set. Before Frederick III died in 1337, after a reign of forty years, he invested his third son, John, aged 20, with the Marquisate of Randazzo. During the preceding century the Calafati family, former feudatories, must have died out or been dispossessed for they vanish from the pages of history. The town had been granted this rank, new in Sicily and ranking after a duchy, following its heroic defence against Robert of Anjou in 1299, when the citizens had attacked the enemy camp by night and forced a precipitate retreat. The Marquisate included Bronte and Maniace, as well as the territories of Montalbano, Troina, Francavilla and Castiglione, which had once formed the Queen's dowry. Moreover as a royal prince, the Infante had the right of *merum et mistum imperium* conceded to him. This 'pure and mixed dominion' in legal parlance conferred the highest judicial powers over life and death or banishment, as well as comprising a lesser criminal and civil jurisdiction. On this basis the holder also administered executive power, including the issuing of regulations and proclamations, the collection of taxes, deputising for higher authority and the policing of the area. Normally the outward symbol of its existence was the erection of a gallows outside the town.

In Radice's opinion, Randazzo had not previously enjoyed these rights. As a periodic royal residence, it had had its own civil code and magistrates, who had exercised a degree of local authority, but it had been administratively subject to Messina. Now the townspeople, profiting from the prevailing anarchy, were to arrogate these privileges to themselves, a source of endless trouble with the local communities and with the Abbey in the future. While the Infante John was alive abuses were held in check. Complaints that the officials of the marquisal court had misused their powers at the expense of the Maniace villagers were forwarded to the Infante by the Abbot with the request that the people should be judged according to their own customary laws. John received his petition favourably, and by letters patent of September 10th 1347 limited the rights of his justiciar, forbidding him to intervene in criminal cases concerning the local population if the indictment was too trivial to require the amputation of a limb or the death penalty. In such cases the plantiff could seek his own redress according to customary law and the justiciar was bound to accept it. Indeed in mid-August every year a tribunal was to sit for a month to hear the people's grievances, during which the officials' powers were in abeyance.

The Infante died prematurely in April 1348, leaving a baby son, Frederick, who was invested with the Marquisate. The child with his tutor was besieged in Catania by the rival Chiaromonte faction, while Randazzo had already surrendered after one assault. In order to preserve the town's loyalty the rights of *merum et mistum imperium* were granted directly to it in the name of the new Infante, an act which lacked any validity whatsoever without the King's express permission. Furthermore, in 1353 a justiciar was nominated for all the Infante's territories, a measure difficult to reconcile with the earlier grant. Lastly at the boy's death in 1355, the Marquisate lapsed, its territory was reintegrated with the royal demesne, and civil and criminal cases came once more under the jurisdiction of the Crown courts. Randazzo was listed again among the royal cities, independent of any other feudal ties. Nevertheless its citizens were to continue to claim their rights had been re-confirmed, and were therefore to try to exercise them.

Unfortunately by this time the Abbey was in no position to protect its vassals. Although Brother Giovanni da Anagni had been elected Abbot in 1307, he probably never took up his appointment owing to the interminable lawsuits, later being given preferment to a see. No successor appears to have been chosen until 1342, when Brother Bonamico di Martino was elected. In that year, Andava Lo Spinola, Archbishop of Monreale visited the Abbey and, finding it in a state of *omni honestate relictum*, expelled the wretched monks. He confided his troubles to his colleagues at Catania, who suggested that a young cleric, Angelo Sinisio be installed as Prior. The Archbishop took Sinisio with eleven other new recruits back with him to Maniace and after recommending them to Abbot Bonamico, returned to Monreale. Of course the Abbot and his disgraced brethren had no intention of accepting the newcomers as events would prove.

A vendetta had begun within a few months. Sinisio complained to the officials of the Marquisate of ceaseless harassment by the expelled monks. Two of the worst of them had lain in ambush for the prior in the wood of Mascali, although having drunk too much they passed out and failed to waylay him. Abbot Bonamico was openly hostile, and the following year, aided by the peasants he drove out the Catanese monks. Some of these attempted to found a monastery in Messina, but the venture quickly collapsed and the survivors sought refuge at Monreale. The Archbishop summoned the Abbot, who was tried, found guilty of a variety of crimes and stripped of his dignities. Ever thereafter Bonamico continued to intrigue to have Sinisio murdered, and he only repented on his deathbed. The next Abbot, Brother Garcia died in 1346 after a mere two years in office, and although his ineffectual successor, Brother Salvo lasted until 1367, the spiritual authority of Maniace steadily deteriorated.

Frederick IV, who had been forced to pawn his Crown Jewels, so empty was the Treasury, finally succeeded in concluding peace with Naples by the payment of an annual tribute, while the Papacy lifted decades of Interdict. But this came too late. The island's prosperity had vanished, all revenues raised had been spent on the war and such was the general poverty that the *collecta* when levied produced virtually nothing. The irrigation works created in a happier age had been neglected so that many valleys in the interior had become dustbowls or malarial swamps, while thanks to the endemic insecurity many peasants had deserted the land and fled into the towns. After the King's death in 1377, Sicily was divided between four rival overlords and complete anarchy was only averted by a Spanish invasion in 1392 to put his son-in-law, Martin of Aragon on the throne. Despite being a strong and determined ruler, Martin faced a titanic task to reassert the Crown's authority, and, not surprisingly, he failed. A fresh feudal register was drawn up, with the stipulation that major criminal cases must be tried by the royal courts alone, which could also hear appeals from baronial justice. Inevitably many of the nobles and towns like Randazzo ignored these reforms, continuing their excesses unchecked.

Spasmodically the Abbey did now attempt to protect its vassals, as the villagers of Maniace had actually become since their community was formally enfeoffed to the monks in 1355. Brother Alberto Rocca had succeeded Abbot Salvo in 1367, and for twenty-three years tried his best amid impossible conditions. At his request in 1392 the King reconfirmed the limitations imposed on the Randazzese officials by the letters patent first issued by the Infante John. This mark of royal favour did not however imply approval of the luxury and indiscipline of the monks. Abbot Alberto died in 1393, and Brother Nicolo di Maddelena, who was elected in his stead only lived for three years. In 1396 Martin decided with the tacit approval of the Papacy to grant the Abbey *in commendam* (ie holding a benefice in trust in the absence of a regular incumbent) to one of his favourites. The first such lay appointee was Giovanni Ventimiglia, who was granted Maniace together with the Castle of Castiglione, 'for having well defended the throne'. He was ordered to pay the Crown 32 ounces of gold per annum, and to provide sustenance for three monks, a number which signified that the Abbey's religious life was almost extinct.

At some point early in the 15th century the village of Maniace ceased to exist altogether. The last mention of it in official documents occurs in 1402, when the King sent a justiciar as usual to Maniace, Bronte and the neighbouring villages to hear the grievances of the people. Thereafter, official records are silent, and subsequently mention only the Abbey, which is also described as 'the fort' (presumably alluding to the towers which formed part of the monastic buildings) and the village of Bronte. The latter had gradually grown up once more, sufficiently for it to be assessed to pay seven ounces of gold to the royal exchequer in 1375; which if divided by the amount payable on each family dwelling implies 70 households or, taking each to have five members on average, a population of 350. The Abbey still maintained a dominating influence in Bronte, for its powers comprised the election of Captain-at-arms, the jurors and the other officials of the 'University' (ie administrative entity), in addition to receiving the income and rents from the various fiefs cultivated by the villagers.

But what happened to Maniace? The question cannot be conclusively answered for lack of firm evidence, but it would appear that the village was abandoned, most of its inhabitants moving to Bronte, where they settled in a quarter known as *Borgo Nuovo* for centuries thereafter. The most likely date is following the earthquake of 1408, when Etna erupted continuously for ten days, and the chronicler Simon of Lentini noted that fire and lava destroyed much of the surrounding countryside. There is no specific mention of Maniace here, so perhaps it was gradually abandoned until another disastrous earthquake in 1444 completed its ruin. It now suffered from a malarial climate, being so near to the river, an exposed position which made it vulnerable to attack and considering the total decay of the Abbey it must by the 15th century have become a site with few attractions. Its inhabitants who moved to Bronte, a location more favourable in every way, were simply following the dictates of reason and good sense.

Sicily was certainly no haven of stability in the early 15th century. King Martin's death in 1409 betokened further chaos, and the island's Parliament, convened at Taormina, tried to place Sicily under Papal protection. The Spaniards however solved the problem by selecting Ferdinand, a prince from the ruling dynasty of Castile, to occupy the vacant throne. Henceforward the King would be a permanent absentee, ruling through foreign Viceroys. In 1416 he was succeeded by Alfonso, who was to reign for 42 years, during which time life in the island became a degree more tranquil and secure. The price paid was the recognition of all baronial privileges, while any attempts to curb them were abandoned. If the feudal overlords infringed age-old rights over communal lands or water supplies, few peasants had the courage or resources to challenge them in the Crown Courts. Rural depopulation continued, and once fertile Sicily began to suffer from periodic famines. Only in the largest towns was any illusion of civic freedom maintained, while the germ of urban revolt, which was to recur with such frequency was being slowly nurtured. The government's financial position remained shaky; revenues from the diminished royal demesne no longer covered expenses, the *collecta* or the *donativo* to use its Spanish name, was levied regularly, and royal prerogatives went on being sold for ready cash.

Thus a rich benefice like Maniace came to be viewed as a useful sinecure to be bestowed on someone important to the government. Occasionally the Abbot was nominated by the Church, the Antipope Benedict XIII appointed Brother Nicolo di Cipro from Messina in 1415, but the latter was deposed by the Papacy, which four years later

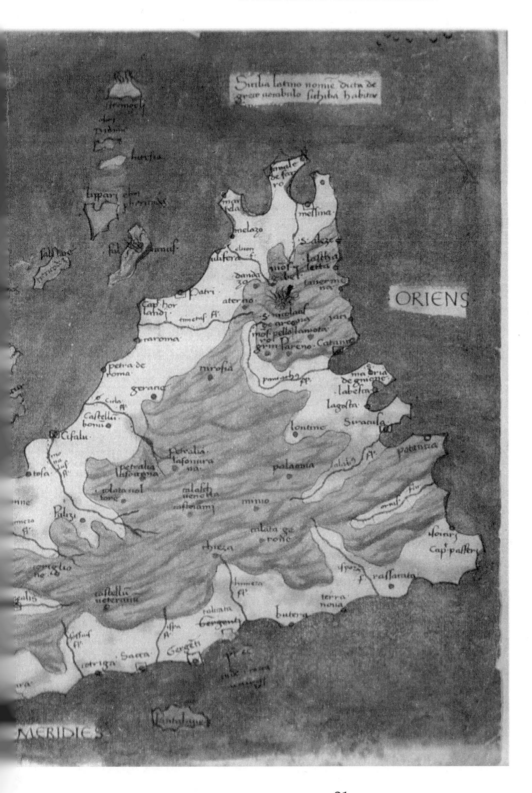

ordered a Spaniard, Brother Gonzalvo Roderigo to fill the post. More normally it was given to some great prelate, like the Cardinal del Conte in 1423, followed by the Patriarchs of Jerusalem then of Aquileia. Any pretence of election had been discarded and the Abbey was usually administered by clerical procurators general like Nicolo Tedesco (the German), a master of canon law and a priest from Catania, who proved so effective that he was appointed Abbot himself before being promoted Archbishop of Palermo in 1434, after which the Abbey was granted *in Commendam* once more. Sometimes lay castellans resided at Maniace, responsible for guarding the monks and their property. Their reports show the state of dilapidation into which it had fallen; one wrote in 1475: '*Il Monastero e pervenuto oggi in tanto sterminio che in tutto e ruinato, et il loco di santificazione e fatto ricettacolo di ladri.*' (The Monastery has reached such a state of decay now that everything lies in ruins and the consecrated places have become a haunt of robbers.) The Abbey was now quite unable to pay its taxes; two assessments of 94 ounces of gold in 1456–57 had to be suspended.

The Crown had by no means renounced all interest in Maniace. In 1423 the Viceroy ordered the captain of Randazzo to release 'the Abbey's vassals and freemen whom he had unjustly imprisoned' and to hand over the property to the Cardinal del Conte's representative. But unfortunately the pretensions of the citizens of Randazzo were bolstered in 1435 when the King approved the petition, asserting their *merum et mistum imperium* over the neighbouring communities (which remained unspecified), on the condition that their judicial powers were exercised to a minimal extent. Insofar as he was able, Alfonso was determined not to prejudice his rights of patronage or the scope of central authority.

State and Church clashed over Maniace in 1443. The King had nominated Domenico Xarech, Bishop of Girgenti as Abbot *in Commendam* with a procurator-general. Simultaneously, the monks of San Placido di Calonero at Messina petitioned the Pope to allow their union with Maniace, on the grounds that it was rich and almost deserted, while their monastery was poor with numerous hospices and obligations to maintain. By a Bull of December 30th 1443, the Pope ordered the union to take place, and the destruction of Maniace *propter aeris intemperiem.* The combined monasteries were instructed to elect a new Abbot, and another Bull of October 25th 1445 confirmed the appointment of Matteo di Marco. The King however had no intention of climbing down. The Abbey was occupied by his troops, and his episcopal nominee was sternly warned to defend his rights against all comers.

For four years the dispute raged, and eventually the Crown emerged victorious. Domenico Xarech was recognised as Abbot, the election of di Marco was declared void and the proposed union was cancelled.

The most famous or perhaps infamous of all the Abbots *in commendam* was also the last. In 1471 Cardinal Roderigo Borgia was appointed to the benefice of Maniace. As the future Pope Alexander VI, and the father of Lucrezia and Cesare Borgia he was to create for himself a niche of especial notoriety. A vineyard on the far bank of the Simeto is known as the Vigneto Borgia to this day. It is doubtful that he took much interest in the Abbey or indeed that he ever visited Sicily, but it did provide a welcome source of revenue. Under his aegis the union of Maniace with the monastery of San Filippo di Fragala, its rival for centuries, took place, for Borgia was the absentee Abbot of both, and this measure boosted his income by reducing the administrative expenses. Nevertheless his extravagance left him frequently desperate for money, and led him to think how he might commute some of his sources of revenue for a capital sum. The consideration that as Abbot *in commendam* he was merely entitled to the rents of Maniace and not to decide its future in any way he might choose is unlikely to have worried the Cardinal.

Although the Abbey had originally been a royal foundation, the Sicilian government was extremely unlikely to exercise its authority in the matter. King Alfonso had died in 1458 leaving the throne to his brother, who reigned without distinction for 21 years. On his death he was succeeded by Ferdinand of Aragon who, through his marriage to Isabella of Castile, was to unite the entire Iberian peninsula. Thus the insignificance of the island, as a distant part of a large empire, increased, and the viceroys were more concerned with keeping the country quiet, ensuring cheap bread for the masses and paying the army's wages than in challenging the actions of any vested interests.

So in 1491, 'with the consent of the King and the good pleasure of the Apostolic See', the Cardinal sold all his rights over both monasteries to the Rectors of the Ospedale Grande e Nuovo di Palermo. This had been founded sixty years before under the patronage of King Alfonso and the city council of the capital, and was housed in the great palace once the property of Matteo Sclafani, Count of Aderno. Since 1431 seven other hospitals had been incorporated with it, so that it ranked as one of the foremost charitable institutions of the kingdom. Borgia received 2,000 gold crowns from the Rectors, or Governors to use a more appropriate word, additionally reserving for himself an annual pension of 700 gold crowns which reverted to the Hospital at his death, although in 1497 he commuted this too for a further 2000. The sale was ratified by Pope Innocent VIII in a Bull of 8th July 1491 and was recognised by the Crown, which solely retained its rights as supreme feudal overlord. So after little more than three centuries the independent existence of Queen Margaret's Benedictine Abbey came to an end. The results of this rash deed was a further three centuries of nearly incessant quarrels between the local population and the unfortunate new feudatories of Maniace.

CHAPTER V

The rule of the Hospital

The Ruin of the Abbey

'In the condition I was in, our whole Sicilian trip did not present itself to me in a very rosy light. After all, what had we seen but the hopeless struggle of men with the violence of Nature, the malice and treachery of their times and the rancours of their own rival factions?' This rather jaundiced view of the charms of the island was expressed by Wolfgang Goethe in his *Italian Journey*, written as he sailed back to Naples in May 1787. Although he was writing at the end of the period under review in this chapter, his remarks could equally well apply to the entire period from about 1500 to 1800.

Despite popular misconception, the Rectors of the Hospital in fact took over both monasteries with the best intentions. They believed they could repopulate the depleted communities, (for San Filippo di Fragala was in almost as bad a state of decay as Maniace), provide adequate food for the monks and maintain all the Abbey's traditional functions, while collecting their feudal rents and dues. Such enthusiasm was sorely needed, for a string of absentee abbots had appropriated the revenue, spending nothing on Maniace, so that all its buildings, especially the church, were badly in need of repair. Their illusions were soon shattered as it rapidly became apparent that the local people now regarded the monks with contempt.

During divine services at Easter 1502 some Brontesi insulted the monks, and when the latter responded, physically assaulted them. Not content with this outrage, they broke into the Abbey the following night, lay in wait for the monks as they left their cells to say matins and beat them up, leaving one for dead. Similarly during January 1511, a party from Randazzo, including a Justice, scaled the

35

walls of the Abbey store-house and began stealing grain. Any monks who protested were abused and threatened with the painful punishment of being tied to the horses' tails and dragged to Randazzo. On the Abbey's petition the Crown courts ordered the arrest of the guilty men who asserted their innocence, claiming they were acting within their own jurisdiction. However they were tried, found guilty and imprisoned.

The Hospital appointed either an abbot or a prior to supervise the monks, but the community normally numbered fewer than ten. The reputation of the contemplative life enjoyed at Maniace did not improve either, and the Rectors gradually abandoned all ideas of reform. In fact the main advantage of owning the Abbey appeared to be the right it conferred of sitting in the fifteenth place in the ecclesiastical estate of Parliament – and the monks became merely an incidental nuisance. So during the 16th century the buildings remained dilapidated, as the Rectors were much more concerned about cutting the 285 ounces it cost them a year to maintain the community. However, they were not out of pocket. In 1553, historian Tommaso Fazzello estimated the Abbey's income to be 464 ounces in money, 480 measures of wheat and 100 of barley, proof that the land was still productive.

Maniace's main function by the late 16th century was as a guest-house, but the Rectors considered the Benedictine monks unfit even for this task. They therefore applied to the Pope for permission to install priests or monks of any order in the Abbey, which was granted in 1585. For the next twenty-five years one community succeeded another at Maniace with such bewildering rapidity that the only coherent way of describing these changes is to present them as a list:

1585 – Benedictines expelled and replaced by Basilian monks.

1586 – Basilians expelled in favour of the Hermits of St Augustine.

1589 – Hermits superseded by a Convent of Franciscan friars.

1592 – Abbey handed over to local priests, and a prior, Don Antonio Collera da Naso, installed. Before the end of this year, however, Maniace had been handed over to Pauline friars.

1593 – Basilians returned, although their tenure remained shaky. The Pope, wishing to stop these ceaseless changes, recommended the Abbey be amalgamated with the parish of Bronte, but the Rectors refused consent.

By 1602 – Conventual Franciscans returned.

1603 – Franciscans driven out, and Collera da Naso reinstalled.

1604 – This arrangement was unsatisfactory, and the Abbey was entrusted to the clergy of the parish of Cesaro.

1609 – They were replaced by more priests from Palermo under a prior, Nicolo Pamplone.

1611 – Basilians finally came back. Now a monastic order in the Latin Catholic Church, they had always occupied San Filippo di Fragola, and were to stay at Maniace for the remainder of its existence.

There is little to say about the Abbey's subsequent history. For the next few decades it continued to exist at an even lower ebb, if that were possible, than during the preceding century. The disastrous earthquake of January 11th 1693 destroyed the ruined church and the monastic buildings. The remaining Basilian monks moved to Bronte taking their relics and treasures with them. Four monks lived for a few years in a rented house in the town, as a virulent outbreak of malaria had made the Abbey and its environs uninhabitable. Finally, at the request of the Abbot, the Archpriest of Bronte and his colleagues agreed to cede the chapel of San Blandano to them. A church had stood on the site, one of the best positioned in the town, since 1574. The Basilians agreed to maintain the church at their own expense, in return for permission to build a hospice, to celebrate their own services there and bury their dead in the graveyard.

The move to Bronte was recognised in 1698 by the Rectors and by the Archbishop of Monreale. The archbishop, however, demanded the construction of a new monastic building; but as there were no available funds, nothing was done about it. Agreement was reached with the Hospital about both the choice of San Blandano as the new church and how much the Rectors would continue paying the monks. In 1715 the parishes of Bronte also accepted custody of the ruined buildings at Maniace. Interestingly enough, now that the monks were actually living cheek by jowl with local people, relations appeared to improve miraculously, and as the 18th century advanced, they can be found supporting the Brontesi in their fight against feudal abuses by the Hospital.

In 1743, the Royal Vicar-General, Gianangelo de Ciocchis published a report at Palermo on the monastic visitations he had made in North-Eastern Sicily. Among others he included his findings on the communities of Santa Maria di Maniace and San Filippo di Fragala. Painstakingly he enumerated the details about their foundations, their statutes and their obligations. He appended a list of their properties and fiefs with an inventory of their relics, plate and assorted valuables. De Ciocchis noted that the Basilian monks had taken over several of the houses adjoining their chapel and had built a dormitory with six cells. There were, however, only four monks in residence, of whom one served as the Prior. Indeed he considered that San Filippo di Fragala was in a much healthier condition, for he assessed its income at over 216 ounces per annum as opposed to Maniace's bare 127, while its plate was also more valuable being worth 112 ounces to the other's 90. But its community, of only four monks and two deacons, could hardly be reckoned as flourishing either.

The monks grew increasingly restless at their subjection to the Hospital. In 1769 they applied to have the Abbey directly incorporated into the royal demesne, and offered to assign half their produce and income to the Crown. The Rectors had no wish to lose an asset, which still managed to bring more in revenue than it cost in upkeep and strenuously opposed the petition. Not surprisingly, being somewhat nearer to the court, they prevailed. The case did, however, remind the government of the Abbey's existence. So when the following year the Archbishop of Monreale demanded its suppression on the grounds that it no longer fulfilled the monastic purposes embodied in its foundation, the Prior, Gregory San Filippo appealed directly to the Crown. This gambit proved successful – an official despatch confirmed that Maniace was under royal patronage, while in 1784 the King authorised the construction of new monastic buildings. Again, these never materialised, although the church of San Blandano was eventually almost entirely rebuilt in 1824. And a monastic community lingered on at Bronte throughout most of the 19th century, until its final suppression in the United Italy of 1870 along with most other religious houses.

So the history of the Abbey – although not that of Maniace or Bronte – comes to an end. In the last three centuries of its existence, its records cast scant credit on its monks or on the Rectors of the Hospital who engrossed its revenue. The buildings on the site lay in ruins. The earthquake had demolished the east aisle of the church, although some of the arches of the nave and west aisle still stood. The austere Norman-Sicilian façade with its magnificent portico had remained largely intact. But Maniace had to wait to be restored to its former glory by its next, and very different, owners.

The struggle for sovereignty

'Successive Spanish administrators realised that the cheapest way to hold the islands with only a small garrison was to introduce few changes and as little challenge as possible to local susceptibilities and privileges'. (Denis Mack Smith, *History of Sicily*) This policy remained the cornerstone for the conduct of almost every Viceroy until Spain's possession of the island temporarily ended with the Treaty of Utrecht in 1713. It explains why the struggle of the Brontesi against the pretensions of Randazzo and against the exactions of the Rectors of the Hospital was so long and painful that the scars of it are still apparent today.

The Emperor Charles V was the first sovereign to visit Sicily for a century, and the last to do so until 1714. On his way back from campaigning in North Africa he stopped for some weeks on the island in autumn 1535 and was warmly received. In late October he visited Bronte on his way to Troina and later stayed at Randazzo. Here he was offered the keys of the town on a golden cushion, and he granted a diploma formally entitling it to the designation of 'city'. Charles was greeted by specially erected arches and fountains playing multi-coloured jets of water, while every building en route to the castle was draped in brocade. The window from which he appeared to the crowds was subsequently walled up to prevent anyone else ever using it.

During his stay, the Emperor had expressed his wish to enable communities to return to the royal demesne, free of all feudal ties save obedience to the Crown. Thus encouraged, the Brontesi began to agitate against the jurisdiction of Randazzo. That town's officials had grown increasingly high-handed in their behaviour. They forbade the monks or the villagers to take their grain to Messina or elsewhere, as they had often done in the past, but made them sell it locally for lower prices. Reserves stored in the Abbey's or in Bronte's granaries were often seized and payment was refused on the pretext of some minute infraction of Randazzo's privileges. Unfortunately its claim to exercise *merum et mistum imperium* was bolstered by the Viceroy, Lopez de Vega, in 1555 who confirmed various rights claimed by the Randazzesi in neighbouring fiefs, especially over the sowing, harvesting and sale of crops, although no mention was made of any earlier grant.

That same year the people of Bronte petitioned to be allowed to revert to the royal demesne, and at their request an official enquiry into the misconduct of the Randazzese captains-at-arms was ordered. Typically nothing happened, except for vague and intermittent promises of redress. Bronte had now grown into quite a sizeable place; the 1548 census showed a total of 709 households with a population of 2,825, a fact which made their servile status the more bitterly resented. On September 3rd 1595, 115 heads of families gathered in the main square and formed a committee 'to recover their liberties', while an annual subscription of 160 ounces was voted towards the cost of litigation. The committee claimed that Randazzo made a profit of 400 ounces per annum from its exercise of the *merum et mistum imperium*. It cited numerous instances of injustice: a six ounce fine for slaughtering a cow without witnesses, a twenty-four ounce fine for not having registered the sowing of a field, a five ounce fine and gaol for a piece of beef, allegedly stolen, found in a poor man's pot. People had spent weeks if not months in the gaol without trial, where they had to pay for their board. However when officials came to Bronte 'to administer justice', they had refused to pay for their keep or even for items bought. The Brontese captain-at-arms had been flogged for trying to restrain his colleague from Randazzo, who was trying to batter down the door of an honest family's house. The list of grievances was lengthy, and when the case came before the courts, litigation proceeded even more slowly than usual.

Simultaneously Bronte was embroiled in wrangles with the Hospital. Accusations of agreements annulled, rights usurped and new taxes levied were hurled at the Rectors, who displayed no desire to compromise. In September 1553 the people appealed to the Viceroy, on the grounds that the Hospital was now trying to acquire a monopoly of sales of their produce by forbidding them to sell to anyone else, while various fields which they had always used for pasture were now closed. The government sent Dr Giovanni Nicolo da Procida to Bronte as president of a council to judge the matter. The council was held on April 19th 1554 in the church of St Mary, where, amid considerable excitement two-thirds of the population had gathered. Yet apart from electing forty-three syndics to represent the people's grievances, nothing was achieved. The Rectors counterclaimed that two farms had been wrongfully occupied and the Abbey woods devastated by flocks of sheep and goats. The council was adjourned in confusion; the Viceroy then sent a deputy, who managed to turn 500 of the townspeople off their plots in favour of others prepared to pay an annual rent to the Hospital. In 1558 the court in Messina further ordered anyone still in arrears to settle immediately.

Frequent plagues and famines beset Sicily in the 16th century and high taxation exacerbated the general misery. Brigandage was a widespread problem, according to official reports. It was caused by a combination of the growth of vagrancy, inflation, poor harvests which drove some peasants off the land, and the denial of justice to the poor. Every attempt to persuade the barons to organise a local militia failed, while many captains-at-arms merely summoned their levies to receive bribes to let them go home again. The insecurity of the coastal areas, where the raids of the Barbary Corsairs struck dread into the population (in 1535 the Viceroy at Taormina had witnessed the seizure of his own galley before his very eyes), and were rivalled by those of Christian privateers, led many people to flee into the decreasingly fertile interior. Feuds flourished; the poor revolted against the rich; aristocratic families conducted vendettas with gangs of hired *bravi*; and the enmity between rival towns, Palermo and Messina in particular, grew fiercer. The strongest cement holding society together was loyalty to the Crown, for almost everyone feared social revolution more than the rule of Spain.

Is it surprising in such an unsettled climate that petty local quarrels were magnified out of all proportion, and became an obsession with some of the protagonists? In 1604 De Pasquale, one of the Rectors, contrived to get himself appointed collector of customs and excise as well as captain-at-arms of Bronte. That July he published a proclamation prohibiting the townsfolk from cutting trees in the Maniace woods. Transgressors were threatened with a twenty-five ounce fine and if they persisted, with three years in the royal galleys. Despite complaints to the Viceroy, De Pasquale's exactions went unchecked, though he was officially rebuked. So in May 1606 Bronte once more petitioned the Crown for reintegration into the royal demesne. Their rights were formally restated: of sowing in the Abbey's fiefs, of paying only a tenth of the wheat, barley or vegetables they harvested, or of any pigs kept there, of freely cutting firewood and watering their livestock without payment. They disputed the Hospital's attempts to let the land to other tenants at a higher rent or to forbid the sale of wine to any third party. The Rectors denounced the petition as seditious, and a hearing took place at Palermo. On this occasion the Brontesi partially succeeded: their rights were reaffirmed and the charge of sedition quashed. However the Court pronounced no judgement that could finally have settled matters.

Breaking point came first in the struggle against the oppressive sway of Randazzo. A major famine afflicted Bronte in 1636 and the Viceroy sent Captain Andrea di Gregorio to the town to buy grain. On April 6th he met there with Randazzese officials whose obstructive attitude enraged the people. Words, then blows were exchanged and the captain-at-arms of Bronte, Matteo Pace, mounted his horse and galloped through the streets, crying: 'Let us cast out our evil governors. Long live the King of France!' The mob rose and the officials precipitately fled.

After this riot, in which no one had been killed, peace returned but the government was determined to stamp out all sedition. A proclamation declared the Brontesi guilty of treason and urged those who had not joined in the riot to denounce its instigators. A strong body of royal troops arrived; many people were arrested and taken to Messina, while all arms found in the town were confiscated. Pace and his friend, Luigi Terranova were executed, some others sent to the galleys for life, while lesser offenders were whipped and put in the stocks.

The worst incident of this protracted struggle was paradoxically to be the last. Anxious to raise money for the Thirty Years War, in which Spain was heavily engaged, King Philip IV had ordered the sale of many royal assets and prerogatives in 1629. It had already been formally conceded by the government that private jurisdictions could be bought as of right, and that they could be held by both ecclesiastical and lay bodies. Seeing their chance the Rectors offered a small sum to acquire the *merum et mistum imperium* over Bronte, set against a debt they were owed by the Crown. The Brontese councillors responded with the much better offer of 8,000 scudi in cash. The citizens of Randazzo were alarmed. Invoking the earlier privileges conferred on them, they offered 4000 scudi 'from pure goodwill', and a further 6000 to have their grant reconfirmed. The largest offer won the day, and there for the moment the matter rested.

In 1637, with the government even more strapped for cash, the Brontesi decided to try again. They offered the Crown a total of 14,000 scudi – 10,000 to buy the jurisdiction and a further 4,000 to obtain pardon for their recent rebellion. Even by loan the town could not raise such a sum unaided, so that October they turned to the Rectors for help, stipulating that they wished to pay half the sum so they might retain the right to nominate their own officials. After protracted bargaining an agreement was signed on November 19th 1637 between the Rectors and Dr Paolo Ortale, acting as procurator for Bronte. It stated that:

i) The captain-at-arms, the judge, jurymen and tax collector must all be native-born Brontesi.

ii) The Town Council would assemble annually during the three day public holiday of Pentecost and elect eight men of good reputation. These in turn together with the existing office-holders would recommend three literate candidates for the post of captain-at-arms, three lawyers for the post of judge, and twelve reputable citizens for jurymen.

iii) Every year the list must be sent to the Rectors by June at the latest. They would then select from this list of eligible candidates: one judge, one captain-at-arms and four jurymen for the next twelve months.

iv) The tax collector was to be appointed for life from a similarly chosen list of three candidates.

v) He, the judge and the captain-at-arms could be appointed by the Hospital from others not on the lists, provided they came from Bronte, and this would happen anyway if the lists did not reach Palermo on time. The agreement was signed by both parties.

Seriously worried at the prospect of losing its privileges, Randazzo increased its offer to 15,000 scudi that December. The following May the Rectors retorted with a sum of 22,000, 9,000 of which would come from Bronte, 5,000 from the Hospital, while the balance of 8,000 represented the debt still owed by the Crown. Ignoring the previous agreement with Randazzo, the government accepted the last offer. Bronte was pardoned for its rebellion, those who had been imprisoned or exiled were permitted to return, and confiscated property and arms were restored. The townspeople believed themselves free at last of the old abuses of the *merum et mistum imperium*, although they saw its visible embodiment – the gallows – now erected in their own square. Time was to show they were deluded, for in reality they had fallen victim to the *pieta usuraia* (holy money-lending) in Radice's phrase, of the Hospital.

Aside from their other troubles, this period was one of natural disasters for the people living around Maniace and Bronte. Between 1500 and 1800, no fewer than forty major eruptions of Etna were recorded. In March 1536 the volcano erupted in terrifying fashion. Fazzello, the historian who watched it happen, described two rivers of fire flowing down the mountain, one heading towards Randazzo, the other towards Bronte and Aderno. Fields and livestock were destroyed by the lava as it steadily advanced, although fortunately it halted before engulfing any of the towns in its path. A violent earthquake followed; the tremors were felt throughout Sicily, while volcanic dust was borne by the wind over the mainland and even as far as Crete. The reflection lit up the surrounding countryside as brightly as daylight, and the eruption continued for a full month until late April. The memories of horror it left behind were such that the serious eruption of 1559 was dismissed as relatively insignificant.

The mountain was however to cause still greater damage in the 17th century. On February 4th 1651 a flow of lava travelled down the western slopes at great speed, covering sixteen miles in twenty-four hours and only stopping on the banks of the Simeto. It continued to smoulder for three years, forcing many of the local people to abandon their homes. The Rectors complained at the consequent loss of revenue from their fiefs, while the Brontesi appealed to the royal courts to be excused their taxes, as the catastrophe had bankrupted so many of them. Shamed into making a charitable gesture, the Rectors then offered the farm of Gollia, fertile, well-watered and indisputably the Abbey's property, as the site of a new town. The government, delighted, sent officials from Messina to study the feasibility of the project and to draw up plans. The Hospital was ordered to build a church and a prison at its own expense, and offer a free plot of land for a house to every settler. The new community was to be exonerated from all taxes for five years and from civil debts for one, but no one might leave it on pain of three years' imprisonment. Proclamations were posted in Bronte; 3,000 people volunteered to move but typically of Sicily, nothing ever happened.

The famous eruption of 1669, which devastated hundreds of square miles of forest and agricultural land, luckily occurred on the far side of Etna. A river of lava over a mile wide flowed down towards the sea, crumbling the walls of Catania into ashes and only halting in the water after it had filled up part of the harbour. According to popular belief the miraculous veil of St Agatha – taken from the Cathedral in procession through the streets – alone saved the city from total destruction. Those who lived west of the mountain largely escaped this time, but the next eruption affected almost everyone on the island. On January 11th 1693 a violent seismic shock was felt throughout Sicily; tens of thousands of people fled in panic from the towns, most of the buildings in nearby cities such as Messina and Catania were destroyed, and up to five per cent of the island's population perished. Small wonder that the Basilian monks, seeing their decayed Abbey at Maniace virtually razed to the ground, felt their only hope lay in a move to Bronte.

The Hospital has frequently been accused of hard-heartedness in its dealings with its feudatories at Bronte. Indeed after the disasters of 1651 had left the townspeople unable to pay the 400 ounces of interest owing on the loan, the Rectors had demanded compensation in the form of the community's lands. Subsequently the arrears were paid and the land returned but this left further bitter resentments. It was also alleged that the Rectors had not observed their side of the 1637

44

agreement, and that officials were appointed ever more arbitrarily. The government had to find another peacemaker, and on 6th March 1661, both sides signed a new agreement.

Yet in fairness to the Hospital it must not be forgotten that its financial position as a landowner had dramatically worsened since the end of the 15th century. The Crown now frequently defaulted on interest payments on its debt, which in turn affected the landowners and charitable institutions, all of whom derived income from government bonds. The costs of the war had caused export taxes to be raised so high that the sale of wheat was now unprofitable; cultivation of the land had declined as a result of inflation, famine and insecurity, weakening the agricultural economy. The lack of incentive to make agrarian improvements, the primitive tools used, the simple rotation of crops and fallow which reduced the yield and sometimes left the land lying idle for two years out of three, the near mono-culture of wheat and the system of share cropping which encouraged neither party all conspired against a return to prosperity. Communications, especially around Messina were appalling, and grain had to be carried to the coastal towns on muleback, which was slow and expensive. Continuing deforestation had seriously eroded the soil and upset the water supplies, while burning the scrubby hillsides to create more arable fields often caused further fires, and after several harvests the newly reclaimed land usually had to be abandoned.

Thus the Rectors had seen the comfortable revenues they thought they had purchased with the Abbey and its fiefs in 1491 dwindle steadily. Obviously as a charitable institution they had obligations which necessitated a rising or at least a steady income. Although their behaviour was scarcely admirable, it can be better understood in this context. For it was the curse of all concerned that the Hospital's falling revenues and need to ameliorate them coincided with the growing misery of their vassals. During the later 17th century food prices increased too, fostering discontent among the urban poor in particular, while the *macinato* or tax on milling flour enraged the peasants. The Hospital's unpopularity at such a wretched period of Sicilian history was redoubled: because Randazzo no longer exercised the *merum et mistum imperium*, the Brontesi had now only one enemy on whom to vent their spleen.

Perhaps the most remarkable fact about the last decades of Spanish rule was that Sicily still showed no real impetus for open rebellion on the Dutch or Catalonian model. The Palermo rising of 1647 triggered some severe riots as at Randazzo, where the mob rose and burned debtors' records and the tax rolls, but it never spread throughout the island, and although the Viceroy had to flee for some months from his capital where the mob ruled unchallenged, the middle classes banded together and restored order, permitting his reinstatement in return for a lot of paper promises that were not kept. Even the revolt of Messina in 1674, when French soldiers garrisoned the city for several years and defied the Viceroy's attempts to recapture it, had more to do with the loss of civic privileges than with any anti-Spanish plot, and never affected the surrounding region, where Randazzo was used as a main rendezvous for royal troops. It was social and economic injustice at home, not foreign politics, that caused the unrest and this could not be cured by a change of masters.

When King Charles II died in 1700, he left Sicily, and his other dominions, to Prince Philip of Bourbon, grandson of Louis XIV. The war of the Spanish Succession would rage for twelve years throughout Europe yet the island remained largely unaffected. The threat of an Austrian invasion from Calabria in 1707 never materialised, although isolated landings were made along the coast. By the Treaty of Utrecht in 1713, Sicily was given to Piedmont, although this arrangement did not last and in 1716 Spain sent an army of 20,000 men to recover its lost dominion. However they were not left long in undisturbed possession, for Austrian troops crossed the Straits of Messina and for the first time serious fighting broke out on Sicilian soil. The interior of the island was ravaged as two large armies fought for over a year. The Battle of Francavilla, which took place in 1719 on the road up from Taormina, was an engagement on a big scale. Randazzo had served as the Spanish headquarters, and in the ensuing retreat 800 casualties were left there to be buried in a communal grave. But the Austrian conquest was also short-lived, and in 1734 the Spanish Bourbons regained Sicily and would hold it until the Risorgimento.

All the Piedmontese and Austrian attempts at reform had quickly foundered, and their regimes had lost popularity in the process. Almost with relief the island reverted to Spanish rule and its new King, the Infante Charles who had been given the combined realm of Naples and Sicily, even bothered to come to Palermo and be crowned. Against a background of hope restored, many people tried to have old grievances remedied. Thus in 1735 the Brontesi again petitioned for their reintegration into the royal demesne and for the interest on the loan from the Hospital to be reduced to five per cent. Their litigation was sustained and encouraged by the recently elected town procurator, Don Antonio Cairone. Locally born, a rich and clever lawyer, he was to devote the rest of his life and fortune to the cause of freeing Bronte from feudal jurisdiction. He reopened all the old law suits, alleging that the office holders were conniving with the Rectors in the abuses practised, and he even offered the crown 36,000 ounces to buy back the *merum et mistum imperium*. Eventually he aroused such fury that the government stripped him of his rank of notary and imprisoned him. From 1751 to 1754 he was banished to Messina, yet he went on bombarding the King, the Viceroy and the courts with memoranda reiterating the justice of his case. Cairone's fanatical persistence split the Brontesi for while many supported him, others considered he was damaging their best interests. He died, impoverished but still fighting, aged eighty-three in 1758 after a fall from his horse. The litigation, however, was to drag on for another century.

One victory had already been gained. In 1765 the Court of Royal Property cancelled the debt owed by the town to the Hospital since 1638, and ordered the return of goods taken in lieu of the interest due. The Rectors unwillingly acquiesced – after failed attempts to have the judgement reversed though bribery – but they did not mend their ways. Proclamations were issued in 1786 placing restrictions on the fields to be used for pasturage; the dispute became so bitter that the government had to send officials to agree the boundaries. Further restrictions on the cutting of wood and taking of water followed in 1786; these were widely ignored. Some of the offenders were gaoled, yet the Brontesi remained impenitent and many refused to pay their rents. By the end of the century impasse seemed to have been reached by both sides.

Ironically, while the wrangles of Bronte and the Hospital appeared to offer no promise of solution, central government was at last moving in the direction of reform. The Bourbon regime had soon discovered that all the traditional problems of Sicily remained unsolved if not insoluble. During the 18th century the hegemony of Palermo grew so much that it engrossed most of the wealth of the island, while Messina, the chief commercial city, was in decline after a terrible plague in 1743. Food shortages in 1773 led to serious riots, and a determination that something must be done. In 1781 a new Viceroy, Marchese Domenico Caracciolo, arrived to initiate a radical programme of reforms. A far-reaching attack on feudal privileges and baronial jurisdiction was mounted, and the nobility was sharply reminded that all fiefs were held from the Crown and could revert to it. Expenditure was reduced, and a thorough survey of landholdings begun, which was to be accompanied by an effective land tax and cheap agrarian credit to help peasants to buy their own holdings.

Caracciolo's policies did of course arouse much opposition, and he was recalled in 1786 to be replaced by a more easy-going Viceroy, the Prince of Caramanico. He too was a reformer however, albeit a more tactful one, who even persuaded the Sicilian Parliament to consent to revised taxation and a new land survey. It was restated that fiefs were held in return for duties performed, and could not be bequeathed or alienated like allodial land; a judgement which in theory should have reminded the Hospital of its obligations. An edict in 1789 scarcely worked at all: it was supposed to divide up much common and ecclesiastical land where the King was patron, including Maniace, to be granted on copyhold (ie held on special conditions of tenure) to peasants in exchange for them surrendering their rights of pasturage and wood cutting. No one listened to theorists like the Abbe Balsamo, who said that improvement was possible with technical advances, longer leases and better working conditions. Caramanico's death in 1795, and the start of the French Revolution stifled further attempts at reform.

As the 18th century drew to a close, Sicily was still pretty much unknown to the outside world. Gradually however a few adventurous travellers, attracted by the sights and the eccentricities of the island, ventured to explore it – and write about it. Patrick Brydone's *Tour through Sicily and Malta* (1774) is a fascinating account. While climbing Etna, he engaged in conversation with a group of peasants near Nicolosi and records the following story. They told him that English visitors often came to the volcano, as one of their Queens had been burning inside it for many years, and they thought her name was Anna. 'I could not conceive what Queen Anne had done to bring her there, and was puzzling myself to find it out, when one of them soon cleared up the matter; he told me she was wife to a King that had been a Christian, and that she had made him a heretic, and was in consequence condemned to burn for ever in Mount Etna. In short I found it was none other than poor Anne Boleyn. So soon as I mentioned the name; "*Si signor*," said the fellow, "*l'istessa, l'istessa, la conosce megho che noi*". ["Yes, Sir, the same, the same, you know her better than we."] I asked if her husband was there too, for that he deserved it much better than she; "surely" he replied "and if you are of that number, you need not be in such a hurry to get thither, you will be sure of it at last". I thanked him and went to join our company not a little amused with our conversation.'

In fact Etna had proved somewhat more tranquil than in the preceding century. The only serious eruption took place in February

1763 and continued intermittently for a month. A meteor was seen in the sky, to the terror of the population, and several fresh craters were formed. The peasants still held the mountain in superstitious dread and legends continued to gather around it. The Brontese shepherds passed down another tale of Hell: how every Friday towards 8pm a black bitch puppy with eyes like glowing coals could be seen running along the paths towards the crater, and jumping into it, to reemerge still howling. This was supposed to be the soul of Don Ignazio Caraprino, which had migrated into his favourite puppy. He was condemned to make this terrible journey as he had left his estate to a rich neighbour, who had corrupted him with sweetmeats, rather than to his abjectly poor relations. When the shepherds crossed themselves, the puppy abruptly disappeared.

Sicily did not escape all natural disasters during the 18th century. A violent earthquake largely flattened Messina in 1783, killing 12,000 people, and its devastating effects were observed by Goethe when he visited the city four years later. 'For a good quarter of an hour we rode on our mules past ruin after ruin until we came to our inn. This was the only house which had been rebuilt, and from its upper floors, we looked out over a wasteland of jagged wrecks.' A barrack town had been hastily erected to house the 30,000 homeless, but the building was incredibly shoddy. One hut he was shown reminded him of 'those booths at a fair, where wild animals and other curiosities are exhibited for money'. The grand sweep of the palazzata, the crescent of palaces along a mile of the harbour waterfront, did not impress him either, for he detected behind the crumbling façades that almost every building had collapsed. Indeed he found the island primitive and unattractive on the whole, although not lacking in amusement value. In one inn he found an inscription on the wall in perfect English which read: 'Traveller, bound for Catania, whoever you may be, beware of staying at the Golden Lion; it is worse than falling into the clutches of the Cyclops, the Sirens and Scylla.' Yet Goethe was captivated in retrospect: 'I carry in my soul a picture of Sicily, that unique and beautiful island, which is clear, authentic and complete.'

Remote though it was from the world of the Enlightenment, Bronte was becoming more civilised. Communications from the interior were still poor; it took three days to reach Messina and four to Palermo, while the road to Catania was frequently impassable and infested by bandits, even if some, like Gian Giorgio Lanza of Randazzo with his gang of 500 horsemen, had acquired the reputation of being veritable Robin Hoods to the poor. Yet a few Brontesi had managed to make their mark in a wider world. Ignazio Capizzi, who died in Palermo in 1783, was the first to foster painting in his native town. Even after he had left to live in the capital, the old priest continued to send back pictures and pieces of sculpture to adorn the churches, while his own religious paintings were widely copied. His younger fellow-artist, Nicolo Spedalieri, studied at Monreale under the famous master, Martorana. His self-portrait, painted in 1773, is a competent work, and when he moved to Rome he was elected a member of the Arcadian Academy where he met Winckelmann, Mengs and Canova. As a keen music-lover he encouraged its development at Bronte by sponsoring several music students.

By the late 18th century the town's population had grown. After falling by a third from the 1640 total of over 9,000, it rose again from 6,936 in 1714 to 9,153 in 1798. Similarly the balance sheet showed a net deficit of 200 ounces in 1748, but forty years later, the books nearly balanced. Under the Bourbons Bronte was included in the military district of Taormina, and was supposed to contribute thirty infantrymen and a small troop of cavalry to the government levies, which did provide a degree more security in the area. Wheat production was beginning to revive; the bountiful 1520s – when in one year the town had exported 14,350 salme of grain – had been succeeded by decades of agricultural depression and a string of disastrous harvests in the 17th century. Now at last, despite many problems, in particular an inadequate water-supply, there was some hope of reversing this dismal trend and restoring prosperity to the local people.

The slowly rising tide of expectations and enhanced material well-being was encouraged by the French Revolution with its emphasis on the Rights of Man. It is doubtful that news of its doctrines really filtered through to the Sicilian countryside, although the authorities took the threat of revolution very seriously. Ferdinand, who had succeeded to the throne in 1759 aged eight on the death of his father, King Charles, had an almost paranoid horror of Jacobinism. In 1798 the Sicilian Parliament exploited this to refuse the grant of further *donativi* unless Caracciolo's reforms were annulled. But it was undeniably true that the island was increasingly polarised between the 'haves' as represented in the Parliament, and the 'have-nots'. This situation was reflected in Bronte by the position of the Hospital, which seemed to the simpler-minded the sole obstacle frustrating their aspirations, while over two-and-a-half centuries of sporadic litigation remained unresolved. It was indeed a minefield for any uninitiated outsider, yet

an accident of history would ensure that a family entirely foreign and
ignorant of Sicily and its problems was to be left in the middle of it. The
result would be bewildered irritation on the one side and irrational
anger on the other.

Nelson's Duchy

CHAPTER VI

The hero's reward

'A legend of the slipper of Queen Elizabeth I of England is known among the shepherds of Bronte. Queen Elizabeth, in order to overcome the difficulties that stood in her way to gain the English throne, invoked the Devil's aid. He appeared to her in person, and they made a pact that she would reign for forty-four years. When she was near to death, Satan and his demons came to her bedside. Hardly was she dead when they carried her away. They flew over the sea, across France and Italy beset by storms. Tired from the journey, they placed their royal prey on the Calanna Rock, between Bronte and Maletto, facing Etna. When they renewed their flight, a slipper encrusted with gems fell from the Queen's foot and embedded itself in the rock.

A shepherd, tending his flocks, saw a woman clasped between Satan's arms disappear, amidst whirling flame and smoke, into the crater of Etna. He fell to the ground almost dead with fear. When he recovered, he saw something glittering on top of the rock. It was the Queen's slipper, but when he tried to pick it up, it burned his hand. Returning to the village he told the story to an abbot, versed in witchcraft, who put on his stole and vestments and went to the spot carrying a bowl of Holy Water and a 16th century Bible. However, he too could not tear the slipper from the rock, so they entreated the help of Sister Colomba of Bronte, a nun possessed by an evil spirit, who spoke every language. She read the Queen's name, which was written in golden arabesque on the slipper. The abbot started his exorcism once more; the slipper lifted itself into the air, and emitting flames the while, came to earth near the Monastery of Maniace, built by another Queen. It is said that Queen Elizabeth had come to put this land under the protection of England.

When Admiral Nelson, during feasts and orgies at Palermo, was created Duke of Bronte, a richly-dressed lady presented him with a gilded casket. On opening it, the Admiral was dazzled by the sight of this same royal slipper, glittering with gems. He turned to question the lady, but found she had disappeared. Nelson always carried the slipper with him as a talisman in all his battles. Just before the Battle of Trafalgar, the lady of the golden casket, regally apparelled, appeared to him in a dream. She asked him where the slipper was. He replied that before embarking he had given it to Lady Hamilton. "Why have you given it to another?" she said. "You will die in this battle." And so it came to pass.'

Thus Benedetto Radice, the local Brontese historian, recounts in inimitably Sicilian fashion the legend connecting the new Duke of Bronte with one of the most outstanding English monarchs. Indeed so remote was the connection between the great Admiral and the tenants he had acquired with his Duchy that a mythological explanation might have seemed to them the most convincing. To understand why Nelson was given an estate in Sicily, it is necessary to look at a wider historical canvas, and to examine the backgrounds and careers of a variety of figures far removed from Maniace, whose actions brought about the creation of the Duchy.

Horatio Nelson certainly appears at first sight an unlikely figure to have become a Sicilian Duke. Born in 1758, son of a Norfolk vicar, he had inherited a love of the sea from his mother's family, the Sucklings, and had been rated midshipman with his uncle Maurice when aged only twelve. After gaining nautical experience on voyages to the New World, the Arctic and the East Indies, 'although mindful of the many difficulties I had to surmount and of the little influence I possessed,' he yet decided to dedicate his life to the service of King and Country. He had proved himself a zealous officer on the West Indian station in the 1780s, suppressing smuggling, exposing peculation by royal officials, and marrying Fanny Nisbet, widowed niece of the President of the Council of Nevis. Five years of inactivity on half-pay, mostly spent with his aged father at Burnham Thorpe, ended with the outbreak of war with France. In February 1793 he took command of his first sail of the line, the 64-gun *Agamemnon*, and was straightaway ordered to the Mediterranean.

The British Mediterranean Fleet was under the command of Admiral Samuel Hood, a distinguished naval officer under whom Nelson had already served in the West Indies, and whose family will soon reappear in this story. Hampered by a shortage of sailors and seaworthy ships, Hood was only on station by midsummer, when a close blockade of the French coast was instituted. By August Marseille and Toulon, fearful of further revolutionary excesses, had offered to negotiate terms of surrender. The Jacobins quickly recaptured the former, but the Toulon commissioners requested British protection and declared for a limited monarchy. Hood promptly landed men to secure the citadel and forts, while sending Nelson off with despatches to HBM's Envoys at the Courts of Turin and Naples. At dawn on September 12th 1793, Nelson had his first glimpse of a unique landscape. 'We were in the Bay all night becalmed, and nothing could have been finer than the view of Mount Vesuvius.'

For the first time too he was about to meet several people whose lives were to become closely entwined with his own. Sir William Hamilton, then 63 years old and British Envoy at the Neapolitan Court since 1764, was a remarkable man. The grandson of the Third Duke of Hamilton, and a penniless soldier he had married a considerable heiress, Miss Catherine Barlow of Lawrenny Hall, Pembrokeshire. He had originally sought the embassy at Naples because of his wife's delicate health, but was soon enthralled by the charm of what was after Paris the largest city in Europe, and by the classical splendours revealed by the new excavations at Pompeii and Herculaneum. Abandoning all ideas of a more glamorous posting, absorbed in his collecting and archaeology, Hamilton became an institution, invariably visited by all travellers to Naples. Sadly, his wife's feeble health was deteriorating. 'I feel my tottering frame sinking and my spirits fail me; my only regret in leaving this world is in leaving you. Were it not for that I would wish the struggle over.' In August 1782 she died, and the next year the grieving Hamilton returned to England, bringing his wife's body for burial in Pembrokeshire.

Much of his leave was spent with his nephew, Charles Greville, Lord Warwick's younger son and later the celebrated diarist. The latter had recently acquired a beautiful eighteen-year old mistress. Born the daughter of the village blacksmith in Neston, Cheshire, in April 1765, Miss Amy Lyon soon came to London with her mother, who had assumed the name of Mrs Cadogan (although fifty years later her daughter was to refer to her in her will as 'Mary Doggin'). She rapidly became a 'model' at the Temple of Health on Royal Terrace of the Adelphi, run by a bogus doctor, where anyone could see her after paying five shillings. Here she had been picked up by Sir Harry Fetherstonhaugh, and installed as his mistress at Uppark. Yet in less than a year, finding herself pregnant, she was sent packing. She turned for protection to Greville, who promptly installed her with her mother in Paddington, whereupon she changed her name to Emma Hart.

Sir William saw much of this ménage, and on his return to Naples, began to his surprise to receive letters from Greville suggesting that his uncle should take charge of Emma, to give a penurious younger son a chance to find a suitably rich bride. Hamilton was certainly lonely; indeed en route back he had proposed in Rome to a widow, Lady Clarges, but had been rejected. Nevertheless it took a long time to convince him, until November 1785 in fact. Emma was only persuaded to go out to Naples that following spring, as her lover promised to join her there. Accompanied by Mrs Cadogan, she arrived in April 1786, celebrating her twenty-first birthday simultaneously. She soon captivated the ageing diplomat, becoming his mistress within a few months. Sir William remained unreceptive to her hints of marriage until 1791, when on leave again in England he obtained the consent of his old friend, George III, and the couple had a quiet wedding in London. The King had, however, stipulated that in view of her past, Emma could not be received by the Queen, and hence could not occupy the official position of ambassadress.

Back in Naples this scarcely seemed to matter. When Emma arrived from Paris bearing a letter for the Queen from her sister Marie Antoinette, she was received, albeit privately, by Maria Carolina. Thus began the friendship which was to prove so fatal to both parties. A balanced judgement of Emma's character would suggest a barely educated young woman, generous and impulsively warm-hearted, but also shallow and histrionic. Her principal qualities were an animal vitality combined with great physical beauty and considerable force of character. She had been a faithful mistress to Sir William, but had always resented her lowly position. Her new-found marital status soon went to her head, and the Queen shrewdly appealed to Emma's vanity and *folie de grandeur*, fostering the illusion that she was playing an important political role.

The first Lady Hamilton had perceptively summed up Maria Carolina. 'Quick, clever, insinuating when she pleases, she is too proud and too humble. There is no dependence on what she says, as she is seldom of the same opinion for two days.' This Habsburg princess, who among all her sisters most closely resembled their mother, the Empress Maria Theresa, had married Ferdinand in 1768. Wilful and convinced she had been born to rule, she usually dominated her husband. Increasingly appalled by the news from France – enthusiastically spread by the horde of emigrés who had arrived in Naples – the Queen now saw in England a bulwark against revolutionary excesses, and in Emma a convenient confidante, who could be relied on as a channel of communication to the British government, bypassing the King and his ministers. The execution of Louis XVI, then of her sister, had vastly increased Maria Carolina's francophobia and it was no thanks to her that an overt breach between both countries had been averted.

The credit for this must go to the Prime Minister, General John Acton. Descended from an ancient Shropshire family, this English expatriate with a French mother had been in the Tuscan, and since 1778, in the Neapolitan service. Successively Minister of the Marine and of War, reputedly the Queen's ex-lover, and since Caracciolo's death, Prime Minister, Acton was an able and determined administrator, who had however been impotent to impose his ideas of reform and good government on a country where corruption was endemic and justice went to the highest bidder. Nevertheless it was he who had persuaded an unwilling King to receive the French Republican envoys, and when a French squadron had anchored in the Bay in December 1792, he had granted most of their demands, well knowing the city was in no state to resist. Acton was quietly working in 1793 to promote an English alliance while averting a total break with Paris – an ever more difficult task.

Last, if hardly least, of this odd quintet of personalities came the King. He had already reigned for thirty-four years and would do so for another thirty-two. Yet although he had been a bright and intelligent child, his education had been shamefully neglected. Ferdinand had been encouraged to amuse himself with sports and games in the company of illiterate servant boys rather than of those who could have cultivated his mind. Years before Hamilton had described him as 'ambitious to come out of his minority, but more desirous of becoming his own master to follow his caprices rather than to govern his kingdom'. His brother-in-law, the Emperor Joseph thought him 'puerile and indolent; he is quite ignorant of the past and present and has never thought about the future'. Convinced of the divine right of Kings, he still preferred to leave business to his Queen or ministers, who incurred the odium for unpopular decisions, while Ferdinand, the lazy, pleasure-loving sportsman, nicknamed *Il Re Nasone* (King Nose) by his subjects because of his enormous proboscis, remained the idol of the *lazzaroni*, the Neapolitan mob.

Such was the situation into which Captain Nelson stepped. Sir William, sensing the importance of the occasion, invited Nelson to stay at the ambassadorial residence, Palazzo Sessa. The King and Queen, thrilled by the capture of Toulon, paid him every attention. He was placed on Ferdinand's right for the banquet at the Palazzo Reale, was received again at the country palace of Portici, and as a final compliment the King proposed to visit the *Agamemnon* on the Sunday, September 15th. Hood's request for 6,000 troops to help garrison Toulon was duly granted. Nelson's brief visit had been a resounding success. Moreover the Ambassador, his wife and the naval captain had liked each other immediately, while Emma had been especially kind to Josiah Nisbet, the awkward midshipman stepson, taking him round the sights of the city. It had been unfortunate that on the Sunday morning the *Agamemnon* received news that a French convoy had been sighted off Sardinia, which caused Nelson to put to sea forthwith. He retained many happy memories of his four days in Naples, writing home to Fanny: 'Lady Hamilton has been wonderfully kind and good to Josiah. She is a young woman of amiable manners, who does honour to the station to which she is raised.' As yet there was definitely no trace of the infatuation which was to gain them both such notoriety in the future.

Five years elapsed before Nelson set foot in Naples again. During that time much happened. Toulon was evacuated by the Allies before Christmas 1793, mainly thanks to the exertions of a young French artillery officer Napoleon Buonaparte. Nothing had been achieved, and 600 Neapolitan soldiers were among the dead. In 1796 Napoleon had led the Army of Italy on its whirlwind campaign of conquest, causing every regime in the peninsula to sue for peace, even if neither side had any intention of keeping it. Maria Carolina fretted that Acton had lost his grip, and conjured up the wildest horrors to which they would all soon be subjected. She became Buonaparte's reluctant admirer: 'If he dies they should reduce him to powder and give a dose of it to each ruling sovereign and two to each of their ministers. Then things would go better.'

In fact the situation in Naples was by no means so hopeless. In 1794 the police did uncover a plot to seize the forts, massacre the royal family and raise the mob, but in the end only three of the conspirators were hanged, although many of the nobility were found to be implicated or to have revolutionary sentiments. Hamilton gloomily summed up the situation, finding the King 'widely loved, neglectful of affairs of state, although certainly not deficient in understanding', the Queen 'unpopular but feared', while Acton 'even if capable and honest is unable to delegate, hence half the business is conducted by corrupt clerks'. The Queen was now on intimate terms with '*ma bien chère Milady*', as she termed Emma, and passed on her woes as well as much confidential information to the British Embassy (for example that Spain was intending to treat for peace with France). The strains of the times had made both Hamiltons quite ill; Sir William was beginning to feel his age and to look forward to retirement, and Emma was getting fat. One acute observer, Sir Gilbert Elliot, noted: 'her person is nothing short of monstrous for its enormity and is growing every day . . . Her face is still beautiful; she is all nature yet all art, that is to say her manners are perfectly unpolished, of course very easy, although not with the ease of good breeding, but of a barmaid.'

More Napoleonic victories overshadowed everything else in 1797, compelling Austria to sue for peace at Campo Formio that October. In February 1798 Berthier's army occupied Rome, sending the octo-genarian Pope to exile in France, where he soon died. With the occupation of the Papal States, the enemy was at the very frontiers of Naples. Ferdinand's ministers did not however dare be anything except conciliatory. 'Nominally neutral, but never in our feelings,' Maria Carolina had written to Emma, yet the Court had to receive France's aggressive and egalitarian ambassador. Sir William felt his prospects of leave were receding indefinitely. Fearing the worst, he catalogued his considerable collection at Palazzo Sessa; 347 pictures altogether and innumerable classical objects. It would have been an understatement to say that a saviour was much needed at Naples to deliver them from the French.

Since 1793 Nelson's career had progressed by leaps and bounds. He had lost his right eye in Corsica, and had distinguished himself by his vigour in pursuing the enemy off the coast of France in 1795, although his cautious commanding officer, Hotham, had twice missed the chance of a general fleet engagement. It was at this time that he met Commodore Francesco Caracciolo, captain of the Neapolitan warship – the 74-gun *Tancredi* – who took umbrage at Nelson's headstrong tactics. Hood had been replaced by Sir John Jervis, but it was not until February 1797 that a major naval battle took place, against the Spanish fleet now allied with France. The glorious English victory off Cape St Vincent was largely due to Nelson, whose brilliant action in putting his ship clean across the bows of the largest Spanish man-of-war, broke the line and forced a general engagement. Although his ship was badly mauled, he had proceeded to lay alongside, board and capture two more Spanish vessels. At last promoted Rear Admiral of the Blue, Nelson was also given a Knighthood and the Order of the Bath. After an unsuccessful attack on Tenerife that summer, in which he lost an arm, Nelson was sent home for some overdue leave.

He returned to England to a hero's welcome and to a warm reunion with Fanny, receiving the Freedom of London and of Norwich and finally finding a home, Roundwood, in Suffolk. However the Admiral was not to enjoy his leave for long. Within six months Lord Spencer at the Admiralty had offered him fresh employment. In March 1798, Nelson broke his flag aboard the *Vanguard*, and stopping briefly to consult with his commander, Jervis, who was lying off Lisbon with the Mediterranean fleet, he sailed on to blockade Toulon. Unfortunately the *Vanguard* was dismasted in a gale, and while repairs were being done, Buonaparte slipped out of the port with thirteen warships and 400 transports bound for an unknown destination. Although lacking his frigates, 'the eyes of the fleet', Nelson set off in pursuit with thirteen sail of the line – for Troubridge had just brought up reinforcement.

On June 17th the British squadron rode at anchor in Naples Bay and the Admiral immediately contacted the Hamiltons, for he urgently needed frigates and the use of a port to revictual his ships. Emma sent him a formal letter of welcome, and another which contained a note from the Queen which he was asked to kiss! Nelson did not go ashore, but his emissaries, Hardy and Troubridge, were conducted by Sir William to an unsatisfactory interview with Acton and the Foreign Minister, the anglophobe Marquis de Gallo. The government was terrified of infringing its fragile neutrality, but Acton gave unofficial assurance that the British ships could be provisioned at any port in the kingdom, 'under the rose'. With this the Admiral had to be content; it was clear that no frigates would be provided.

The unpleasant news that Napoleon had seized Malta and evicted the Knights of St John reached Nelson on June 22nd. Guessing the French were making for Egypt, he immediately set out in pursuit. Arriving off Alexandria on June 28th, he found the roads deserted, and after chasing around the Levant coasts for three weeks, he was back at Syracuse empty-handed on July 20th. Nelson had twice missed the French fleet by a couple of hours although lacking any frigates he could not have known it. Now he rested his exhausted crews, some of whom had had no fresh provisions for two-and-a-half months. Needless to add the governor, personally courteous enough, denied ever having received any orders from Acton, but lacking the force could not oppose the reprovisioning and rewatering. Reports of a hugh French army at sea had spread as much alarm in Sicily as in Naples, and the local population flocked to greet the English. A month of fruitless searching had deeply depressed Nelson. 'The devil's children have the devil's luck,' he wrote to Sir William.

Nevertheless, he was at sea again by July 23rd, and within a week at last heard some definite news. The French fleet had been seen four weeks earlier steering south-east from Candia. Convinced that Napoleon really had invaded Egypt, the Admiral followed with his ships under full sail. At last his patience was to be rewarded, for on August 1st seventeen French warships were sighted anchored in Aboukir Bay. In the preceding three weeks, Napoleon had captured Alexandria, won the Battle of the Pyramids, and after a triumphant entry into Cairo he controlled all of Lower Egypt. But nothing could have deterred Nelson. At 5.30pm he gave the signal to engage. Admiral de Brueys had not expected a night attack and his ships were strung out across the bay, the oldest and weakest in the van near the island. It was however possible, to any clear-sighted naval tactician, for the English to break the line.

Captain Samuel Hood, a relation of the old Admiral, asked leave to lead into battle in the *Zealous*. Within an hour eight British men-of-war were engaging five French vessels, all undermanned with their port guns loose and their decks obstructed by baggage and mess furniture. At 8pm Nelson was hit in the face by flying shot above his good eye, and was carried bleeding profusely to the cockpit. Fortunately his wound was superficial. By 8.30pm the French ships had begun to strike their colours, and at 10.05pm their flagship, the 120-gun *L'Orient*, blew up with a deafening explosion. Although firing did not cease until 3am, and broke out again at dawn, the battle was over. Of thirteen French ships-of-the-line, nine had been taken and two burned; only Villeneuve with two men-of-war and two frigates had escaped. British casualties were estimated at 200 dead and 700 wounded, while the French had lost 5,225 men. Nelson's calculated risk in entering strange waters in the dark, with neither charts nor pilots, to perform a tricky naval manoeuvre, had paid off and resulted in a magnificent Victory.

'My Lord, Almighty God has blessed His Majesty's Armies in the late Battle,' ran the despatch to London. It took over two months to reach England, and such was the relief it brought that Lord Spencer on hearing it fainted in the Admiralty corridor. The good tidings reached Naples much sooner – by September 3rd – occasioning general rejoicing and the departure of the French envoy, unhappy at the court's ingrained hostility. By then the British fleet was already on its way there to rest and refit; a slow voyage indeed with so many prizes in tow and so much damage to rectify, plus contrary winds the whole way. And as reports of the Battle of the Nile slowly percolated round

Europe, Nelson, 'with his one lame arm and gallant fighting spirit', won for himself a lasting place in history.

On September 22nd Nelson's ships dropped anchor in Naples Bay. A mass of pleasure boats came out to greet them, followed by the Ambassador's barge, which drew alongside the *Vanguard* to a 13-gun salute. 'Up flew her Ladyship and exclaiming: "Oh God, is it possible?" she fell into my arm more dead than alive,' as the Admiral wrote a few days later to his wife. An hour later the royal galley came alongside and the King came aboard. In his suite was Commodore Caracciolo, who supervised nine-year old Prince Leopold's nautical education. After a further three hours the *Vanguard* finally reached port, and Nelson went ashore with the Hamiltons and their guest, Miss Cornelia Knight, the spinster daughter of distinguished parents and long resident in Italy. They drove to Palazzo Sessa, the first night that the Admiral had spent off his flagship for six months.

Soon, however, the incessant round of entertainment began to pall. Unquestionably Nelson was still in love with Fanny at that time. When asked if the day of Aboukir could now be accounted the happiest of his life, he answered: 'No, the happiest was that on which I married Lady Nelson.' He had to sit through banquet after banquet in his honour at the Palace or the Embassy. Maria Carolina received him privately, calling him the Saviour of Italy. Gifts poured in: the Sultan sent a silver canteen and a 'chelengk' (a diamond ornament taken from an imperial turban) among other presents; many sovereigns sent bejewelled boxes and miniatures; the East India Company voted him £10,000. Only his own government's grant of a barony and of a pension of £2,000pa for three lives was considered inadequate by his friends. And on September 29th Emma gave a party in honour of the hero's fortieth birthday, where the 1,800 guests were all presented with buttons or ribbons bearing Nelson's name. While a rostral column with the inscription *Veni, vidi, vici* was unveiled, Emma sang a new verse to the National Anthem:

> 'Join we great Nelson's name
> First on the roll of fame,
> Him let us sing,
> Spread we his fame around,
> Honour of British ground,
> Who made Nile's shores resound
> God Save our King!'

Both Hamiltons revelled in these festivities. In fairness it must be said that they were still happily married. Emma had been a faithful wife to Sir William and had not as yet exposed him to the ridicule he had feared. If he, in failing health, had not been a demanding husband, she had certainly worked hard for him, translating despatches and correspondence into French and Italian, carrying the Queen's messages and supervising endless diplomatic entertaining. But her enhanced position had not correspondingly enhanced her intellect, and her self-criticism had vanished as her self-dramatisation had grown. 'I am almost sick of grandeur,' she wrote to Greville, but in truth she merely hankered after a larger stage for her activities.

Very different was Nelson's reaction. On the day after his party he could write to Jervis: 'I trust My Lord in a week we shall be at sea. I am very unwell and the miserable conduct of this court is not likely to cool my irritable temper. It is a country of fiddlers and poets, whores and scoundrels.' On top of all this, his stepson had got drunk at the party and had accused him of paying attentions to Lady Hamilton which were properly due to Josiah's mother. Moreover, to compound his irritation, all his and Sir William's efforts to persuade Ferdinand's vacillating ministers to march against the French seemed in vain. The Austrian General Mack, who pleasantly surprised Nelson by his business-like approach, was appointed to command the army. Yet no encouragement came from Vienna, whose government was determined to make France appear as the aggressor. After waiting another fortnight for his ships to be refitted, the Admiral sailed off in mid-October to blockade Malta, whose garrison showed no signs of surrendering.

By October 31st Nelson was back in Naples, and attended Mack's review of the royal troops, 30,000 strong. This was held at Caserta, the immense palace built by the Bourbon kings to outdo Versailles, and still being improved. The Admiral stayed at the Hamiltons' villino at the gates, and at various councils of war offered to transport 4,000 Neapolitan infantry to Leghorn to take the French in the rear. Ferdinand remained pusillanimous as ever, and the exasperated Nelson told him 'either to advance, trusting in God for his blessing on a just cause and prepared to die, sword in hand, or remain quiet and wait to be kicked out of your kingdom'. Perhaps these blunt words achieved something, for on November 22nd, the King and Mack marched off to Rome at the head of the army, while the English ships sailed for Leghorn.

This part of the campaign was totally successful. The troops were landed, the town quickly surrendered, and by December 5th the Admiral was back in Naples. Ferdinand's advance was equally swift; despite the shortcomings of his commissariat his troops were in Rome within six days. The French had already evacuated the city and the King made a triumphal entry. His triumph was, however, short-lived. General Championnet moved to counterattack and the Neapolitan army dissolved as chaff before the wind, some of them running thirty miles without stopping. The retreat became a rout, while many of the officers demonstrated that their sympathies lay with the enemy. 'They have not lost much honour, for God knows they had but little to lose, but they lost all they had,' was Nelson's sardonic comment. On December 13th Ferdinand made an ignominious return to his capital with the horrified Queen rightly predicting that, although war had still not been declared, the French would soon follow him. Quite hysterical, Maria Carolina begged the English not to desert her or her children in their hour of need. Nelson reassured her that nothing could have been further from his thoughts.

Plans had already been made to evacuate the royal family, the British residents and sundry French and Corsican emigrés, for whom two polaccas had been chartered. The difficulties were in reality considerable, as the Admiral had solely the *Vanguard* at his disposal, every other ship of his squadron being on station off Leghorn, Malta or Egypt. Although the prospective invasion aroused deep feelings of patriotism, the mood of the Neapolitan mob was uncertain. Only Egidio Pallio and his lazzaroni swore undying devotion to their King. Furthermore the Queen, as well as bombarding Emma with daily missives, insisted on loading aboard all the Bourbon jewels, bullion and treasure, to an estimated value of £2,500,000. Apart from the one British man-of-war, there was a small Portuguese squadron which Nelson discounted, and two of Ferdinand's ships, commanded by Caracciolo, the *Archimedes* and *Sannita*, whose crews' loyalty he considered dubious.

On a stormy night on December 21st, ten members of the royal family, the Hamiltons and a mass of others were secretly embarked. December 22nd dawned so rough that any communication between the various ships – with 2,000 refugees crowded aboard them, rolling at anchor in a heavy ground-swell in Naples Bay – proved impossible. The next day the wind abated a little, and several deputations sailed out from the capital to beg the King not to abandon his people. Ferdinand's mind was however set on going to Palermo, his resolve strengthened by the appearance of Mack, a defeated wraith, begging him to flee before the French arrived. At 7pm on December 23rd the *Vanguard* and a large convoy set sail for Sicily. It was a terrible voyage. The crossing lasted nearly three days, during which they were battered by a violent tempest. Most of the refugees, convinced their hour had come, spent their time in prayer, and on Christmas day, six-year old Prince Charles Albert died of convulsions in Emma's arms. Only she, Mrs Cadogan and one steward had remained on their feet during the voyage. Before dawn on December 26th the *Vanguard* anchored off Palermo mole and the exhausted royal party tottered ashore 'to the loudest acclamation and apparent joy' of their Sicilian subjects.

The Colli Palace, damp and gloomy, was hardly in a fit state for visitors, but the royal party nevertheless lodged there. The Hamiltons and Nelson were accommodated in the charming Villa Bastioni on Marino Parade. Unfortunately in Palermo's wintry drizzle it was cold and draughty, 'lacking chimneys and calculated only for summer,' grumbled Sir William to Greville, adding: 'the Admiral is not in robust health'. The Queen was sunk in the depths of depression, writing to Gallo in Vienna: 'Remember with compassion the unhappiest of mortals'; only the King, looking forward to new sport, seemed impervious to the disasters that had befallen them all.

The situation could actually have been far worse. The Bourbons still possessed part of their realm, and had saved many of their treasured possessions from what would have been certain confiscation by the French. In Naples, disaster had rapidly ensued. General Pignatelli, left as Regent, had tamely surrendered to the French, although the Portuguese had managed to burn all warships in the Bay. On learning the ruinous terms of the armistice dictated by General Championnet, the city mob rose and seized the forts. Pignatelli fled to Sicily and the lazzaroni put up a hopeless, although fierce, resistance, sustaining 3,000 casualties for 1,000 enemy dead, and halting the French advance for three days. Luckily Championnet was a good diplomat, and he soon reconciled the Neapolitans to the newly-proclaimed 'Parthen-opean Republic'.

News of this did little to alleviate the despondency of the exiles at Palermo. Lodgings were hard to find; there was only one hotel in the town (in Sicily, quipped the cynics) where Miss Knight and her mother had been fortunate to find rooms. Emigrés were scattered throughout Palermo in crumbling, uncomfortable palazzi. The Queen was convinced she would be assassinated by republicans, while the King presided over up to three councils a day, which never decided anything. Harassed by correspondence with half-a-dozen foreign governments, trying to supervise sixteen ships-of-the-line scattered throughout the Mediterranean, infuriated by the pretensions of Sir Sidney Smith, whose aspirations to an independent command in the Levant occasioned several furious letters to the Admiralty, Nelson felt none too cheerful himself. His greatest consolation lay in the Hamiltons' company. The previous December he had written home innocently enough to Fanny: 'What can I say of her and Sir William's goodness to me? They are in fact with the exception of you and my beloved father the dearest friends I have in the world.' But by now, so it seemed to many observers, his sentiments could no longer be described as innocent.

With the coming of spring the weather improved, as did people's spirits. The ménage à trois, or 'Tria Juncta in Uno' as Emma wittily nicknamed them (that being the motto of the Order of the Bath which both men wore), moved to the Palazzo Palagonia nearer the mole, where the Hamiltons were again able to entertain in grand style. The expenses of this establishment were so great that Sir William could not have afforded it had the Admiral not generously offered to share them. Even after two other English families, the Nobles and Gibbses had, with their children, moved in as paying guests, there was still plenty of space. Splendid parties were thrown, followed by heavy drinking and gambling in mixed company – the Sicilians were only too glad to part the exiles from their money. Nelson seemed happy in this incongruous environment, and when in spring Fanny wrote to say she wanted to join her husband if he did not return home soon, he replied sharply: 'If you had come, I would only have struck my flag and carried you back again, for it would be impossible to set up an establishment at either Naples or Palermo.' He claimed that only the national interest kept him abroad and that if the King was restored he would be back in the summer.

Comments on the behaviour at Palazzo Palagonia and Emma's theatrical antics grew increasingly acerbic. Young Charles Lock, who had just arrived as Consul-General, a post secured for him by his powerful relations, was a particularly bitter critic. He had been kindly received by Sir William, who had found scarce lodgings for his family at Porta Felice, but he hoped that the ambassador would soon retire – an intention he had publicly announced. 'I shall then be left in the charge of corresponding with ministers in England.' As spring advanced without this happening, his impatience grew along with his homesickness and scorn for the social scene in Palermo: 'The King gives a superb gala in the evening in honour of Acton's birthday, and a great bore it will be.' Not surprisingly relations between Emma and Charles and his wife Cecilia were frigid. At one banquet a Turkish emissary of the Czar, who had brought Nelson a snuff-box from his master, brandished a scimitar with which he boasted he had decapitated twenty French prisoners. Emma, exclaiming: 'Oh let me see the sword that did the glorious deed', then kissed the blade encrusted with Jacobin blood and handed it to Nelson. Thereupon the pregnant Cecilia Lock fainted and had to be carried from the room. 'Her Ladyship said it was a piece of affectation, and made no effort to assist her guest; the truth is she was jealous of her beauty and insinuated that being a sister of the late Lord Edward Fitzgerald (an Irish nationalist killed in the 1798 Rising) she must necessarily be a Jacobin herself. The toadeaters applauded, but many groaned and cried "shame" loud enough to reach the ears of the Admiral, who turned pale and hung his head . . .' Such imbroglios reflected scant credit on anybody, as Emma publicly paraded her conquest of Nelson, while Sir William, ever the 18th century rationalist, turned a diplomatic blind eye.

The inactivity prevalent at Palermo had sapped everyone's energies. The Queen complained furiously of Ferdinand's indifference: 'As far as he is concerned Naples might be in the land of the Hottentots', but the truth was that the King had lost faith in her judgement and he blamed her for the employment of Mack and the march on Rome. Having suspended the viceregal administration, and made the ex-Viceroy, Prince di Luzzi, his Minister for Internal Affairs, the King became suddenly convinced that he must end the light taxation of the aristocracy. The 1798 session of Parliament was stormy, with the Houses demanding that Caracciolo's reforms be annulled before they voted further *donativi*. Sicilian delight at the King's arrival had given way to grumbles at the cost of maintaining the court and at their lack of participation in government. They remained fanatically franco-phobe, however, and when a ship carrying 120 French refugees from Alexandria put in at Augusta, they were promptly butchered.

One bright spot, indeed the only one, had been provided by Cardinal Fabrizio Ruffo. This militant prelate, scion of a great Calabrese family, had landed in his native country in February with only eight companions to raise the Southern provinces for the Bourbons. His 'Christian Army of the Holy Faith' made astonishing progress. Soon he led 17,000 men and most of Calabria was in revolt. French attempts to democratise the masses and abolish primogeniture, ecclesiastical titles and the cult of saints, had been ill-received, while the middle classes, originally Jacobin in their sympathies, were disillusioned with their foreign occupiers and the leech-like Republican agents and contractors. Ruffo's men sacked Crotone with gusto when it resisted, although their excesses were no worse than those committed by the French and Republicans in Puglia. General MacDonald, who had replaced Championnet at Naples, began to grow alarmed, but whenever he tried to crush one popular uprising, another, hydra-like, arose in its place.

Nelson's spirits began to rise. The arrival of dynamic General Sir Charles Stuart with two regiments from Minorca ensured that Messina was properly garrisoned. Troubridge with his squadron was closely blockading Naples, and could report by early April that all the neighbouring islands had rehoisted the royal standard. The Vicar-General's undisciplined horde, now strengthened by Turkish and Russian troops, was fast approaching the capital, Although Ferdinand had forbidden Ruffo to assault it before the English fleet arrived, he also held a private letter from Acton authorising him to re-take it independently if he could. Austria had at last declared war on France and an Austro-Russian army under Marshal Suvarov was advancing into Northern Italy. Its leaders might continue to pass Utopian laws; they even instituted a mini-Terror, shooting some royalist prisoners without trial, but the Parthenopean Republic was on the brink of collapse.

'I ever preach that rewards and punishments are the foundation of all government,' wrote Nelson, whose political views were simplistic in the extreme, while Sir William – old, ailing and utterly disheartened that the *Colossus*, bearing his precious collection of Greek vases, had foundered off the Scillies – did nothing to correct them. Yet obviously some practical accommodation with the rebels had to be devised, despite some several cases of treachery. Commodore Caracciolo, for example, had always resented the King's decision to travel to Palermo aboard a British ship rather than his own (whose crew had been so short-handed they had anyway to be supplemented by twenty-five English sailors). He had come to Sicily 'looking utterly miserable and scarcely speaking,' in Miss Knight's words, but had left again in February on the plea that the Republicans would seize the estates of absentee landlords. In fact evidence showed incontrovertible evidence that on returning to Naples Caracciolo had signed proclamations describing Ferdinand as a vile tyrant, and was given command of the rebels' navy. In an attack on the island of Procida, he had even fired on the *Minerva*, his old flagship. To Nelson it was more important to deal with such a man in exemplary fashion than to seek to regain his allegiance.

His plans to escort their Sicilian Majesties back to Naples had to be shelved abruptly on the news that nineteen French ships had escaped from Brest and were heading for the Mediterranean, perhaps to join up with the Spanish fleet. On May 19th Nelson put to sea with heartfelt regrets, sending Emma a message on embarking: 'You and good Sir William have spoiled me for any place but with you.' Three times during the next month he put to sea on orders from Lord Keith, now commander in chief, but the enemy never materialised. Meanwhile, after MacDonald's troops had withdrawn to Caserta, Ruffo's 'Christian' army entered Naples, indulging in an orgy of revenge which the Cardinal was powerless to prevent. The remaining Republicans retired into the forts, except St Elmo, whose French garrison refused to admit them.

On June 14th, Ruffo signed a capitulation with the enemy, which was both humane and sensible, although his emissary, Micheroux, exceeded his instructions by agreeing to a general pardon and liberty for any rebels that chose to do so to leave for France, terms which were unlikely to have proved acceptable to the Court. The Cardinal's reasons for signing were in part humanitarian – he wished to avoid any further bloodshed and looting – and in part practical, as he wanted the forts to surrender speedily, hourly expecting the French fleet to arrive before the British. Captain Foote of the *Seahorse*, temporarily in charge of the small English flotilla, also signed the document.

Hearing the reports that Naples had surrendered, Nelson re-embarked on June 21st, taking the Hamiltons with him. Aboard the *Foudroyant*, to which the Admiral had shifted his flag, all three laboured under some mental strain – Nelson because he was disobeying Keith's orders by sailing to Naples rather than in search of the French fleet, Sir William because he felt unwell and shaken by the loss of his amphorae, and Emma in euphoric mood because she knew that her infatuation with Nelson was now mutual and she also believed herself to be the Queen's emissary.

The *Foudroyant* dropped anchor in the Bay on the afternoon of June 24th, and Foote was summoned aboard immediately. He was bluntly told that he had blundered by signing the capitulation, and 'had been imposed upon by that worthless fellow, Cardinal Ruffo, who was endeavouring to form a party hostile to the interests of the sovereign'. That night, at Emma's urging, Nelson gave a large quantity of arms to Egidio Pallio, the ruffianly leader of the lazzaroni. Riots promptly broke out all over the city. The next morning the British ships approached Naples in line of battle, a summons was sent to St Elmo demanding unconditional surrender from its French garrison rather than the three-week armistice previously agreed to, while the Republicans in the Castelli Uovo and Nuovo were refused permission to embark, and the Cardinal was sent the Admiral's written opinion 'of the infamous terms entered into with the rebels'.

That afternoon Ruffo came aboard to explain matters and a long dispute followed. Nelson's contention 'that no power on Earth has a right to stand between Rebels and Traitors and their gracious King' was countered by the argument that clemency provided the best hope for re-establishment of the monarchy. Ruffo also threatened to withdraw all troops if the truce was broken and to make the English complete the reconquest themselves. Impasse was soon reached, while the Hamiltons, acting as interpreters, made no effort to help find a compromise. Convinced 'that an Admiral is no match in talking with a Cardinal', Nelson then committed his views to paper: that no treaty could be approved without the express sanction of the King and the British Commander in Chief. Early on June 26th, however, Sir William handed Ruffo a note to say that the Admiral had resolved not to interfere with the terms of the capitulation until explicit orders had arrived from Palermo. Thereupon the Republicans in the castles surrendered, albeit without the honours of war, and were confined aboard vessels that were not allowed to sail. Fort St Elmo was closely blockaded by land and sea.

Orders at last arrived from Palermo on June 28th. Acton's letter disavowed the capitulation and demanded that no terms save unconditional surrender were to be made with the Neapolitan Jacobins. Disgusted, the Vicar-General tendered his resignation and declined to support further operations against the French. Nelson considered arresting him, then decided against it. The prisoners' transports were brought under the guns of the British ships; all rebels who had gone home were told to submit to the King's clemency within twenty-four hours. Foote was sent off to Sicily with a request that Ferdinand, the Queen (thrice underlined) and Acton should embark forthwith for Naples. Maria Carolina's presence might have been deemed a mixed blessing. She had just written to Emma: 'Finally, dear Milady, I recommend to treat our capital as if it were an Irish town in a similar state of rebellion.'

Precisely at 10am on June 29th a court-martial assembled on board the *Foudroyant* for the trial of Commodore Caracciolo. The latter had

1. Interior of the Chapel at Maniace.

2. Icon of the Virgin, reputedly painted by St Luke.

3. Capitals from the portico of Maniace Chapel.

4. Fortified street houses in Randazzo.

5. The basilica of S. Monica at Randazzo.

6. View of Collegio Capizzi at Bronte, founded 1642.

7. View of Piano della Sconfitta.

8. Palazzina Cinese near Palermo, where Nelson received the King's grant of the Duchy of Bronte.

9. The Palazzo Palagonia, the house in Palermo where Nelson and the Hamiltons stayed in 1799.

10. King Ferdinand IV of the Two Sicilies.

11. Queen Maria Carolina of the Two Sicilies.

12. Emma Hamilton in 1791.

13. Embroidered panel of the death of Nelson.

14. Death of Captain Alexander Hood:
from a painting at Maniace.

15. Nelson: print from a portrait by Beechey.

16. Nelson's decanter and glasses from the wardroom of HMS *Victory*.

17. Portrait of Admiral Lord Hood.

18. Portrait of Admiral Lord Hood's brother, Admiral Lord Bridport.

19. Exterior of Trafalgar Park [www.trafalgarpark.com] (courtesy of Michael Wade).

20. Portrait of 2nd Countess Nelson (courtesy of Michael Wade).

21. William, 1st Earl Nelson, brother of Horatio Nelson (courtesy of the National Portrait Gallery).

22. Portrait of Don Federico Gravina,
Commander of the Spanish fleet at Trafalgar.

23. Charlotte Mary Nelson, the future Lady Bridport
(© National Maritime Museum).

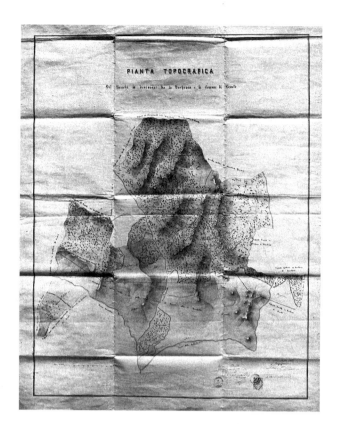

24. Topographical map of the Duchy at the time of its presentation to Nelson.

25. Map of the original land grant of the Duchy to Nelson.

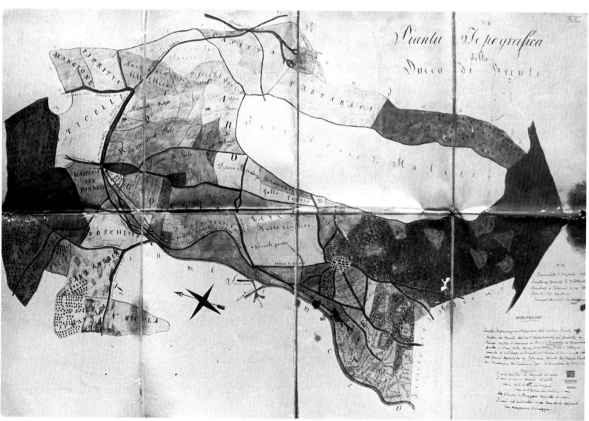

(Left) **26.** Aerial view of Maniace (courtesy of Speer Ogle).

(Below left) **27.** The 2nd Viscount Bridport, Alec Nelson Hood's father.

(Below right) **28.** Bust of Alec Nelson Hood.

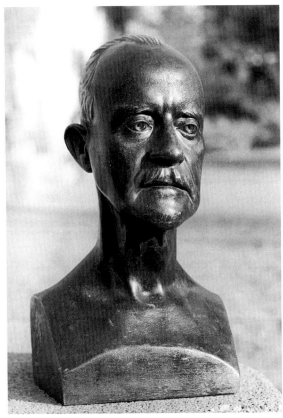

29. General view of the private family cemetery at Maniace.

30. Spy cartoon of Alec Nelson Hood, "a little bandbox duke".

31. A view of Otaiti, the summer house in the hills to which the Duchy administration moved every summer.

32. The tomb of Philip Thovez, administrator of the Duchy, in the chapel at Maniace.

33. George Woods, the Duchy administrator, with the *campieri*, or forest guards, in their uniforms (courtesy of the late George Woods).

34. The Duchy administration in 1938. From L. to R.: Giuseppe Ciraldo, clerk; Dott. Alfio Nicolosi, technical director; George Woods, administrator of the Duchy; Niblett, his successor; L Hughes, superintendent of the forests; Mario Carastro, accountant. (courtesy of the late George Woods)

been recently captured, hiding down a well, by Ruffo's men, and had been handed over to the English. Remembering the Admiral's belief that condign punishment was the foundation of good government, it appears likely that he had made up his mind in advance. Caracciolo was arraigned before a tribunal of five senior Neapolitan officers, presided over by Count Thurn, an Austrian in Ferdinand's service. The trial lasted two hours, during which no advocate or witnesses for the defence were allowed, while the defendant's request to be tried by British officers was refused. At midday the verdict, a foregone conclusion, was announced; four officers, including Thurn, had found him guilty of high treason and had voted for the death sentence, two against.

Nelson ordered that Caracciolo be hanged from the yard-arm of his former flagship, the *Minerva*, at 5pm that day, ignoring all pleas for an appeal or for the sentence to be changed to a firing-squad. Attempts by Thurn and Sir William to have a 24-hour stay of execution granted were brushed aside, and the sentence was carried out. Although only 47, Caracciolo looked 'wretched, old and grey-haired', but an observer noted 'his countenance denoted stern resolution to endure that misery like a man'. At sunset the rope was severed, letting the body fall into the sea.

Probably no single action in a great, if controversial, career has earned Nelson so much opprobrium from posterity – although the storm over Caracciolo's death had yet to break. Lord Spencer explicitly approved the Admiral's conduct: 'The intentions and motives by which all your measures have been governed have been as pure and good as their success has been complete.' And undeniably in the heated atmosphere engendered by a recent counter-revolution, the prime consideration had to be that justice, however summary, must be seen to be done to traitors to their sovereign, especially as royal judges sent earlier to try such cases had balked at the task.

Humanity had certainly been lacking: all extenuating circumstances (such as Caracciolo's assertion that he had been offered the choice of taking command of the Republicans' navy or of being shot) had been disregarded, while the propriety of using an English war-ship for a foreigner's court martial was dubious. His outburst that he was not guilty of treason as the King had already deserted him and other loyal subjects was not unjustified. Moreover, the callousness shown by the principal parties concerned did little good to their reputations; Emma was alleged to have watched the execution and then to have had herself rowed round the *Minerva* in a barge while the corpse was still dangling.

Of course all the critics could not be called impartial. Charles Lock was furious that he had not been asked to join the *Foudroyant*'s company; 'I underwent a severe mortification in not being invited to accompany Sir William or receiving any intimation of their designs, which I relied on as it had been promised me . . . but for this I may thank that superficial, grasping and vulgar-minded woman, whose wish to retain her husband in a situation his age and disinclination render him unfit for, has made her use every endeavour to keep me in the dark.' He castigated Nelson too: 'his extravagant love for her has made him the laughing-stock of the whole fleet'. Yet Lock's prime reason for getting to Naples was apparently: 'to obtain a house and accrocher a little of the loads of furniture, which the plunder of the wretched Jacobins has occasioned to be sold as cheap as dirt.' Thus when he did arrive in Naples several weeks later, his comments can scarcely be described as unbiased: 'You will hear with grief . . . of the stab our English honour has received in being employed to decoy these people, who had relied on our faith, into the most deplorable situation.' Thus also when Charles James Fox rose in the House six months later to regret that 'the atrocities of which we hear so much . . . do not, I fear, belong exclusively to the French . . . Naples, for instance . . .', it must not be forgotten that his probable informant was the husband of his first cousin, Cecilia Lock.

The King accompanied by Acton finally arrived in the Bay on July 10th, and for the next month Naples was governed from a British man-of-war. Ferdinand was too nervous of his newly regained subjects to go ashore once, although the Hamiltons paid one nostalgic visit to the plundered Palazzo Sessa. Loath to leave his excellent hunting in Sicily, he was in no mood for leniency. Although the Queen, who had reluctantly stayed behind in Palermo, daily bombarded Emma with instructions, she was not primarily responsible for the White Terror that followed. Nearly every night for the next nine months public executions continued on the Piazza del Mercate. The gruesome story that Caracciolo's corpse floated to the surface directly before the gaze of the horrified King is probably true. Sir William diplomatically suggested he had come to beg his sovereign's pardon, and Nelson is said to have arranged for a Christian burial in the church of Santa Lucia.

The Admiral's temper was not improved by another row with Lock. That rash young man had solicited the revictualling of the fleet, normally a Consul's prerogative, 'as the profits were large', and was unwise enough to add that the pursers were busily defrauding the victualling board by falsifying the price for stores purchased. An angry Nelson demanded his proofs, shouting to Hardy: 'Here, take him off from me. I am afraid, by God, he'll strike me!' Knowing that he could not reveal his informant's name, Lock was in an invidious position. The pursers wrote him a joint letter asking for proofs or a public retraction and, much chastened he more or less climbed down, although that was not to be the end of the matter. On top of this, Nelson received a despatch from Keith telling him, once the St Elmo garrison had surrendered, which it had on July 11th on receipt of a hefty bribe, to send part of his fleet to reinforce Minorca. When he ignored this request a second peremptory note resulted in the departure of three ships-of-the-line and one corvette.

On August 5th the *Foudroyant* sailed for Sicily, with the Admiral and the King aboard, the latter delighted to take passage in an English ship. After docking at the mole, the entire royal family came aboard to dine. Then, to a 21-gun salute, the party went ashore to a specially created landing-stage on which waited the assembled senators of Palermo, sweating in their togas in the midday sun. This heralded the start of weeks of festivities. Munificent gifts poured in for those deserving royal gratitude. Emma received a diamond necklace and Maria Carolina's portrait in miniature to wear round her neck, inscribed 'eterna gratitudine'; two coaches full of dresses replaced those she had lost at Naples. Sir William was given the King's Portrait set in jewels among other mementoes; indeed the Hamiltons' presents were reputedly worth £6,000.

In the next two days Emma passed on to Nelson several discreet hints from the Queen that the King was about to make him a splendid gift. On August 13th he received an official letter from the Prince di Luzzi offering him the Duchy of Bronte. After some hesitation he accepted, to be told that Ferdinand would write to George III for permission for him to use the Sicilian title and settle the succession to it as he chose. On reflection the Admiral felt this should pass to his father, then to his brothers and their children, and lastly to his sisters and their children. He took to signing his correspondence 'Bronte Nelson', changing that to 'Bronte, Nelson of the Nile', and finally settling on 'Nelson and Bronte'. Simultaneously a more tangible present arrived; the King sent him the diamond-hilted sword that Ferdinand's grandfather, Philip V, had received from his grandfather, Louis XIV, on departing from Paris to assume the Spanish throne.

The feast of Santa Rosalia, patron saint of Palermo, began in sultry summer weather on August 16th. It usually lasted for around five days, but this time the Queen had devised a spectacular finale over a fortnight later. At midnight on September 3rd, she gave an enormous *fête champêtre* to which all British naval officers were invited. In emulation of the ancient Romans' triumph for their generals, columns had been erected in the palace gardens, from which fluttered the flags of the allies: Russian, Portuguese, Turkish and English. Underneath the latter was an inscription reading; 'To Nelson, the Hero of the Century'. After a display of fireworks symbolising the blowing-up of *L'Orient*, everyone flocked to see 'the Temple of Fame', crowned by a trumpet-blowing goddess and occupied by waxworks of Nelson, Sir William and Emma, 'Britannia's Pride', crowned with laurel wreaths and grouped under the motto 'Tria Juncta in Uno', a wry comment, some thought, on their domestic situation.

A cantata, 'La Concordia Felice', commissioned for the occasion was sung, then little Prince Leopold solemnly thanked the Admiral, 'the guardian angel of his Papa for recovering his throne.' Nelson wept with emotion as bands struck up *See the Conquering Hero Comes* and Maria Carolina dressed as Juno with Emma dressed as Venus led him by the hand to the King's throne. Here he knelt while Ferdinand presented him with a diploma formally granting him the Duchy of Bronte. The fête was only marred by the behaviour of some of the more ebullient English midshipmen, who charged the royal guards waving their dress dirks and got a discharge of musketry in return. But everyone present agreed it had been a splendid and memorable evening, a fitting celebration of the heroic deeds Nelson had wrought for his mother country and its allies.

CHAPTER VII
Duke of Bronte

'It will be my aim for the rest of my life to follow that same conduct which has led me to obtain the royal favour, so that I may deserve its continuation,' the new Duke had written back to Luzzi when accepting the King's gift; while he assured Ferdinand: 'The bounty of Your Majesty has so overwhelmed me that I am unable to find words adequate to express my gratitude.' All his stipulations had been granted, and the normal provisions of inheritance by the nearest male, and thereafter by the nearest female relative were dispensed with in his case. 'His Britannic Majesty has consented that the Dukedom of Bronte and the estate with it should be absolutely given to Lord Nelson and will be entirely at his disposal without any restriction to relatives as his will may direct,' was the reply from London. The diploma creating the Duchy of Bronte was dated October 10th 1799, and after taking his oath of allegiance Nelson was formally granted the estate, the title of Duke, and the right to a seat in the House of Peers in the Sicilian Parliament, as well as the *merum et mistum imperium* previously claimed by the Rectors of the Hospital. Normally a large sum was payable on investiture, but after application to Ferdinand this too was waived.

There had initially been a choice between three possible estates for Nelson: the territory of Bisacquino, belonging to the Cathedral of Monreale; that of Partinico, belonging to the Abbey of Santa Maria d'Altofonte – both of these near Palermo; or that of Bronte. The King, who was interested in mythology, observed: 'Questa terra di Bronte è la piu adatta al caso,' ('This territory of Bronte is the best suited to the case'); and thus the decision was reached. He had also insisted that the estate should produce an annual income of not less than 6,000 and not more than 8,000 ounces, plus another 100 ounces from the exercise of *merum et mistum imperium*, some adjacent land would be added to it – and its owners suitably recompensed. The estate was to be a feudal domain, carrying the title of Duke.

The King lastly directed that the Rectors of the Hospital should be paid exactly the equivalent of their lost fief, free of all encumbrances and in perpetuity. The Rectors in no way resisted; they were delighted to be rid of their troublesome fief, which in 1791 they had petitioned the Crown to be allowed to convert into a long lease. Accounts of how the Brontesi received the news vary. Naturally Radice claimed they saw with dismay that they were to be subjected to a new tyranny, but an earlier and less prejudiced historian, Gesualdo De Luca, recorded that the news was received with joy; certainly the Basilian monks, formerly of Maniace, were delighted, for they hoped that the Duke would pay them their 200 ounces per annum more punctually than the Hospital had ever done.

Nelson at first viewed the prospect of his country estate and of the £3,000 annual income it was meant to produce with relish. Writing to his father from Palazzo Palagonia he offered him an immediate £500 a year, explaining he could not do more until he had heard if the Admiralty would pay all the debts he had incurred in entertaining the royal party aboard the *Foudroyant*, for he had refused to take any payment from the King. Busy as he then was at Palermo, and aware that at any moment he could be called away on his naval duties, he realised he must appoint a reliable agent to oversee affairs at Bronte, particularly after Ferdinand had also conceded in January 1800 the right of administering the municipality, which he promptly delegated to four appointed magistrates. Nelson complained of the lack of information he had been given about his new estate, yet the job of agent seemed an attractive proposition to offer somebody.

That same month he received a description of the Duchy which began thus: 'Bronte, an opulent and populous city at the foot of Mount Etna . . . is situated on an easy declivity towards the west,' continuing: 'The territory is fertile in vines, mulberries and all kinds of orchard fruits, it is well watered and produces excellent pasturage. The sheep are in such abundance that the cloth manufactured from their wool not only serves for the apparel of the inhabitants, but is exported and esteemed the best in that part of the country.' This fanciful account also described the town's principal Church of the Holy Trinity, with 24 priests under an Archpriest, seven lesser churches, five convents or monasteries and a hospital for the poor.

Fortunately, a suitable candidate was to hand. Back in the 1780s Sir

William had interested Maria Carolina in establishing an English garden at Caserta, and on the recommendation of Sir Joseph Banks, eminent botanist and President of the Royal Society, a skilled gardener, John Graeffer, had been sent out in 1786. Lacking any knowledge of the country, Graeffer and his family had taken some time to settle down, but by April 1787 he was reporting that everything should be finished within eighteen months, while the Queen, madly enthusiastic, was spending £50 a week on the project. In Naples, initial energy soon flagged, and work continued spasmodically, Graeffer's excellent English foreman being turned by the climate into 'a drunken dog'. The garden nevertheless survived, despite the King's belated desire to sow the site with Indian corn or turn it into a maze, and it had become a favourite place of royal relaxation by the 1790s. Subsequently Graeffer had received several commissions from the Neapolitan nobility and had fled to Palermo with the Court in 1798. Now short of work, he readily offered his services and left with his family that autumn for Bronte.

All too soon, disillusionment set in. Graeffer discovered that La Fragilia, a medium-sized farmhouse, was the sole habitable dwelling on the entire property. The Abbey buildings at Maniace were a picturesque ruin, roads simply did not exist. Moreover he found the Brontesi exercising their traditional rights of cutting wood and pasturing their animals without payment or permission all over the estate. They had ploughed up the Nave fief, only paying one-tenth of the crops by way of rent. His proclamations forbidding these abuses were ignored. Undeterred, Graeffer set about putting the buildings at Maniace into a habitable state. He was, however, becoming depressed. On April 22nd 1800, he wrote to Nelson: 'Your Lordship's letter of the 2nd inst. has damped my spirits very considerably, because it has deprived me of the pleasure of seeing you at Bronte before your intended departure for England.' He went on that he intended to go and live in the partially finished buildings among the bricks and mortar. His gout and bilious fever had abated, but Graeffer was appalled by the roguery he found everywhere. 'The lawyer, Don Gennaro Minessale, has turned out to be one of the greatest villains existing, the Vicar of Bronte, a most pious priest whom Mrs Graeffer took to be a saint, is really a cunning hypocrite and an avaricious scoundrel.' Finally he begged his employer to obtain a decree from the King annulling the leases on two farms, which would augment the estate's income by 100 ounces per annum.

In the intervening six months, Nelson had much else on his mind.

They had been full of quarrels with his allies, his civilian colleagues and his commanding officer. On the Sunday following his investiture, a major riot had erupted at Palermo between some Turkish seamen and the mob, leaving 120 dead and 80 badly wounded. Forbidden a hearing of his grievances, the enraged Ottoman Admiral forthwith set sail for the Bosphorus. The Portuguese squadron was recalled to Lisbon; it was announced that the Russian ships would be laid up for the winter. The dilatory King, who showed no wish to return to Naples, even after the recapture of Rome had removed the last obstacle to his doing so, maddened Nelson. He openly deplored his 'inactive service' at a corrupt court.

Meanwhile gossip about the ménage at Palazzo Palagonia was widespread. The Elgins, en route to take over the embassy in Constantinople, were disgusted by it. Lady Elgin reported: 'they say there was never a man turned so vainglorious in the world as Lord Nelson,' adding: 'I am told the Queen laughs very much at her to all the Neapolitans, but says her influence with Lord Nelson makes it worthwhile making up to her.' They considered Sir William long overdue for retirement, and found the investiture party at Palazzina Cinese a ridiculous extravagance; it had reputedly cost £6,000.

On October 5th Nelson weighed anchor for Minorca to protect an outward-bound British convoy 700 strong from a rumoured French fleet. This transpired to be Spanish and had in fact already turned back to Ferrol. He returned empty-handed to Palermo. All that autumn he worked feverishly to get supplies for the siege of Malta, even pledging his diamonds from the Czar and the income from Bronte as collateral. However the blockade proved unsuccessful and Valetta did not fall.

The feud with the Locks continued, Charles Lock writing home: 'We have in Lady Hamilton the bitterest enemy imaginable,' so when Sir William suggested he bury the hatchet: 'I answered His Excellency that it depended upon Lord Nelson alone whether I should be on a footing of coldness or of friendship.' Thus when the Admiral heard of Lock boasting of the thanks he had received from London for saving the Victualling Board 40 per cent in the purchase of fresh beef at Naples, he exploded. A stormy interview followed, after which Lock, while maintaining: 'that I consider myself wholly independent of military authority in the civil capacity of consul,' wrote what amounted to an apology in front of Sir William. Peace was ostensibly restored, and Lock, although complaining: 'I am totally in the dark if I have to take up the business,' still hoped that he would be left in charge when the Ambassador went home. Surely he was better than the Embassy's

Dutch secretary, whose English was so bad that he had once reported: 'His Sicilian Majesty is gone to Caserta, but from motives of economy has only taken a few of his courtesans'?

With the advent of winter, Nelson afforded fresh food for scandal by accompanying the Hamiltons to the rooms at La Nova, where heavy gambling took place. Even the faithful Troubridge remonstrated about 'the bad publicity from your nocturnal parties'. In January 1800 Lord Keith returned to the Mediterranean from leave. Nelson was told his acting command was ended, and was summoned to meet his chief off Genoa where, at a chilly interview, two temperamentally incompatible characters strove to be polite to each other. Both admirals sailed on to Palermo, where Keith spent 'eight long days'. They continued towards Malta, off which Nelson captured the *Généreux*, one of the French ships which had escaped him at Aboukir. He had however no intention of obeying Keith's orders to base himself at Messina or Syracuse, and requesting a fortnight's sick leave, he returned to Palermo.

In his absence the thunderbolt had struck. Sir William had been notified by the Foreign Office that he was being replaced by the Hon. Arthur Paget, who had already begun his journey out in a fast frigate. Unclear whether after 36 years service he 'was being kicked up or down out of my post', Sir William was very upset, although Emma was blithely planning her return to Naples after a season in London. The Queen professed herself mortified, but the King refused to interfere or solicit their reappointment through his own ambassador. He was sick of being castigated for his lethargy, petty meanness and despotic temper, and had come to see Emma as Maria Carolina's evil genius. 'The fatal Paget' arrived in Palermo to a very cool reception, Sir William petulantly refusing to present his own letters of recall until the day before he left. The conduct of state business had anyway almost ground to a halt, as the Prime Minister, aged 64, had decided by special dispensation to marry his 18-year old niece during Carnival.

Convinced that his work in Sicily was done, Nelson decided to return home with the Hamiltons, and Keith, relieved to see him go, raised no obstacles. First the trio embarked on the *Foudroyant* for a visit to Malta on April 23rd. Emma was now openly living with her lover, while Sir William was using his ill health as an excuse for avoiding public humiliation. Indeed to judge from subsequent events it was on this voyage that she became pregnant. At the end of May the party returned to Palermo for a week of leave-taking ceremonies. Nelson had intended to return to England as fast as possible, but now the Queen announced she wished to visit her imperial son-in-law in

Vienna, and requested their company en route. Frustrated at seeing her influence over the King steadily diminish, she wanted to repair relations with her children instead. The *Foudroyant* set sail again on June 10th, bound for Leghorn, with Maria Carolina, her three unmarried daughters, Prince Leopold, Miss Knight and a party of fifty aboard. Ferdinand was so evidently delighted to see them all go that his expressions of regret were no more than perfunctory. They reached Leghorn to the news that Napoleon had just crushed the Austrians at Marengo, and an armistice had been signed. Keith arrived, 'to be bored by Lord Nelson for permission to take the Queen back to Palermo, and princes and princesses to all parts of the globe'. He adamantly declined, remarking according to one source 'that Lady Hamilton had had command of the fleet long enough'.

In early July the entire party therefore set out overland to Ancona, on a route which took them perilously near the French. Here they embarked for Trieste, thence proceeding overland again to Vienna. The journey back to England was to take four months, severely taxing Sir William's health. The lovers were mainly preoccupied with each other and with Nelson's triumphal progress through Europe. In Vienna they took leave of the Queen who assured Emma, 'her friend and sister', that 'my attachment and gratitude would terminate but with my existence.' Unkind observers compared the trio to a senile Pantaloon, an anguished Harlequin and a posturing Columbine. Mrs Melesina St George, who met them in Dresden, commented that Emma was 'more stamped with the manners of her first situation than one would suppose after having represented Majesty, and lived in good company for fifteen years'. 'Anthony and his Moll-Cleopatra' travelled down the Elbe, but finding that no frigate awaited them at Hamburg, they were forced to catch the mail packet, reaching England after a stormy crossing on November 6th.

Nelson never visited Sicily again. Intermittent letters from Graeffer followed him to London. On May 16th 1800, the agent reported on the old monastery buildings that he had already started improving: 'The house is a simple one, and the old walls run the whole length, except that the windows are new. The south end or front is part new and part old; it comprehends three rooms for Your Lordship and one for an attendant, an open lodge (ie balcony) from these rooms, and a most perfect view of Etna presents itself.' He went on: 'Every tawdry show shall be avoided, and neatness as far as our blundering bricklayers are able, alone attended to ... I wish Your Lordship a happy voyage, a speedy and safe return to Sicily, and a long visit to Bronte.' By that

December he had prepared a survey of the estate. The land amounted to 8,003 salme (ie 13,975 Hectares, or roughly 34,500 acres in modern terminology), comprising:

3,469 salme of arable land
1,964　　„　of woodland
　702　　„　of hill pasture
1,861　　„　useless for any cultivation
and only 7 salme of irrigated land.

He listed twenty-seven farms or parcels of land let to separate tenants, three mills and eleven other sources of income derived from tithes, the gaol, the customs house and the notary's office. On paper this produced an annual income of 6,405 ounces, 71 tari, or well over £3,000 sterling. Graeffer did not mention that these estimates bore only the faintest resemblance to the revenue he was actually receiving.

Graeffer continued to perform his duties diligently for some time. When the Duchy was threatened by a demand to provide men and money for the royal army in 1801, he addressed Sir John Acton requesting some reduction in the assessment: 'Your Excellency's attachment towards the welfare of Lord Nelson has emboldened me to transmit the enclosed memorial, craving in the name of His Lordship, Your Excellency's assistance to ease the demand.' Sir John replied: 'I shall ever be ready to promote whatever may be useful to our worthy and most excellent Lord Nelson', promising that the Duchy's obligations would be no heavier than any other estate in Sicily. In fact the original quota of horses for the King's use, which the Duchy had to support, was reduced from twenty to two or three.

That September Graeffer informed Nelson: 'I feel proud to have the honour of being thought worthy by Your Lordship to take upon me the principal management of the Duchy of Bronte. I shall always think it a glory to sacrifice both life and health for your advantage: I flatter myself that in a very few years you will find that my time has not been foolishly employed in the improvement of your estate.' He did, however, continue to complain that 'rural amusement alone can be the diversion here', and before any English family settled down to farm they must build a decent house, as there were nothing but hovels on the land, thanks to 'the accursed custom in Sicily of living in the towns where 'the farmer lounges half the day about the market place,' while the labourer 'stands in the street to listen to a cock and bull story.' What was needed in his opinion was a colony of English agriculturists to raise the whole standard of land management. But after this enthusiastic outburst, his energies waned. Over the next few months correspondence from Bronte grew increasingly spasmodic and by mid-1802 had ceased altogether.

Nelson's subsequent career is far too well-documented to require a detailed description here. His return to England aroused a popular enthusiasm that was not echoed in official quarters. He and Emma were referred to as 'a pair of silly sentimental fools', and the cynics were in no doubt as to the nature of their relationship, while Miss Knight hastened to distance herself from her travelling companions. When the Admiral attended a levée with Sir William, George III was extremely curt to him; it was also made clear that Emma could not be presented at court. Relations with Fanny worsened rapidly, although their reunion in the middle of a thunderstorm in a London hotel lobby had been frosty enough. Poor Fanny, who had been naively looking forward to a visit to Bronte, having read glowing reports of its Elysian charms in the British press, was left in no doubt as to her position of abandoned wife. She broke down at dinner at the Admiralty and fainted in her box at Drury Lane. In January 1801, William Haslewood, Nelson's solicitor, witnessed the culminating scene at their house in Dover Street, after which Fanny moved out. The couple never lived together again and their country retreat at Roundwood was put on the market.

Despite the scandals, Nelson was promoted Vice-Admiral of the Blue, and by February 1801 was at Torbay where he was made second-in-command of the fleet that was to be sent to the Baltic under Sir Hyde Parker. Here he received the news that Emma had borne him a daughter, and taking three days' leave 'on my private affairs' he rushed to London, sending first an ecstatic letter: 'Now, my own dear wife, for such you are in my eyes and in the face of heaven, I can give full scope to my feelings . . . I never had a dear pledge of love until you gave me one.' Fortunately he seemed unaware that Emma had a previous daughter, the result of her liaison with Sir Harry Fetherston-haugh, who was by now nineteen. The baby was christened Horatia, and Nelson was consumed by a mixture of paternal pride and frustration at his marital situation. Writing to Emma: 'I have been the world round and in every corner of it, and never yet saw your equal or even one which could be put in comparison with you. You know how to reward virtue, honour and courage . . . I hope one day to see you in peace before I set out for Bronte, which I am resolved to do.' But all too soon his brief leave was over, and he had to rejoin the fleet.

The brilliant tactics that Nelson devised and imposed on his unwilling commander for neutralising the Danish fleet have added to his legend, as did his famous gesture in raising the telescope to his blind eye, when Sir Hyde signalled to break off the action. But the battle of Copenhagen on April 2nd was not followed by any further engagement, and Denmark sought peace after news of the assassination of Czar Paul had undermined the Confederation of Northern Powers. Even when on duty, Nelson's personal problems pursued him. He had written to Fanny: 'Living, I have done all in my power for you, and if dead, you will find I have done the same; therefore my only wish is to be left to myself,' and indeed he had treated her handsomely, giving her the income from a capital sum of £20,000 in his will. Thereafter he never saw or directly communicated with her again, underlining his other attachment when on April 24th two dozen officers including Sir Hyde gathered on his flagship to toast Emma's birthday. The next day he wrote to her in high spirits: 'I have so much to tell you that I cannot know where to begin. I think we shall have a general peace, and then nothing shall stop my going to Bronte.'

After his return to England in June 1801, Nelson was to stay there until May 1803, and enjoy a relatively peaceful period of his life. Apart from a few weeks in command of a flotilla of light vessels, protecting the south-eastern coastline of England from a French invasion, he was out of uniform. The preliminaries of the Peace of Amiens were signed that October and a weary naval officer was finally permitted a return to civilian life. He had told Emma to begin looking for a country house in which to install his ménage, and during August she had found one. On Haslewood's advice, Merton Place in Surrey had been bought fully furnished with a small 70-acre farm, for £9,000, and the Hamiltons were already ensconced there. Nelson's first sight of his purchase delighted him, and he hoped to see 'my little charge' lodged under his own roof. Most visitors found the household distasteful; Sir Gilbert Elliot commented acidly: 'She is in high looks but more immense than ever. She goes on cramming Nelson with trowelfuls of flattery, which he goes on taking as quietly as a child does pap.'

Except for his aged father, most of the Admiral's family had abandoned Fanny's cause and established friendly relations with Emma. She even managed to inveigle the old clergyman into a visit to Merton, during which she successfully set out to charm him. The least contented resident was Sir William, who was maintaining one virtually unused London house and paying half the bills in someone else's. As a veteran diplomat, however, he preferred to let sleeping dogs lie, taking refuge in his aesthetic interests and his angling, maintaining to Greville: 'Nothing at present disturbs me but my debts and the nonsense I am obliged to submit to here to avoid coming to an explosion ... However I am determined that my quiet shall not be disturbed, let the nonsensical world go on as it will.'

1802 dawned quietly, for Nelson – aware of the gossip he had engendered – would not go visiting, 'for I wish to live retired'. Nevertheless, being only an hour's carriage drive from London, he was constantly posting there for interviews, for numerous public engagements and for his maiden speech in the Lords (he had been created a Viscount after Copenhagen), while any leisure time was spent planning improvements for Merton. His correspondence was busier than ever, although a Christmas letter from Fanny was returned: 'Opened by Lord Nelson but not read'.

At last the first remittance had arrived from Graeffer, albeit for less than £800, accompanied by a list of excuses as to why it could not be more. All efforts to have seed and agricultural implements sent to the Duchy via Malta, now under British occupation, had proved unsuccessful. But Nelson, absorbed in his domestic bliss at Merton, did not seem too worried. That summer he accompanied the Hamiltons on a six week tour to Sir William's estates in Pembrokeshire, attending many banquets in his honour and receiving the freedom of several towns on the way. Straight after their return Emma decided she wished to go to Ramsgate for the sea-bathing, which provoked an explosion from her long-suffering husband. With his patience failing he asked her in a letter: '... if really one cannot live comfortably together, is a wise and well-concerted separation not preferable?' The ultimatum had its desired effect, and life continued unchanged through autumn until Christmas, when there was a large gathering of Nelson's family and a ball given by Emma for the children.

By early 1803, it was evident that the storm clouds of war were gathering again, and the Prime Minister received a reminder of one distinguished naval officer's zeal for his country's service: 'Whenever it is necessary, I am your Admiral.' Before the summons came, however, Sir William died. In feeble health for some time, he went into a sudden decline, and on April 6th he died in Emma's arms, with Nelson holding his hand. His will contained a few surprises. Emma was left a legacy of £300, and an annuity of £800, of which £100 must be paid to Mrs Cadogan for her lifetime. As expected the residue of his estate went to Greville; the government pension of £1,200 a year ended at Sir William's death, while his claims for compensation for the losses he had sustained during his posting at Naples, amounting to £23,213, remained unsettled. Obviously these legacies would not keep Emma in the style to which she had long been accustomed, nor was there any sign of her tiring of her habitual extravagance. A worried Nelson computed his annual income at £3,400 (excluding the unreliable remittances from Bronte), but after payments to his wife and other relatives, plus interest on the loan needed to buy Merton, he could reckon on only about £750 on which to live. His need for some prize money gained on active service was indeed pressing.

He had been given command of the Mediterranean fleet, and on May 20th, after war had been declared once more, he sailed from Portsmouth in the *Victory*, sending Emma a fond farewell. After brief stops at Gibraltar and Malta he continued through the Straits of Messina – his only glimpse of Sicily – to Naples, where he anchored in the Bay on June 25th. 'Dear Naples, if it is what it was. God send me good news!' he noted. The Royal Family had come back about a year before, Ferdinand to a rapturous welcome from his *lazzaroni*, Maria Carolina on her return from Vienna to a much cooler reception. On his arrival, Nelson received warm messages arrived from the court, especially from the Queen, although she did not mention Emma. Nelson commented in a letter home: 'I am vexed that she did not mention you! I can only account for its being a political letter . . . I trust my dear Emma she has wrote to you. If she can forget Emma, I hope God will forget her! But you think she never will or can. Now is her time to show it.'

On his Welsh tour the previous summer, Nelson had heard of Graeffer's death. A letter from Naples of August 21st 1802 informed him that poor Graeffer had died suddenly on the 7th, and although Mrs Graeffer had applied for the post herself, Acton had decided that 'a proper person', the Cavaliere Forcella, should be appointed. Perhaps a farmer should be sent out from England with the necessary implements, 'as the former ones were mostly lost or spoilt'. Nelson had then commented: 'This embarrasses me a little, but I must endeavour to make the best of things, and it may possibly turn out to my pecuniary advantage. I have his full account of my estate; rather more than £3,000 a year net, and increasing every year in value.'

He had applied for information to his friend Abraham Gibbs, a Palermo-based banker, with whom he had once shared Palazzo Palagonia. A month later Gibbs replied, promising to do anything he could to help, but the report did not reach Nelson until late that autumn. Gibbs had reached Bronte having completed the last thirty miles of his journey over very rough country. There he found extensive if incomplete rebuilding of the monastery of Maniace, although La Fragilia was a perfectly adequate residence for occasional visits. Chaos reigned: the tenants had not paid their rents; the workmen were clamouring for their wages; and Mrs Graeffer was demanding £200 a year pension to support herself and her child. Small wonder that virtually nothing had come in for three years, although Gibbs estimated that with careful management the estate might produce a £2,000 rental by 1805. After reading this gloomy report, the Admiral noted: 'As for getting anything for Bronte, I cannot expect it, for the finances of Naples are worse than ever. *Pazienza*, however.'

By this time Nelson was feeling thoroughly disillusioned. He had spent several months fruitlessly blockading Toulon, without the French fleet venturing out of port once; furthermore some monotonous cruising round the Mediterranean had not resulted in engaging the enemy either. The much needed prize money had not materialised, and even 'living as frugal as my situation will permit', he was saving nothing. Despite the friendly noises emanating from the Court at Naples, he considered they were too frightened of the French to abandon their neutrality.

In fairness the King had shown himself still interested in the Duchy: a diploma dated October 13th 1801 had reconfirmed the grant, listing the fiefs and rights attaching to them; a royal decree of March 27th 1803 had exempted the estate from payment of all taxes, a privilege not previously enjoyed by the Hospital. Gibbs' report, however, shattered Nelson, and in response to Gibbs' enquiry whether a sale would not be the best solution, Nelson's reply was an unequivocal 'yes'. He had given up the idea of settling there, adding a melancholy postscript to his letter: 'I told Graeffer on first setting out that I would give up two years' rent for fitting up a house and improving. I paid more attention to another Sovereign than my own; therefore the King of Naples' gift of Bronte to me, if it is not now settled to my advantage and to be permanent has cost me a fortune,' and then: 'I did my duty to the Sicilifying of my conscience, but I am easy . . . All I beg is that the just thing may be done immediately; I shall never again write an order about the estate'. Nevertheless, the very next day he was again addressing Gibbs about a Mr Broadbent who had made 'a sort of offer to hire the farm'. Although nothing definite had been proposed, perhaps there was a vague chance of renting out the estate for a decent sum for the next few years. He also needed the Duchy arms 'for the Heralds' College' and wondered if they could be drawn at Bronte.

Indeed for the remaining two years of the Admiral's life, there are few mentions of the Duchy among his surviving correspondence. Occasionally he allowed himself a little fantasy about his Sicilian dignity, writing to Emma: 'I hope that one of these days you will be my own Duchess of Bronte, and then a fig for them all!'; but on the whole he seems to have put the whole matter out of his head. The estate was not sold and Gibbs was left with an ill-defined role of looking after its administration, in so far as that was possible from distant Palermo.

At first Nelson had tried, without success, to involve Gibbs more closely in the day-to-day running of the Duchy. In autumn 1803 he fired off several more letters instructing him to get in the year's rents and sell off the stock on the farm to pay off all debts as soon as possible, refusing to continue an annual pension of 65 ounces granted by Graeffer to one of his protégés or to spend a penny more on Maniace: 'They say the house which is fitted up is ridiculous. Instead of a farm house it is a palace – quite a folly in Graeffer.' Gibbs, however, refused to commit himself, although he remained helpful. He wrote back: 'Allow me to assure Your Lordship that I regard the Bronte estate as if it belonged to myself . . . the old accounts are under examination, part of the unnecessary expenses diminished and the debt of 4,000 ounces to the Archpriest of Bronte ordered to be discharged from this year's rents.' Unfortunately Graeffer had used all of three years' income on the rebuilding, while 8,000 ounces of debts were outstanding. Broadbent had been asked to repeat his offer. Nelson commented sourly to Emma: 'Do you know the King never heard of my wish to resign Bronte; it is said Acton dare not tell him, and now I fear the French will have Sicily, so that I shall be worse off.'

In 1804 Gibbs devised a new system of management of the Duchy; a lawyer, Cavaliere Antonio Forcella, was to be regularly consulted and charged with legally representing the Duchy's interests as well as supervising the production of annual accounts, although by 1805 this had never been done. Matters at Bronte were brought to Nelson's attention periodically; both his agents and the townspeople had appealed to the government on the vexed question of pasturing livestock and taking firewood from the estate. A memorandum of June 1804 stated that the King had bought 'the fief of Bronte' for £60,000 sterling from the Rectors of the Hospital, and had given it to Nelson free of all encumbrances. It was therefore up to the Rectors to pay, from interest received on the purchase price, the 800 ounces per annum to the Benedictine Convent at Bronte, which was demanding it from the Duchy as of customary right. Gibbs added that a stream had been discovered in the mountains, which could irrigate 100 acres of grassland, that two water mills were already built and 'the foundation of Nelson town is laid'.

Encouraged by this, the Admiral wrote to Emma from aboard the *Victory* in August 1804: 'I am settling my Bronte affairs and next year my net income from thence will be as sure as any estate in England. But I have very much to weed away; the gross amount is large, but the salaries for Governor, '*campieri*', the college fees and Mrs Graeffer's pension will not be less than £800 sterling a year ... in case of any accident happening to me I have given you £500 sterling a year out of the estate, although I hope we shall live many years.'

Overall, however, the Duchy occupied little of its owner's attention, although he remained on friendly terms with Gibbs, admitting: 'He is doing I believe all he can for me at Bronte', agreeing to the latter's request to send his motherless nine-year old daughter, Mary, back to England in a man-of-war. Within a few months the child had become part of the household at Merton. Indeed she stayed closely connected with that peculiar ménage for years, until in 1810 her English cousins offered to take her into their family and see to her education, in order to remove her from Lady Hamilton's influence. She did not rejoin her father in Palermo until 1812.

1804 was a year that brought Nelson little happiness otherwise. As it dawned, Emma was far from well, having just given birth to another daughter, who did not survive. The Neapolitan court now disgusted Nelson. The new British ambassador, Hugh Elliot, reported that Acton was about to be dismissed as Prime Minister to satisfy the French. In their correspondence Maria Carolina persisted in omitting to mention Emma, ignoring Nelson's blunt request that she should write to the British government asking them to grant Sir William's widow a pension. 'Put not your trust in princes,' he noted sourly.

When Spain reentered the war against England, the Admiral heard with fury that Sir John Orde had been given a separate command to blockade Cadiz. This would surely siphon off any prize money that should rightfully have been his. And just as permission had at last arrived for him to go home on leave, Nelson received a signal on January 18th 1805, that the French fleet from Toulon had put to sea. Unaware that a major storm had sent them limping back into port, he spent a month scouring the Mediterranean for them, but in vain, then resumed the blockade. On March 31st, Villeneuve tried again, eluded his adversaries by good luck and escaped into the Atlantic. Immediately Nelson set out in pursuit on a long voyage to the

Caribbean and back, although he never managed to engage the enemy. Hearing that, after an indecisive battle off Finisterre, Villeneuve had fled back to Ferrol, Nelson eventually landed at Portsmouth on August 19th. He had been at sea for twenty-seven months.

The next twenty-five brief days, the last that Nelson would ever spend in England, were far from restful. Pitt's ministry was still eager to employ the nation's most distinguished naval officer, even if he had just written: 'I have brought home no honour for my country; only a most faithful servant.' Therefore most days were spent in conference, while Merton was packed with a host of relatives and friends. A devoted father was able to see something of his infant daughter however. Back in autumn 1803 he had written to 'my dear child' from 'your most affectionate father', explaining to Horatia that in the event of his death he had left Lady Hamilton as her guardian. A few months later Nelson further abandoned the pretence that he and Emma were merely acting 'in loco parentis' for a fictitious Mr and Mrs Thompson (she away, ill in the country, he serving with the fleet). A letter to Emma, intended to be shown to anyone, formally requested her to take under her wing 'the child left to my care and protection'.

In these last weeks of his life, Nelson was still worried about the provision made for his mistress and illegitimate daughter. In February 1801, just after Horatia's birth, he had sent Emma a suggested amendment to his will, by which he left her: 'the entire rental of Bronte for her particular use and benefit and in case of her death, before she may come into the possession of the estate of Bronte, she is to have the full power of naming any child she may have in or out of wedlock, or any child male or female which she may choose to adopt and call her child by her last will and testament.' She had, however, thought the wording and implication of this bequest too obvious to be acceptable, and in the end the only definite legacy left to Horatia was £4,000 held in trust, by a codicil to his will of September 6th 1803, which also expressed the hope that 'if he proves worthy, in Lady Hamilton's estimation, of such a treasure as I am sure she will be', the Admiral's nephew, Horatio, might marry his baby cousin.

During these final few weeks the Admiral had but little time to devote to his personal affairs. Gibbs and Forcella had offered to rent the whole Duchy from him themselves for £2,800 per annum. But Nelson retorted that he wanted £3,200 paid to him in quarterly amounts, out of which he would pay fees and salaries. Moreover he grumbled that: 'You have not told me what has been done with the stock, nor whether the tenants keep the premises in repair nor what the land is let for.'. . . I have spent over £10,000 upon the place, and my net income will be under £2,800. It is enough to make me look about me and think a little . . . I know that it was the good King's intention to give me a fine rental.' Nevertheless, Nelson's final news of the Duchy was more encouraging, for Gibbs wrote that the rents had been increased considerably, so more money would soon be available by way of remittances, although the whole question of an overall deal was left in abeyance.

On September 13th 1805, according to the notoriously unreliable Emma the Admiral left for Portsmouth after an emotional leave-taking during which he had gone up to Horatia's room and prayed by the child's cot. The next day the *Victory* weighed anchor and within a fortnight the Admiral was blockading the combined French and Spanish fleets in Cadiz. Contrary winds kept the enemy in harbour, but Nelson was more than fully occupied in managing a large force, in keeping up morale among his officers and men and in communicating with his own and several foreign governments. At length Villeneuve succeeded in getting most of his ships out to sea on October 20th and by mid-morning next day firing had begun. Within two hours Nelson had fallen on his own quarter-deck, shot through the backbone by a sharpshooter, and at 4.30pm he died surrounded by his devoted chaplain and attendants. The Battle of Trafalgar, one of the most glorious feats of British arms, resulted in the capture or destruction of 18 of the 34 enemy ships, while the French casualties were nearly four times greater than the English losses. But the hero whose genius had accomplished this made his last voyage home stripped of all clothes save his shirt, upended in a cask filled with brandy to preserve the corpse.

There is one further interesting connection between Nelson and Sicily which should be mentioned here. The commander of the Spanish ships at Trafalgar was a Sicilian nobleman, Don Federico Gravina, a gallant and distinguished naval officer. He had met Nelson at Palermo in 1799 – indeed he had attended the investiture festivities at Palazzino Cinese. In 1805 the two comrades found themselves on opposing sides. Gravina fought bravely ensuring his flagship escaped being captured, but he was mortally wounded during the battle and died of his injuries the following year. Legend has it that, on hearing of Nelson' death, he exclaimed: 'God's will be done – I go to join my friend.'

On Nelson's cabin desk in the *Victory*, the faithful Hardy found two letters undelivered. One, written on October 19th, was a loving missive to Emma; the other, a codicil to his will, had been scribbled in his pocket-book that very morning. In it, after setting out once more the services Lady Hamilton had rendered her country before the Battle of the Nile, which he felt entitled her to a government pension, he ended by saying: 'Could I have rewarded those services, I would not now call upon my country; but as that has not been in my power I leave Emma, Lady Hamilton therefore as a legacy to my King and Country, that they will give her an ample provision to maintain her rank in life. I also leave to the beneficence of my country my adopted daughter, Horatia Nelson Thompson; and I desire in future she will use the name of Nelson only.' His dying wishes were not, alas, to be fulfilled, and neither his Duchy of Bronte, nor most of his other worldly possessions, were to pass to those he would have most wanted to inherit them, on that day off Cape Trafalgar.

CHAPTER VIII

The Reverend Doctor

'Large and heavy in his person, boisterous in his manners, his own voice very loud, and he exceedingly and impatiently deaf.' Such was the character sketch drawn by Admiral Sir William Hotham of Nelson's elder brother, William. If he has not appeared so far in this history of the Duchy of Bronte, it is with good reason. William Nelson's entire life was but the mirror of his brother's greatness, or in the words of the *Dictionary of National Biography*: 'The Admiral's glory reflected on the Clergyman.' Nevertheless, as he and his progeny were to succeed to the Duchy, his career and personality warrant some attention.

Born in 1757, William Nelson graduated from Christ's College, Cambridge in 1778, and six years later, having been ordained, he was appointed to the Norfolk parish of Brandon Parva. By no means sure that he wanted thus early to settle down as a simple country parson, he had asked Horatio whether he should join the Navy, and had been appointed chaplain to HMS *Boreas*, the frigate commanded by his brother, recently ordered to the West Indies. A career in the services proved not to be to his taste; after three months on station he was invalided home, indeed he had found the work so distasteful that he refused to draw any pay. After returning thankfully to Norfolk, William married Sarah, daughter of the Revd Henry Yonge in 1786. They had a daughter, Charlotte, the following year, and a son named Horatio after his uncle – in 1788. Country life was uneventful, the rector performed his duties conscientiously and in 1797 was given the richer living of Hilborough. He remained in close touch with his family, indeed 'the interest that attached to him during this time is mainly as the correspondent of his distinguished brother, who wrote to him frequently, freely expressing his opinion of men and affairs'.

William saw in Nelson's rise to fame an opportunity to aspire to higher things. In the autumn of 1797, after the Battle of St Vincent had brought his brother national renown, he began his campaign, writing to Horatio: 'A person a good deal connected with the Church assured me he knew it as a fixed and certain thing that you had secured the vacant stall (at Norwich Cathedral) for me, that the Lord Chancellor had promised it and all was settled.' On this occasion he was to be disappointed. 'You may easily guess it was no small mortification to me to be told at Norwich by Doctor Sandby the Chancellor, Mr. Wodehouse and some other church dignitaries that there was no vacancy.' He soon elaborated: 'A prebend in any Cathedral and of almost any value is my wish. When I say a prebend, I mean a Residentiary, for there are many prebends which are not Residentiaries and have only a small stipend of ten or twenty pounds a year and no stall. They are not what I mean, it must be a stall no matter where, only the nearer home and the larger the income the better'.

The news of the Battle of the Nile and the grant of the Sicilian estate further aroused his expectations. On November 2nd 1799, he wrote to his father in great excitement: 'I had received a letter last Saturday from my dear and good brother mentioning particulars of the settlement of the Dukedom of Bronte in the manner you wrote. There is a paragraph I consider of singular importance ... couched in the remarkable words: "You may rest assured that I never have or will forget my family. I think that would be a crime, and if you will tell me to whom and what I am to ask for, for the descent of the Nelson title and the pension that goes with it, I will do it".' Evidently his saintly father suspected William's fondness for money, for a few months later the latter was writing to him: 'We have been obliged to hear many unpleasant insinuations as if we had made use of an undue influence with dear Aunt Mary (lately dead). Mrs Nelson can say whatever she did was not from a selfish motive to get what little my aunt possessed, as she always understood everything was left to you.'

William and his wife were certainly ready to tack to whatever prevailing wind was blowing in the Admiral's private life. Originally they had been very friendly with Fanny, consulting her about Charlotte's schooling in April 1799: 'Mrs Nelson will write to the governors to know when the school opens again after the Whitsun holidays, but she will first wait your answer, because we shall take no further action unless you fully approve of it.' However, soon after Nelson returned from the Continent with the Hamiltons, they realized the changed state of affairs and promptly switched their allegiance.

Emma was delighted to cultivate their goodwill, both as the first members of her lover's family who had accepted her, and as useful allies in the campaign against 'Tom Tit', as Fanny had been nicknamed. In March 1801 William wrote to her: 'We are very much gratified by your kind and friendly letters: they are most interesting to us, and they give an additional zest to our breakfast; indeed they are the only things that give us any comfort in your absence.' Praise for Horatio was readily accepted: 'I am glad my little Horace (by now at Eton) looks so well, and that you think him so like his great, his glorious, his immortal uncle. Why should he not be like him?'

On the whole, Nelson was fond of his grasping brother. During that summer of 1801 all four were at Deal, where the Admiral was commanding the anti-invasion fleet. He was more amused than exasperated by William's zeal for preferment, as his correspondence with Emma shows: 'What can Reverend Sir want to be made a Doctor for? He will be laughed at for his pains!' And again: 'I have a letter from Reverend Doctor, he is as big as if he was a Bishop, and one from the Beadle of the University to say how well he preached. I hope you ordered something good for him, for those bigwigs love eating and drinking.' Yet William, who had been made Doctor of Divinity by both Oxford and Cambridge Universities, and who was to be presented to a Prebendal stall at Canterbury in May 1803, remained as blatantly self-seeking as ever, writing to Emma: 'If Jove gets a higher title, perhaps things may be settled more to our minds. Now we are already in the patent as Barons, it will be no difficult matter in that case to have our entails advanced to the highest honour if my brother so wishes.'

Despite his status as a man of the cloth, William's principles seem to have been sufficiently elastic to ignore the impropriety implicit in the household arrangements at Merton. In autumn 1802 he sent his daughter Charlotte to live there, while Horatio often visited from Eton. Emma, anxious to give the ménage an air of respectability, was delighted with this arrangement; indeed when Sir William died the following spring she invited her sister-in-law to come and stay for a while as her chaperone.

Charlotte evidently enjoyed her life at Merton, and although young was obviously an acute observer. Writing to her uncle, after the news of the victory of Aboukir: 'We sent to London for all the songs which are published of the battle and had them sung. I am learning them all to play to Your Lordship when I have the pleasure of meeting you, which I hope will be at Bath soon after Christmas.' She soon became an unquestioning admirer of Emma, who took her into circles she would hardly have encountered with her parents, while in her turn Emma realized Charlotte's worth as an asset in her battle to gain an entrée to London society, telling her mother: 'I never quit her for a moment. My whole time is given up with pleasure to this lovely girl.' Mrs William Nelson in turn was not above appealing to her new friend as an ally in gaining patronage. When the Canterbury appointment came up, she wrote to Emma: 'My Lord has a right now to go to Mr Addington and say I expect my brother shall have the Canterbury stall, and something better whenever it is vacant . . . recollect what the Prince of Wales said at your house that when My Lord was afloat again, he might command a Bishopric.'

Another advantage of having Charlotte at Merton was that she provided an excellent alibi for the presence of the 'orphan' Horatia. She dutifully wrote to her uncle about her affection for the baby and received an appreciative reply: 'Thank you very much for your kind letters, and I feel truly sensible of your regard for that dear little orphan, Horatia. Although her parents are lost, yet she is not without fortune . . . I shall cherish her to the last moment of my life. I curse them that curse her and Heaven blesses them who bless her.' By mid-1804 Charlotte, together with young Mary Gibbs, appeared to be a permanent part of Nelson's household, an arrangement totally accepted by her parents. Both William and his wife were at Merton for those famous last few days in September 1805, and when the Admiral departed to join the fleet, they took Horatia and Charlotte off to Canterbury with them. It is ironic to note that these two girls, one the eventual owner of the Duchy, and the other, who surely had the best moral claim to it, should have spent so much of their youth in such close proximity.

The William Nelsons' behaviour had not been copied by the Admiral's other relations. His eldest sister, Susannah, was married to a Norfolk farmer, Thomas Bolton, and had borne five children, leading a healthy, simple life in the country. She was sensible of the kindness shown to her family by Fanny, who for instance after a disastrous harvest had readily lent them £200 in 1799. Thus she was at first wary that a visit to Merton might imply her approval of the ménage to be found there. At last, after all Emma's charms had been exerted, she paid a short visit in June 1802. Gradually Mrs Bolton accepted her brother's mistress, even inviting her to Norfolk, but avoiding too much intimacy. This attitude was echoed by her younger sister, Katherine, married to George Matcham, a handsome and charming gentleman of independent means. Both ladies, however, were to be more than kind to Emma and her unfortunate daughter in their days of adversity to come.

The Revd. Edmund Nelson had behaved most honourably of them all, supporting Fanny in her tribulations, and although he had enjoyed his stay at Merton, he was never to condone what had happened. Alas, his good influence on his children ceased in 1802 when he died at a great age, while his eldest son, Maurice, had predeceased him. It was Maurice, for thirty years an unassuming and comparatively lowly clerk in the Admiralty, who had written to Fanny, having heard about the grant of Nelson's peerage: 'I now declare to you that William may have all the honour to himself. It will be my wish and request to my brother not to put my name in the patent ... I move in too humble a sphere to think of such a thing.' Such humility was certainly not shown by William when the family honours descended thick and fast upon him.

Tidings of Trafalgar reached London in the early hours of November 6th. The *London Gazette* published Collingwood's well-worded dispatch, yet the rejoicing was muted and the capital only partially illuminated, for the nation felt its hero's loss as keenly as the great victory he had won. The Admiralty sent an official communiqué to each member of Nelson's family and to Merton, where Emma was carried swooning to bed. In fairness, 'the Reverend Doctor', as the Admiral had called him, was also moved to tears when the Mayor of Canterbury pre-empted the government messenger by personally going round to break the news. William and his wife left in haste for London; the Matchams rushed up from Bath, while the Boltons were already at Merton.

On November 9th the *London Gazette* published the government's decision to reward the Admiral's services to his country by making his elder brother an Earl while simultaneously, seventeen-year old Horatio became Viscount Merton. Pitt in his letter to William hoped: 'these marks of honour from the Sovereign would mitigate the weight of domestic affliction added to the sense of national loss which pervades the whole country.' That same evening an obsequious reply came 'from a heart borne down by the deepest sorrow for the loss of my good and gallant brother and with gratitude for the munificent intentions of a gracious Sovereign.'

As co-executors of Nelson's estate, his solicitor William Haslewood and the new Earl journeyed down to Merton to read the Admiral's will (dated May 10th 1803) with its seven codicils, to the family assembled round Emma's bedside. As far as William at least was concerned it contained several unpleasant surprises. The legacy of £4,000 to Horatia seemed an admission of her parentage, while the hope expressed that, despite the difference in age, she should wed Horatio, horrified William who was already hatching much more ambitious marital plans for his son.

When the *Victory* finally arrived at Spithead on December 5th, Hardy ensured that the personal relics of Nelson were sent to Merton, although he was legally bound to deliver all documents found in the Admiral's cabin to the Earl as co-executor of the will. Whatever his faults William, after taking expert advice, in no way tried to suppress the famous codicil which bequeathed Emma and Horatia to the generosity of their country. It was anyway obvious that the Prime Minister alone could see that its provisos were achieved. But few people realized how near to death Pitt himself was. On January 23rd 1806, he died, while his successor, Lord Grenville, was to prove far less sympathetic. The Earl also chafed at the annuity of £500 to be paid to Emma from the income of the Duchy; here again, though, he did attempt to fulfil his obligations.

Gradually, however, he disentangled his family from Emma's clutches. Charlotte was removed altogether from Merton in January to the splendid house he had rented in London; visits were only paid on official executor's business; and the correspondence between them grew increasingly frigid. In any case, his time was taken up with arrangements for the state funeral, which took place in St Paul's Cathedral on January 9th. Everyone had to be seated by 9am, yet the huge procession only filed into the Cathedral at 2pm and some of the guests did not escape until after 9 o'clock that night. It had been a memorable occasion, emphasizing the love and respect in which his country held Nelson.

In May 1806, Parliament offered more tangible proof of the nation's gratitude to the Admiral's relations. Following a message from the King, a motion was laid before the House of Commons and debated for an entire day. The Earl was granted an annuity of £5,000 a year for himself and his descendants indefinitely, and a further sum of £120,000 as provision for the family was voted unanimously. It was divided in a curious fashion, £10,000 going to each sister, £10,000 to his widow, Fanny, and the balance of £90,000 to William for the purchase of an estate to be called 'Trafalgar'. All efforts made on behalf of Emma and Horatia were unavailing, for the grants originated from the King, to whom Lady Hamilton had always been anathema.

Relations rapidly worsened. According to Emma's unreliable recollections, the Earl chose the day on which Parliament voted the grants to throw Nelson's pocket book, with an oath, across her own dinner table, exclaiming that now she must do what she could with it. She immediately had it registered, a gesture which availed her nothing, for as it was not a codicil it lacked any legal force. Over the next nine years, after receiving not one penny from the estate or her lover's family, Emma's claims became ever more desperate and inflated, so that eventually even her well-wishers turned against her. In fairness, Nelson's sisters never suspected from her extravagant life-style that she could possibly be short of money, while her false pride and fatal capacity for exaggeration further undermined her credibility.

The Earl, as executor, had the unpleasant task of selling the agri-cultural land around Merton to pay the legacies provided for in the will. Emma had been left the house, grounds and contents, so furiously contested the decision. In fact it would only have postponed the inevitable. By early 1808 her debts amounted to over £8,000, a fact she dared not publicly admit. Her only hope lay in selling Merton, but an auction that spring proved unsuccessful, while her friends had to rally round and make her a loan secured on the sale of the property to prevent her imprisonment for debt. Finally it was sold for £13,000 in April 1809, but the proceeds were quickly swallowed up in the morass of Emma's insolvency. Ministry succeeded ministry, yet her prospects of a government pension did not improve. Canning suggested the best solution was to ask that 'a small pension be granted to the child'.

Indeed Horatia had become her greatest asset. The child's existence was now generally known, although she maintained her 'attitude' as guardian of the dead hero's orphan. The Boltons and Matchams had taken the girl to their hearts, although none of them appeared to believe that Emma was her mother. Emma did little to enlighten them. Indeed she started a rumour that Horatia was really the daughter of the Queen of Naples; 'her mother was too great to be named'. This did not prevent her sending Maria Carolina, via Mrs Graeffer, a long account of her woes. As her circumstances worsened, the pair of them moved from one set of furnished lodgings to another. In a will made in 1811, Emma left all her possessions to Horatia, requesting 'the Prince Regent that he will provide for her in such a manner that she may live as becomes the daughter of such a man as her victorious Father was'.

Nemesis finally struck in 1812. To counteract her fits of depression, Emma had taken to drinking heavily. She never answered letters for fear of betraying her whereabouts, so the Matchams and Boltons had no idea of her plight. The bailiffs still managed to track her down, and at the suit of several tradesmen, she and Horatia were removed to the King's Bench Prison, where she was made 'free of the Rules', which permitted her to live nearby on parole and to bombard ministers with fresh petitions. Her claims had become ludicrous and her fabrications usually evoked disgust. Not until 1814 did her friends manage to effect her release from prison; that June she and Horatia fled precipitately across the Channel to escape her creditors. Bankrupt and bedridden, her letters show the pathetic condition to which she had been reduced. In this wretched state Emma died on January 15th 1815, and was buried outside Calais at the expense of the British Consul. Thus, sadly, ended the life of one who despite all her shortcomings had, thanks to her beauty and vivacity, given Nelson some of his moments of greatest happiness.

No such tragic end awaited the Earl. Within a year or two his and his wife's pomposity and affectations of grandeur had alienated their relations. He insisted on keeping his prebendal stall at Canterbury, claiming he was entitled to it notwithstanding all his other advantages until further clerical advancement was offered him (it never was). Young Viscount Trafalgar, as he was now called, for in January 1807 his father had successfully applied to change the title from Viscount Merton, scarcely saw his Bolton or Matcham cousins at Cambridge: 'Our young peer is always flying about' from one grand house to another. He was reputedly a charming and able young man; his old tutor had just written in glowing terms about his former charge to Lady Nelson: 'His look was that of spirits, health, good-humour and sense. He made all around him happy by his affability and politeness.'

On the day after Christmas 1807 he took to his bed with what the doctors diagnosed as a cold. Complications set in, and on January 17th 1808 he died of typhoid fever. This was a terrible blow to his parents, who had nurtured ever more grandiose hopes for his future. William was for all his ungracious blunt manners, his decided meanness and his incessant social climbing, a very fond father, while six months later his wife was writing to a friend who had just lost her son: 'I know how to feel for you. Not a day passes that I do not shed many tears for my beloved Horace – I always called him from a child by this dear name and to the day of my death I shall feel his loss.'

To compound his grief, his wife was long past child-bearing age, so the title would pass by remainder to his nephew, quiet, studious Tom Bolton, whom Mrs Cadogan had once pronounced her favourite of all Nelson's family. The Earl's brothers-in-law acted with unseemly haste in applying for a licence to change Tom's name to Nelson. This so enraged William that he resolved even if he could do nothing about the title, to cheat them of their inheritance. In fact the licence was not taken out then, but it took many years and much rancour before he could even begin to countenance his nephews as his heirs.

William's gloom was somewhat alleviated when his daughter Charlotte married Samuel Hood at St Marylebone Church on July 3rd 1810. Although not endowed with beauty, Charlotte evidently possessed other qualities. Her godmother, Mrs M. Whyte, had written to Lady Nelson saying: 'I am rejoiced that her looks were not affected by her cold. It is a mind-illumined face and where good nature is depicted there must be beauty . . . I am happy that her disposition is all the fondest parent could desire. I have this account from all who know her.' It was not a brilliant match, for the bridegroom was an undistinguished but pleasant enough naval officer who bore a name recently made glorious in the nation's service. Moreover he was the heir by special remainder to his great-uncle, Lord Bridport's, Irish barony and fortune. The Earl, gratified by becoming the grandfather to six children, was now doubly determined that his Sicilian Duchy should descend in his own line. He had good cause to bless his brother's foresight in stipulating that the original grant of Bronte should allow the current Duke to appoint as his successor whomsoever he wished, a stipulation accepted by both Ferdinand and George III.

In 1814 he had at long last found himself a worthy residence. The trust set up by the government acquired the estate of Standlynch in Wiltshire for £120,000. It had a square, red-brick house overlooking the Avon a few miles below Salisbury, built as a showpiece in 1733 by the city magnate, Sir Peter Vanderput, with a Doric portico, copied from the Temple of Apollo at Delos, fourteen columns wide, with classical embellishments by Nicholas Revett and flanking wings by Wood the Younger of Bath. As the Earl still had to reside for part of each year at Canterbury, he moved only by degrees into what had been rechristened Trafalgar House. It was certainly grand enough, even for his tastes. The splendid plasterwork in the hall, the music room frescoes by the fashionable Cipriani and the capacious library all bore witness to this.

The purchase of Standlynch afforded a measure of reconciliation with his nephews, George Matcham and Tom Bolton, who both came to visit him and on whose advice he relied in running the estate. Ironically, both were to marry the local ladies they met under his roof there, respectively Miss Harriet Eyre and her cousin, Frances, lineal descendants of the first Lords of the Manor of Standlynch. Indeed after the young Matchams married in 1817, the Earl abandoned Trafalgar to them for a year, only thereafter beginning to furnish the house properly. It was intimated to Tom Bolton that his uncle regarded him as his heir; so his first born son was tactfully named Horatio.

This harmonious relationship did not last. In April 1828, the old Countess died, and by his behaviour her husband demonstrated that he had not yet abandoned all hope of begetting an heir. Although almost 72, he started to pay court to a young widow of only 28, Hilaire, third daughter of Admiral Sir Robert Barlow. His wooing provoked general merriment, but the Earl remained undeterred. After being refused several times, he gained her eventual acceptance by an enticing offer of a settlement of £4,000 per annum, the gift of his house in Portman Square as well as the position of mistress of Trafalgar. The match was certainly unwelcome to his daughter, as William's comments to his son-in-law showed: 'I had Charlotte's letter, it is so unkind I shall give no answer to it. If those who make such remarks knew the amiable qualities of the Countess Elect, and how much she is admired and beloved by everyone that knows her, both high and middle ranks as well as the poor, they would spare them.' Alas, it was all in vain. Despite all his efforts the lady did not produce an heir, and after six years of remarriage, William died on February 28th 1835. His funeral took place with much pomp in St Paul's, where the Earl was buried alongside his famous brother and his beloved son. The Boltons did after all inherit Trafalgar, while the widowed Countess quickly remarried George Knight, nephew of Jane Austen and squire of Godmersham Park in Kent, a house often regarded as the prototype for Mansfield Park.

After his initial exertions on her behalf, the Earl had done nothing more to plead Emma's case for a pension with the government, and the unfriendly terms on which they stood precluded any social contact. He had, however, tried to fulfil the legacy in his brother's will by paying her £500 annuity from the rental of the Bronte estate. As will later be seen, this was easier said than done, since for some years the Duchy was to produce a most unreliable income. From 1805 to 1807 the payments were apparently made, minus a property duty of 10 per cent, but payments after that were irregular. In July 1807 on the Earl's instructions, Haslewood had consulted counsel on the subject. The opinion given was that Lady Hamilton was entitled to the £500 annuity from the rents on the Bronte estate, as a first call payable at twice-yearly intervals during her lifetime, but only when the trustees had actually received the money from Sicily. Therefore if no revenue had been received, the payments would lapse. Indeed the annuity and all other income remitted from the Duchy were subject to property tax.

In April 1814 Emma addressed a bitter letter on the subject to the Earl from her debtor's prison. Even allowing for her habitual distortion of the facts, she clearly did have grounds for complaint: 'My Lord, it cannot be more disagreeable to you to receive a letter from me than it is for me to write to you, but as I will not have anything to say or do with lawyers without I am compelled to it, I should be glad to know from Your Lordship whether the first half-year of the Bronte pension which my ever Dear Lamented Friend the Glorious and Virtuous Nelson left in his will I was to receive and which I never have received, I shall be glad to know how it is to be settled, as now from my present situation which has been brought on not by any Crime but by having been too generous to the ungrateful I rather glory in being the injured and not the injurer and as every sixpence is of the utmost consequence to me on account of Horatia Nelson's education the beloved child of my dear Nelson I do not in the midst of poverty neglect her education which is such as will suit the Rank in life which she will yet hold in society and which her great Father wished her to move in. I ask not Alms I ask not anything but right and to know whether I am to receive my due or not.'

This broadside had its effect and '£225 on Bronte' was soon forthcoming, but the Earl refused to pay her annuity quarterly instead of half-yearly, claiming he was too poor. This provoked another outburst that he and his wife had lived with her seven years, that she had educated Charlotte and paid for Horatio at Eton. Wisely William refrained from further correspondence, although when Horatia herself wrote to him from Calais, begging a £10 loan as her mother had 'not one shilling' until her next remittance, he promptly responded.

Belatedly enough the Earl atoned for his hard-heartedness to Emma by his kindness to Horatia. The wretched girl had been escorted back to Dover by the Consul and met by George Matcham senior, who was now her guardian. For the next two years she lived happily with the Matcham family, a marvellous change from the squalid circumstances of her earlier life. Thereafter, as the Matcham parents had decided to settle abroad, she moved to join the Boltons in Norfolk. After an engagement to one curate, which she broke off, she married another, Philip Ward, in February 1822. The honeymoon was spent with the Tom Boltons in Wiltshire, and the young couple were taken over to Trafalgar to be presented to the Earl. Not having seen her since her infancy at Merton, he was reassured by what he saw and put himself out to be friendly.

In 1829 the Earl offered the Wards the living of Tenterden in Kent, which was in his gift as a prebendary of Canterbury Cathedral. They could not move in for some time, as the Rectory was in urgent need of repairs, and thereafter proved uninhabitable. Nevertheless they produced no fewer than nine children within fourteen years, and were very happily married. It was unfortunately at the Earl's instigation that Philip Ward launched a campaign for the commutation of tithes. This resulted in a lawsuit with the landowners of the parish which lasted ten years and left him broken in health and finances. They stayed on at Tenterden, however, until Ward's premature death from heart trouble in 1859. Horatia then moved to Pinner, Middlesex, to live with her son, Nelson, who was still single. Many of her children had married, several of them moved to be near her, and she spent the remainder of a long life surrounded by them and their numerous offspring, dying in March 1881. The inscription on her tombstone read: 'Adopted Daughter of Vice-Admiral Lord Nelson', although 'beloved' was later substituted for 'adopted'.

Over the years Horatia had conducted persistent enquiries to establish her paternity, although Nelson's solicitor, William Haslewood, had been of little help. As more and more books and articles on her father's career were published, her wish to learn the truth grew, and she was encouraged by Sir Harris Nicholas, editor of the seven-volume edition of Nelson's letters in the 1840s. Sadly it was not until after her death that Alfred Morrison privately printed more Hamilton and Nelson correspondence in 1893, finally establishing her parentage beyond doubt. To all who knew her, she was so evidently a throwback to the rural, deep-rooted clerical stock from which her father had sprung. With her courage and dedication to duty she never grumbled at her lot, in striking contrast to her Uncle William, whose moral claim to Nelson's inheritance was so much less than hers.

A Troubled Inheritance

CHAPTER IX

Illusion and disillusion

'I have to request of yourself and the Chevalier Forcella that you will continue in the agency and management of the estate in the same manner as during the late Lord Nelson's lifetime,' William Nelson wrote to Abraham Gibbs in February 1806. It seems unlikely that the Earl knew anything at all about the Duchy of Bronte when he succeeded to it. He had seen little of his brother in the preceding few years, and almost always under the pressure of great events. Moreover Nelson's general disillusionment with his Duchy seems to have largely driven it from his mind after 1803.

William Haslewood, the Earl's solicitor, sent Gibbs the power of attorney with explicit instructions to differentiate in the accounts between the Earl as successor to the Duchy and others who were jointly entitled to Nelson's residual assets. Considering that letters to and from Sicily took an average of two months or so, Gibbs replied fairly promptly. In early June he wrote in optimistic vein: 'The estate is now perfectly clear and money is coming in daily – I expect that at the present favourable exchange it will net near £3,000 sterling.' He enclosed a draft for £900 (which then equalled about 1,500 ounces), pointing out that on December 6th 1803, he had already remitted over £1,057 to Nelson. Moreover the money borrowed by Graeffer for rebuilding work at Maniace plus interest on it, as well as £4,700 of debts (which the Admiral had incurred before leaving Palermo in 1800), had been paid off. He added that he had promised Nelson to remit £2,800 per annum 'free of every charge', and thought this could be maintained 'for a certain number of years'. In November he enclosed another two drafts for £600 each, while noting that he had paid £500, a bequest from the Admiral to Mrs. Graeffer's daughter, who had just married into a Brontese family.

So far so good; although Haslewood complained that he had not yet received any accounts and that the Earl wanted a map and survey of the Duchy and details of its coat of arms. The executors finally wrote Gibbs a stiff letter demanding the accounts and the first hint of trouble came with Gibbs' reply in March: 'The Chevalier Forcella has so many affairs upon his hands that he has not yet furnished me with a statement of accounts, although these should arrive shortly.' He added 'the tenants of the Bronte estate have not been able to dispose of their corn, which owing to the war is fallen to about 35 shillings per English quarter, and consequently are backward in paying their rents.' He added that the Duchy had no coat of arms so far.

Haslewood's angry reply dismissed Forcella's other commitments as an excuse for not preparing the accounts and claimed that only a simple statement of receipts and payments was required. He noted the gloomy forecasts about the crops and the Earl added a postscript . . . regular remittances would be very acceptable, more particularly as I have an annuity of £500 to pay to Lady Hamilton, and it might be inconvenient to Her Ladyship not to receive it.' In a message sent to Palermo that June via the captain of an English frigate, he was less restrained. 'While I do not entertain any suspicion or distrust of the integrity of Mr Gibbs or the Chevalier Forcella, I cannot be blind to the disrespect with which they treat me nor to the irregularity of their conduct as agents.'

This elicited a hurt rejoinder, along with a plan of the estate and the accounts. 'Allow me to add Your Lordship is entirely indebted to Mr Forcella for inheriting the Bronte estate – for had he not attentively examined the Diploma which was put into his hands by your late brother, and added to it the following words: "that His Lordship was at liberty from the very day of the gift by his Sicilian Majesty to cede the estate to whomsoever he pleased", at his death it would decidedly have been appropriated again by the King according to the laws of this country.' A note from Forcella blamed the delay in preparing the accounts on the difficulty of obtaining figures from Bronte, and the lack of rental income on the large amount of unsold wheat. Over the next six months an increasingly sour series of letters from England would have been enough to discourage any agent.

Meanwhile, the widowed Mrs Graeffer's behaviour left much to be desired. She had written to the Earl from Merton, pretending to have important information relating to Bronte, but he had declined to meet her and Haslewood had seen her instead. At the interview she had threatened to stir up trouble among the Brontesi unless she was given a suitable present: 'I am not a gardener's wife, My Lord, Mr Graeffer having been the intimate friend of the late Sir William Hamilton, was placed in the Queen of Naples' service as Intendant of the pleasure grounds. There was not a nobleman or Crowned Head who visited Naples who did not think it an honour to be acquainted with my husband.' She added: 'I have received respect and attention from all ranks of persons except from the brother of our glorious friend. Dear, generous Lady Hamilton has been more than kind.' She had lastly handed Haslewood a petition with many signatures asking that the Duchy repair the church at Maniace.

It must by now have dawned on the Earl that in the Bronte estate he had inherited a very mixed blessing. One difficulty was of course his entire ignorance of the true state of affairs in Sicily. It was far from stable. In the face of Napoleon's stated resolve to eject the Bourbons once and for all from their dominions, Ferdinand and Maria Carolina had fled from Naples again early in 1806. Joseph Bonaparte had entered the city in triumph and assumed the crown. The sole ray of hope lay in fighting a rearguard action in Calabria, but the royal troops were soon defeated, while old Acton, back in office once more, was only concerned to defend Sicily. Lacking any navy or army, the King had been forced to invite in the British to take over the island's defences. Much to the Queen's irritation they occupied Messina and its environs, and an army under General Stuart crossed the Straits and defeated the French at Maida. This was, however, merely a brief stroke of good fortune; soon the mainland was evacuated for good, and a military stalemate ensued.

Maria Carolina had over the years become positively Anglophobe. Although on hearing the news of Nelson's death, she had exclaimed: 'I shall regret him all my life', she did not respond to Emma's anguished cries for help. She blamed the British government for encouraging Naples to stand up to Napoleon, then withdrawing practical help in the hour of need. Soon Acton retired for good, and the policy at court lacked all consistency, veering wildly in one direction, then another at the whim of a volatile Queen. Ferdinand, morbidly convinced of Bonaparte's invincibility, had abandoned affairs of state for the pleasures of shooting. The only solution lay in a closer alliance with the British. In March 1808 an Anglo-Sicilian treaty provided for the maintenance of 10,000 troops on the island, and an annual subsidy of £300,000, rising to £400,000.

Maria Carolina resented this enforced dependence, quarrelling with the English ambassador and generals, and putting her faith in a multiplicity of hare-brained plots against the French which achieved nothing. In the circumstances it is hardly surprising that neither she nor Ferdinand took any further interest in the Duchy they had bestowed upon Nelson. When the Earl had applied to the King in June 1806 for formal recognition of his rights to inherit and permission to use the title Duke of Bronte, this was granted, but the estate's exemption from taxation was revoked.

In the circumstances, therefore, things might have been very much worse. In July 1808 Forcella had written saying he had made every arrangement necessary to collect the annual rents from the Duchy as well as some arrears. Soon afterwards Gibbs mentioned that the eight payments made since June 1806 had totalled 8,030 ounces or over £4,800. He found Mrs Graeffer's conduct extraordinary and agreed that no obligation existed to pay her anything beyond her pension, but that she would undoubtedly make mischief at Bronte. Regarding the petition, there was no need to repair the church as the Brontesi already had plenty of places to worship. In response to the Earl's query whether the Duchy produced any drinkable wine, Gibbs' answer was negative, 'although a Mr Woodhouse, who resides at Marsala, makes a wine which is called Bronte Madeira, but it is not much approved of.'

The easiest way of dealing with the problems of the tenants and their rents was to let the whole estate as one unit, an idea that had already occurred to Forcella. He wrote to the Earl in March 1810: 'Should Your Excellency wish to avoid such delays in and the uncertainties of payment, depending on the prices of produce, taxes and charges, it would be necessary to reduce all the rents into one only.' Otherwise: 'You must be contented to suffer the delays and contrarieties incident to all administrations, and which you may be assured my zeal and care have reduced in yours as much as possible.'

Unfortunately the Earl was never satisfied. The idea of letting to one large tenant had crossed his mind, as had that of selling the Duchy altogether, but he was at pains to deny it to Gibbs. 'There are rumours here that I have agreed to sell the Bronte estate to an Italian gentleman called the Commander di Acuto. If such a report has reached Sicily, I must beg the favour of your contradicting it in the most decided manner.' He continued to niggle at his agents. The tin box sent by Forcella had cost him 'the large sum of seven guineas' and in future such items should be sent via the diplomatic bag to the Neapolitan ambassador, 'in which case they will come free.' The accounts simply did not tally. In July 1810 he demanded that Gibbs rectify the discrepancy between the figures on paper and the actual receipts, by the immediate despatch of a draft for the sum in question. Moreover all moneys retained on deposit against a possible succession tax should be remitted to him too. He concluded rather pathetically: 'I have no intention at present to lease out my estate, so I must rely on the efforts of my agents.'

By 1810 a new hazard appeared to threaten the Duchy. Napoleon, after deciding to replace the Spanish Bourbons with his brother, Joseph, had given the Neapolitan throne to his Marshal, Joachim Murat. The latter had proved an able and popular ruler, and after consolidating his regime was threatening to invade Sicily. A counter-attack whereby an Anglo-Sicilian fleet sailed into the Bay and British troops captured a few islands had accomplished little. Now Murat had massed forces on the other side of the Straits, and seemed about to attack across them.

There was some alarm in London, although Gibbs' letter to the Earl of July 30th dismissed the threat: 'If the Sicilians are but true to themselves as we have little doubt, no apprehensions are entertained of the issue.' Two months later he had to qualify this: 'On the 18th September, Murat succeeded in landing about 4,000 men six miles south of Messina, but they were immediately repulsed by our soldiers and obliged to re-embark for Calabria, leaving behind 1,200 prisoners. Without the aid of the Toulon fleet, which was considered unlikely, his chances of success were deemed to be minimal.' In fact the French did not try their luck again.

A much more real if less apparent danger was posed by the political crisis in Palermo. Ever since Ferdinand's return to Sicily in 1806, opposition to his rule had been far more determined and united. The constitutional movement had begun in the 1780s as resistance to attempts by the Crown to centralise power at the expense of the barons. Twenty years later the nobility and the Church had come to realise that the feudal privileges, which they had been so tenaciously defending, in fact restricted their flexibility in an era of static rents and rising prices. Resentment against the Neapolitan bias of the court was mixed with a hankering for a corpus of common law and a constitution, similar to that to which they naively ascribed British prosperity.

It was at this time that Lord William Bentinck arrived as British ambassador and Commander-in-chief of the garrison. Honest, forthright and energetic, he resembled a Victorian colonial administrator. Finding the Court intransigent he only achieved the release of the five opposition ringleaders imprisoned by the King and a change in the ministry by threatening to cut off the subsidy and deploy his troops. Ferdinand's abdication of power in favour of his son, Francis, was a cosmetic exercise, for the King, a firm believer in Divine Right, had no intention of permanently renouncing the reins of government. In 1811 the new ministry under Prince Belmonte spent several months drawing up a constitution based on the British model. The baronial and ecclesiastical houses were merged in a single Upper Chamber, while the royal and baronial towns together formed a Lower House.

Under the new Constitution, finally passed in 1812, all feudal dues, jurisdictions and privileges were abolished, and fiefs were converted into freeholds. Many of the nobility calculated they could thus dispose of their properties at will, for the 'promiscuous rights', whereby the peasants enjoyed a practical co-ownership of much of the land had been abolished too, while the new middle class and the *gabellotti* ('tax farmers') sensing potential profits were equally enthusiastic. But Belmonte's insistence on allowing a full debate on all these measures proved fatal. An extreme radical party emerged in the Commons, which, against a background of bread riots in Palermo, demanded cheap food, extensive agrarian reforms, the division of church property and the abolition of all entails. They combined with the conservative majority in the Upper House to refuse further supply until their grievances had been redressed.

Against this background, three Parliaments held within two years had accomplished nothing. Moreover the King refused to sign anything, pushing all responsibility on to the weak Hereditary Prince, then early in 1813 suddenly reappearing in Palermo to resume power. In practice, with the British paying half the expenses of government and defending Sicily, ultimate authority lay with Bentinck, who became effective dictator of the island. He wished for: 'the firm and just exercise of our superiority,' although maintaining the fiction of two equal and independent allies. If all concessions were refused: 'to become a province of England would not, I believe, be looked upon as a misfortune by the major part of the population.' Bentinck conferred daily with ministers, raised public loans and controlled both finances and the army.

A titanic battle of wills took place with the Queen. Twice banished to remote places of residence, she reappeared in Palermo to bolster Ferdinand's resolve to resist the Constitution. Armed with evidence that she was also intriguing with the French, Bentinck now forced her into exile, and in June 1813 she sailed off for Vienna, after British Secret

Service funds had been used to pay off her enormous debts and redeem her jewels from pawn. The ambassador's naïve belief that Maria Carolina's exile would solve all the problems was quickly destroyed. That summer the ministry collapsed in the face of opposition from both ends of the political spectrum. Bentinck hurried back from Spain, where he had gone to participate in the British campaign in Catalonia, formed a new ministry, and when Parliament threw out the Budget he dissolved it and himself issued the proclamation to continue collecting taxes after November 1st.

But both the Constitution and its chief instigator soon came to grief. Following his expedition to Leghorn in 1814 where he had once again tried to impose a constitution on the newly-liberated Tuscans, he was recalled to Britain and replaced by Sir William A'Court, a cynical, conservative diplomat who disliked change.

Meanwhile Ferdinand had resumed power; Parliament was deadlocked between the Lower House, which supported the Constitutionalist ministers, and the House of Peers, controlled by 'The King's Friends', which blocked all reform. Then Murat, to whom the Austrians had tacitly agreed to cede Naples, sided with Napoleon after his escape from Elba, and was rapidly deposed. The King sailed for Naples forthwith, ignoring the new statute obliging him to seek Parliament's permission before leaving the island, and reentered his capital in triumph in May 1815. Once restored he abandoned all pretence of liberalism, abolishing the 1812 Constitution and all separate Sicilian institutions, while proclaiming the Union of both his kingdoms. Maria Carolina was no longer there to nag him. Rejoicing at Bentinck's downfall, her preparations to return home were cut short by a major stroke that killed her at Vienna in September 1814. Within two months Ferdinand was remarried to his mistress, whom he created Duchess of Floridia. Pretty, placid and apolitical, she was quite a contrast to her predecessor. Calm seemed to have returned to Sicily, and to Europe with the general pacification, but the frustrated taste for reform had left a legacy of discontent for the future.

The Earl, meanwhile, was at pains to keep on good terms with Ferdinand's representatives. He wrote to Prince Castelcicala, the ambassador in London, to thank him for sending some journals and when he informed Castelcicala of Charlotte's wedding, he was recommended to write and tell the King, to safeguard the position of the future heirs. In March 1811 the ambassador advised the Earl that, after examining Nelson's will, the estate could not be left at whim, but according to Sicilian law it must descend to male heirs or failing them to female heirs. So William wrote to the Consul-General at Palermo asking him to discover the exact legal position, and also whether he was exempted from the double tax recently imposed on absentee landlords. He and his son-in-law raised several other issues, to which the harassed Consul-General replied that in the present disturbed state of Sicily, it was impossible to get answers to these questions but 'as soon as things are slightly more settled' he would endeavour to do so.

Otherwise the Earl seems to have been unconcerned with the implications of the political upheaval in Sicily. A letter from Bentinck however, asking that a suitable proxy for the Duchy should be appointed to the Sicilian Parliament, did bestir him to action. Gibbs advised that Forcella could not be trusted to be the proxy representative of the Duchy in the Parliament, and the Earl wrote to Palermo, proposing that Bentinck himself was the best fitted to appoint the proxy, 'to vote on public matters only', and in no way to interfere with the running of the Duchy.

The most significant feature of the correspondence is the growing distrust between the absentee landlord and his agents. In autumn 1810 the Earl made a list of reasons why the estate should never be let outright to Gibbs and Forcella. He felt the contract would be unenforceable if the Duchy was mismanaged or confiscated; that such a contract would entirely bar its sale; while the 'oppressive measures' they would undoubtedly take to obtain an immediate large return would alienate the local people. Nevertheless the idea of one tenant retained its attractions; in September 1810 the Earl advised Gibbs that he might consider any proposal equal to the improved rental, paid to him quarterly and for a seven year period, but pointing out that he was merely the tenant for life, and that the agreement would not be binding on his successor. Gibbs answered, optimistically suggesting a lease for seven years at £2,800 per annum, to be paid quarterly after all arrears had been settled, thereby for the first time expressing his own interest in the transaction. But the Earl promptly replied that he had 'forgotten' the idea of granting a lease on any terms, and that anyway £2,800, the sum once offered to Nelson, was quite inadequate. There the matter rested.

Suspicion of his agents' motives was fuelled by outside accusations concerning their integrity. For example, an anonymous petition signed 'Your Brontese subjects' was received by the Earl in March 1812. This alleged that Mrs Graeffer had persuaded Gibbs and Forcella to appoint as Governor (ie the Duchy steward); 'a miserable favourite of hers called Don Gregorio Biosa. This adventurer, destitute of merit, on seeing himself raised to such an office gave himself up to all manner of excesses and debaucheries imaginable.' He had reputedly persuaded 'a decent girl', a minor, to elope with him, had been tried and imprisoned, but released thanks to Gibbs' influence. All public offices were sold or bestowed by Biosa and Mrs Graeffer; the Duchy's vassals were forbidden their common right of gathering charcoal; the gate at Maniace had been locked stopping all access to the Abbey church. 'Also your own interests and advantages are going to ruin,' for Mrs Graeffer and Biosa had withheld the fiefs, although there had been bidders at proper prices, blatantly granting them to their friends or supporters for lesser rents. 'Mrs Graeffer, therefore, this old cheat to whom My Lord you pay 100 ounces a year, settled upon her by your generous brother, instead of attending to your interests makes this great profit at your expense by means of plotting and fraud.' The petition recommended that the Earl appoint an independent and reliable person to make secret enquiries; Don Guiseppe Lombardo at Palermo could furnish all the details.

The document was sent on to Gibbs with the comment that some of the allegations might be true, that Lombardo should be seen forthwith and that he had entire authority to hire and fire employees on the spot. Gibbs replied promptly that Biosa had denied all the allegations made against him. The Earl scornfully retorted: 'It was not likely Biosa would acknowledge the validity of the charges made against him.' The allegations must be thoroughly investigated, while it should be announced that Mrs Graeffer had no authority to interfere. Those found guilty must be sacked, while 'not an hour should be lost in recovering any portions of the Duchy that had been criminally sequestered'. The enlarged power of attorney followed, being made out to Gibbs alone; 'You must regulate the whole detail of the administration, reduce and circumscribe the expense and transmit me annually a proper account in the English language.' It disclaimed any wish to offend Forcella but advanced the pretext that only one person could be put in charge. In October a letter from Palermo stated that the charges made in the petition had been investigated by Forcella, who reported they were almost all unfounded. Gibbs warned that they must be careful as: 'Forcella has been frequently on the spot and nothing was done without his approbation.' He promised that henceforward he would attend to every detail of the estate personally, nor would he delegate authority to Mrs Graeffer or other undeserving persons. The Earl professed himself satisfied by this assurance, a satisfaction mitigated by a note from Lombardo. It expressed surprise:

'that Gibbs had been expected to be a person capable of conceiving and giving a suitable opinion on the subjects contained in the petition.' As for Forcella: 'it was useless for me to go to him, it not being likely that the very accomplice should be an impartial judge of the offender.' Lombardo again offered to cooperate with any disinterested investigator the Earl might care to appoint: 'to understand the causes of dissension which have for many years troubled your city of Bronte.'

The nightmare was that as one problem seemed to have been settled, another, hydra-like, arose. Gibbs had smoothly passed on the blame for the discrepancy in the accounts to Forcella, 'who would provide the explanation.' The latter eventually admitted the discrepancy, but pointed out that the duchy was no longer exempt from taxation; it was now taxed at 384 ounces per annum and a further 'donativo' would shortly be issued.

The accounts at last arrived in December 1811 and the discrepancy was indeed explained as monies which had to be kept back against the possible succession tax on the Duchy. In fact the figures were by no means disastrous. However, there were a mass of unspecified outgoings while Gibbs and Forcella had raised their annual charges of 1,200 ounces for looking after the estate's affairs by some 50 per cent. Examining the accounts, Haslewood could only remark: 'At this distance what can you do except complain, and what would such complaints avail?' So in March 1812 the Earl merely congratulated Forcella, who had contrived to have the succession duty waived; he did not mention the discrepancy again, only expressing his concern about fees and costs. He had been asking for a plan of the estate for three years, so that usurped land could be discovered, and the portion covered by lava properly delimited, and this was finally completed. For the next couple of years, this unsatisfactory state of affairs persisted. Surprisingly, even Gibbs began grumbling about Forcella. By October 1814 the Earl was truly exasperated and wrote: 'I have not had a word or a farthing for nine months.' Since the money voted by Parliament for his brother's services had just been laid out on buying an English estate, 'my income is reduced so much that the want of regular payments from Bronte have become a serious and distressing inconvenience . . . I know not how to express my uneasiness and astonishment without offending you.' More than two years' rent was now unaccounted for, while he must continue paying Lady Hamilton's annuity and the 10 percent property tax on it in advance. In late November Gibbs finally answered, belatedly enclosing some more money but saying that he was unable to take on the entire management of the estate. This deflated the Earl, who had little choice but: 'regretfully to accept your inability to undertake the entire management of my concerns in Sicily as you had once proposed.'

Things remained fairly quiet until the late summer of 1816, when a bombshell arrived. A Mr John Skurry wrote from Messina to inform the Earl that Gibbs had committed suicide on July 15th. 'He was found in his chamber early the next morning, a large horse pistol lying by his side, and his head blown to pieces. His debts are rumoured to total three to four million ounces. The creditors at Palermo are very numerous, chiefly among the nobility and gentry.' The truth was that although Gibbs had seemed: 'at the very height of his repute and prosperity', all was far from well with his business. Half-an-hour earlier he had been playing backgammon with his brother, when he received a message that the government had again deferred repaying him several large loans. The shock had been too much for him, particularly as it had later transpired that his confidential clerk had been systematically robbing him and concealing the real extent of the disaster.

Skurry now proceeded to offer his services as the new agent at Bronte. Within three weeks he had extended this to a suggestion that he lease the whole estate for ready cash. If the Earl was a creditor, he must send out a fresh power of attorney straight away. Gibbs' affairs were in chaos; it now seemed that the loss of an unsecured loan of 60,000 ounces was the last straw, but he had been fundamentally insolvent since 1812. Moreover the son-in-law, Colonel A'Court, who had recently married Mary Gibbs, was brother to the ambassador at Naples, and had filed a claim for £30,000, representing the bond he held for his wife's dowry, which Skurry was convinced would be given priority.

The Earl was worried. He had no intention of appointing Forcella as his principal agent, but it was madness to appoint Skurry – an entirely unknown quantity. He had to find: 'some able, intelligent and trusty person to send out to Bronte.' Fortunately Julius Hutchinson, who had succeeded Haslewood as the Nelsons' solicitor, was able to help: '. . . a gentleman named Bryan Barrett, who had some time since practised as a solicitor in London, but was obliged to live abroad on account of his health, applied for the post'. After a meeting with the Earl, it was proposed that he should go out to Sicily as 'Procurator General of the Duchy'. He promptly accepted the offer, giving a bond of £3,000 as a guarantee of his reliability. By September 30th Barrett was ready to start for Sicily with his family, armed with an introduction to the

British Vice-Consul at Messina, to enable him to forward remittances. He wrote optimistically to the Earl: 'Some time, I fear, will be requisite to bring affairs round at Bronte, but nothing shall be wanting on my part to forward to the utmost the best interests of Your Lordship.'

Barrett's first letter to England, written from Naples in January 1817 was pessimistic. He believed that the chances of recovering anything from the deceased's estate, even at a creditors' rate of 20 percent, were highly dubious. When he wrote again from Bronte, a fortnight later, Barrett was still more depressed. Forcella, 'who begins now to be fearful as well as suspicious,' had handed over some money, but half of it must be used to pay outstanding taxes and so avert a threatened sequestration of the Duchy. The chances of recovering anything from Gibbs' estate now seemed even more remote; every day a fresh horror was exposed: 'I verily believe that if Your Grace had delayed for two years more the sending out some person from England to look into your affairs, the estate would have been brought in debtor to Gibbs and Forcella.' Barrett reported he had persuaded Biosa to come out of his sanctuary at Messina and make a full confession of his misdeeds. 'I expect a pretty tale of villainy to be unfolded'; although the steward might well run away again and could not be rearrested: 'there is no benefit of law here but for the thief.' Meanwhile, the house and garden had fallen into a ruinous state, while: 'the exhalations arising from the low ground and some larger pools and marshes along the river render it very dangerous during the hot months of summer'. Proper drainage might solve the problem, and Barrett was prepared to live there nine months of the year: 'it is certainly most desirable to undertake it, for the house stands in the middle of the greatest parts of the lands which are at lease and have not been granted anciently in perpetuity'. He proposed hiring two masons and two carpenters in Catania to fell the timber and see to the estate's running repairs.

As to rectifying the abuses perpetrated: 'to discover deeper villainy every hour that cannot be punished is heart-breaking. There is not a single man among all the servants of the Duchy who was honest, or dared at least to be so.' Mrs Graeffer had died in the autumn of 1815, having taken six months' pension in advance, yet for all her plundering she and Biosa had been nearly destitute. Forcella on the other hand had, in Barrett's view, made a fortune out of the estate. The Earl must resign himself to a low income for some time, although eventually the Duchy could become profitable. However Barrett had grave doubts regarding the local people: 'The three 'campieri' (estate guards) are three as consummate thieves as any in the Kingdom of Sicily.'

In reply the Earl reluctantly agreed with Barrett that they must shut their eyes to the past, although if gross misconduct could be proved against Forcella he was keen to prosecute. He was happy for Barrett to purchase cattle and hire builders. Mrs Graeffer's death had removed one troublemaker, while as to the Duchy officers: 'Of course their salaries will cease. I cannot continue to pay useless people as hitherto and receive nothing for myself. I had better give up all at once otherwise.' In concluding, he did concede there could be little chance of remittances until the outstanding problems had been resolved; 'fully relying on your judgement and economy in all that may lead to my advantage.'

Silence ensued once more for the next nine months. As in 1816 it was to be broken by a bombshell. On March 1st 1818, a Mr George Wood wrote from Palermo informing the Earl of Bryan Barrett's death there at 5am that morning. 'He arrived here about fourteen days ago from Bronte; the fatigue of the journey had weakened him very much.' Wood promptly offered his services as the new agent: 'My long residence here, my knowledge of the country and people may perhaps entitle me to the confidence of Your Lordship.' A letter from Signor Ognibene, counsel to the Duchy, soon followed, explaining that Barrett, foreseeing his death, had given his wife a general power of attorney and had left everything in order. Enclosed was a recommendation from another of the lawyers, Rosario di Martino, that Mrs Barrett be appointed her husband's successor to be aided at Bronte by his brother, Joseph.

In a lengthy communication Martha Barrett lamented: 'the irreparable loss, I and four fatherless children have sustained.' To add to her misfortunes, 'a most violent shock of an earthquake has so shattered the house we are in belonging to Baron Meli, that we must if possible remove to another . . . We still sleep in one vaulted room, myself and females with the children on a billiard table in the middle, Mr di Martino and the menservants round. Different families have erected temporary wooden shelters on the plains about the town.' She asked for instructions, offering her own services as agent, adding: 'I confess I do not want to see another person in Sicily engaged in these affairs.' She entertained fears with regard to Ognibene's honesty, but extolled the virtues of the di Martinos, especially 'their activity and fidelity'.

Once she had reached Palermo, Mrs Barrett addressed the Earl again. She requested a year's trial, promising to write every two months. On hearing that Martha Barrett was willing to become the agent in her husband's stead, the Earl responded enthusiastically: 'it

121

will afford me the gratification to befriend the widow and the fatherless'; moreover the fact that she had been left in charge during her husband's absences combined with the recommendations he had heard of her abilities, encouraged him to appoint her to the post. Mrs Barrett was implored to send accounts and letters regularly and to practise 'due economy', although the building projects were sanctioned.

She expressed her gratitude fulsomely, promising her fidelity and zeal, even offering to come to England if required, provided she could travel overland. She admitted problems in finding suitable staff, describing Spedalieri, Mrs Graeffer's son-in-law, as 'the only rational person . . . at Bronte', but he was too deeply implicated in earlier frauds. As to the others, 'we are surrounded by starving lawyers and physicians, not a respectable person amongst them'. Only the poor she believed regretted her husband's death. Now she would solely employ people whom he had approved of, and would supervise everything herself.

The immediate problem concerned the agent's residence. After much deliberation, she finally decided to settle on restoring the house at Maniace; repairs on it and on the church had begun under the steward Antonio's direction. Having now taken a three year lease on Baron Meli's house, she would stay there in the summer for four months, and live at Maniace for most of the remaining eight, 'when the malarial vapours of the evening and before sunrise are not found so hurtful'.

On receiving Mrs Barrett's plans, and the accounts, the Earl's lawyer Hutchinson wrote a chilly letter, saying that he found it most unsatisfactory that all the balance of Duchy income over expenditure, some 2,000 ounces, should have been retained. Even if the dilapidated state of the buildings had required the entire sum, Mrs Barrett must remember that the Earl had received no remittances at all since early in 1815, and these had merely represented arrears. The proposal that the buildings at Maniace should be repaired was agreed to, although Hutchinson could not see the need for her to lease a residence at Bronte as well. He doubted also whether Antonio, 'although a very honest character, was the proper person to superintend the repairs'. Indeed he professed his amazement at a country where people could freely cut wood on someone else's land; in England this would be tantamount to robbery.

At the end of that year an interesting document reached London. Mrs Barrett had prepared 'a list of persons employed by the Duke of

Bronte' and to this was appended a note of current expenses and taxes. There were 38 employees altogether, and these included: 6 *'campieri'* (or Duchy guards), paid 36 ounces a year, the oldest of whom was seventy-six. Each was allowed a best outfit every three years and 'a common suit every year.'

In addition there were: 3 gardeners,
3 muleteers,
1 butterman,
9 labourers, each paid
33 ounces a year,

1 pigkeeper,
1 caretaker,
9 shepherds, each paid
barely 14 ounces a year.

There was also one cowherd and two other men listed as 'having no particular duties to perform', whose wages were unspecified. Twelve men had already been sacked; five more were to go, including the carpenter, 'to be discharged in six or eight months if he is kept constantly at work.' There was no mention of the other building staff, who were supposed to have been hired. In toto the wages absorbed 1,250 ounces per annum, state taxes took another 1,710, while payments to the monks at Bronte and San Filippo di Fragala, with various other local causes, cost a further 715 ounces.

The clerical staff included a notary and the chaplain, whose emoluments, plus payments to no fewer than ten lawyers, amounted to 380 ounces. Counting in Mrs Barrett's salary of 600 ounces, plus another 600 incurred under the heading of 'house', the grand total of Duchy expenditure exceeded 5,250 ounces. Meanwhile, in a reasonable year, rents brought in 5,400 ounces, and the sale of corn another 2,400. Thus the owner of the estate might count himself lucky to be left with a net income considerably smaller than Gibbs had promised to Nelson fifteen years before.

On top of the unsatisfactory financial situation, allegations concerning Martha Barrett's behaviour and honesty poured in to trouble the Earl. In an anxious letter Hutchinson wrote that he hoped that: 'your conduct is and will continue to be the exact reverse of what is imputed to you'. Naturally if she had come to feel the job was beyond her strength: 'you should express yourself without reserve'.

Eventually, on hearing in March 1819 that contrary to his express orders she had dismissed Joseph di Martino, the Earl decided to act. Afraid that Mrs Barrett was likely to marry Antonio Pratese (her husband's former steward), 'which would necessarily lead, contrary to my determination, to my affairs being placed in the hands of a foreigner', the Earl decided he must send someone out to investigate the numerous complaints, while the Duchy's management must be entrusted ad interim to some responsible deputy. Hutchinson was instructed to look for suitable candidates for both these tasks.

Considering that a post at Bronte was only likely to appeal to a very small cross-section, it is amazing how rapidly people were always found prepared to travel to Sicily and try out the prospects. Yet again the Earl was lucky. Within a few weeks Mr Philip Thovez, a purser in the Royal Navy and then Secretary to Captain McCulloch of the Revenue Service at Deal, had applied for the job of going out to investigate the abuses. Simultaneously a Mr James Smith, formerly resident in Sicily as an agricultural adviser to the British Commissariat, was engaged to go out in that capacity to Bronte and, temporarily at least, to take charge of the running of the estate. Thovez seemed vigorous and articulate, so after several interviews, it was agreed that he should be sent out to examine the state of affairs at Bronte on the Earl's behalf. He was only to be paid the expenses of the trip, while his application to take over from Mrs Barrett as agent was to be considered in the meantime. Smith's salary was however fixed at £100 per annum, plus a right to some of the estate produce. Both men were ordered to begin their journeys to Sicily in May 1819; Smith was to travel out with his family and possessions.

Before their departure, Hutchinson drew up voluminous instructions, primarily for Thovez's benefit, which ran in all to some 23 pages. He was enjoined to write constantly to the Earl, to consult with Rosario di Martino at Palermo, and to beware of seeming to condemn Mrs Barrett or 'of satisfying impertinent enquiries'. If the connection between her and Antonio Pratese was as disreputable as had been alleged, she was to be dismissed as painlessly as possible.

The accounts from 1815 onwards were to be thoroughly examined; as for the income: 'it is only necessary to observe that His Lordship has received nothing for himself for four years past', so he would expect remittances again from 1820 of £3,000 per annum with a considerable increase in prospect thereafter. On no account should Thovez stir up a hornet's nest during his visit to Bronte, and he must return with all speed to England to report personally to the Earl. Finally both men were cautioned to devote their whole time to the discharge of their duties, and 'not to be concerned in any speculations or traffic on their own account' on pain of instant dismissal. On past evidence, this was a pious hope indeed.

CHAPTER X

In search of a solution

'I have been reduced to the most shameful and painful circumstances to which any person who took the interest of an employer was ever subjected,' wrote Mrs Barrett to the Earl in spring 1820. The brief history of the Duchy to date had been marred by fraud, misconduct and scandal. It might now seem to its harassed proprietor that, after a string of unpleasant rows, he had found a reasonably satisfactory solution to its problems, with several honest and diligent men in charge of the estate. Alas, the next decade was to show this to be largely an illusion.

Philip Thovez arrived at Bronte in midsummer 1819, and was immediately inundated with a flood of claims and counter-accusations from everyone.

That autumn, he reported back to the Earl and Hutchinson. The latter wrote that Thovez's investigations acquitted Mrs Barrett of deliberate fraud, but found her expenses for house, furniture and 'other extraordinary items' to be exorbitant. Joseph di Martino's integrity remained unimpaired. The final proposal was that the new agent's salary should be limited to 1,000 ounces (then equivalent to £540), while he should be officially allowed estate produce, to which he would help himself anyway. As the expenses Thovez submitted seemed reasonable, only £225 altogether, following further negotiation he was appointed General Agent to the Duchy, providing a bond for £2,000 himself as a guarantee.

Back in Sicily, James Smith was busy chronicling the gloomy state of affairs. Late in October he wrote: 'We have many dubious characters about us that we cannot discharge without proper orders.' He had been commissioned to make an agricultural survey of the entire estate, to report on the state of the woods and on possible improvements, and to take charge of the harvest. Also he was supposed to survey the land in the Boschetto earmarked by the Barretts as the site for the agent's house and to advise whether this was practical for a year-round residence. Yet he complained that no instructions had been left and he had no idea what his precise duties were. Hutchinson retorted that Smith's long silence had almost led the Earl to dismiss him, so his letter had arrived in the nick of time. Sympathy for the malarial attacks he had mentioned was proffered, while the promise of an early remittance was gratefully accepted. In December, after another long illness, Smith's letter recommended that the Duchy should let the two farms in hand and sell off the 700 sheep and 100 pigs which cost far more than they ever brought in, as he had already done with the cows. The vineyards and olive plantations could, however, profitably be extended. He reiterated his opinion that if the same economy as practised in the preceding six months could be maintained, the estate should produce a net revenue of 4,000 ounces during 1820. Finally he offered to resign on Thovez's return if his services were no longer deemed to be needed. Meanwhile, a serious cause for concern arrived in the form of a letter from Bronte signed Nunzio Negozia. This was decidedly strong meat: 'I speak through the mouth of an entire population about the injustices done to her [Mrs Barrett]. During her administration all your farms, houses, vines, fields and woods were well cared for. It was through God's omnipotence (ie the earthquake) that they were ruined. It is now in contemplation among us Brontesi to take from you your commons and waste lands which originally belonged to us ... I am really the more astonished that a man professing religion as Your Excellency does can commit such an outrage against innocence ... Learn too that Smith only knows how to eat, drink and sleep. He keeps the best wine for his table, and with these talents he has ruined the Duchy.' The letter concluded melodramatically: 'We are even ready to sacrifice our lives for so worthy a person as Mrs Barrett.'

The Earl was outraged and wrote to Thovez: 'This appears to me to exceed in audacity and insolence even any former communications of the Brontesi.' He wanted the author's real identity discovered, and a prosecution brought for libel and conspiracy. Thovez must discover the truth; if Mrs Barrett and Pratese were behind it, he should try to get them expelled from Sicily by the authorities.

Mrs Barrett vehemently denied to Hutchinson that she had sent the Earl any anonymous letters. She enclosed a letter to the Earl which was overtly offensive: 'Surely there must be some fascination which draws

128

Your Lordship and your advisers towards di Martino?' The accusations against Pratese were despicable, for he had meticulously supervised all the building work, while for the loss of her husband, 'my reward has been injustice and calumny.'

In late spring 1820 a long report from Thovez, dated April 9th, arrived in London. He had left for Sicily with his wife and children on January 2nd, and had a rough midwinter journey. At Bronte he had found a morass of problems. Firstly Smith had hired labourers from Castiglione to plough up between the vines, although the local farmers swore this was a method of cultivation unsuited to the neighbourhood, which would damage the plants. As yet their argument remained unproven, but Thovez had grave doubts as to the wisdom of this innovation. Moreover he saw no prospects in 1820 of making the remittances earlier promised by Smith. The accounts were so chaotic that no proper statement of the Duchy finances could even be prepared. Briefly there was about 1,000 ounces in hand, with a further 1,200 still uncollected from the 1819 rents, most of which should be written off as bad debts. Even had he all the money owing, the estate's expenses until August with salaries, taxes and building costs would more than absorb the whole. 'Mr Smith could not have considered the necessary disbursements to be made, or he would not have written such nonsense.' Want of money had delayed starting the repairs at Maniace. A few weeks later Thovez added that even a good harvest would do no more than balance the books, as so much revenue went in taxes. It was pointless to press too hard upon the tenants in arrears, as, if he evicted them there was not the smallest chance of letting the land to anyone else. After that year he felt no part of the estate should be kept in hand, for Smith's efforts had yet to prove successful. Therefore all the remaining livestock should be sold except for the mules and a few oxen, while only vines and fruit trees, 'as opportunities offer', would be cultivated in future.

As to the real identity of Nunzio Negozia, no such person existed at Bronte and all attempts to find him had been in vain. Di Martino opined that Mrs Barrett had been the author of the memorial, but the judge at Bronte was so hostile that he would suppress any evidence. Thovez had paid her 300 ounces owing, as she had been artfully broadcasting her distress, and only subsequently had recommenced abusing everybody. However they need not worry, for she could do little harm: 'I can assure you the Brontesi have entirely abandoned her; they are ready to enlist under any banner that can give them a good dinner and that she cannot offer to do.' She had now turned Catholic and was still determined to marry Pratese, although the latter, charged by di Martino with assault, had escaped arrest by flight. With any luck all this should make her leave Bronte quickly, although a month later he reported she would stay there until she settled her debts.

In June 1820 the Earl replied to Thovez in deep depression. He agreed they had best cease farming. The planting of vines could be continued, provided it did not interfere with an annual remittance of at least £2,000. Smith should not be dismissed for another year anyway, as he might be useful as a deputy agent and to oversee the labourers.

These interminable epistolary ping-pong matches were suddenly interrupted by outside events. Once safely reinstated at Naples, and supported by Austrian bayonets, Ferdinand had had no qualms about abolishing the 1812 constitution, or separate Sicilian institutions even including the flag, while freedom of the press was suppressed. The two countries were formally amalgamated into the Kingdom of the Two Sicilies; laws and an administration based on a centralised French model were imported from the mainland, and the island was divided into seven new provinces with intendants in charge. Royal absolutism had returned, and many of the nobility now saw in separation from Naples the best hope of retaining their privileges. An economic slump had accompanied the return to peace; and when British expenditure of some £12 million per annum ceased in 1815, local wheat prices fell by three-quarters and land values plummeted correspondingly. The government had not however abandoned all ideas of land reform; in 1818 it was proposed that some of the most inefficient *latifondi* should be split up into more viable smaller units. Meanwhile the King's minister, Luigi Medici, who ruled supreme over the kingdom, only wanted peace and quiet, ignoring the intrigues of the revolutionary Carbonarists, whose numbers had grown significantly by 1820. Sicily still appeared tranquil, for Ferdinand's son, the Duke of Calabria, had been a conscientious Viceroy.

In July 1820, however, revolution erupted in Naples, and the Carbonarists, led by General Florestano Pepe, forced the King to promise to publish a constitution within a week. News of this had immediate and violent repercussions in Sicily. Bourbon troops were attacked in the streets of Palermo, the garrison then withdrew from the capital, and a separatist junta was formed. In the countryside many landless labourers reoccupied plots from which they had been excluded since 1812, and brigand gangs terrorized the interior. Eastern Sicily, following the lead of Messina, largely opposed Palermo and supported Naples.

A sizeable army commanded by General Pepe landed to crush the rebellion, while the Palermo junta did not scruple to bolster their position by fomenting social unrest in the countryside – and in many places – open civil war.

With its turbulent past it would indeed have been surprising if Bronte had not become embroiled in the troubles. At the end of August the town mob took up arms in support of the Palermo junta, refusing to pay any more taxes and setting fire to the houses of those loyal to the government, including the mayor, Gioacchino Spedalieri, who fled to Randazzo. As the timorous Committee of Public Safety which they had formed did nothing, the mob offered its allegiance to the leader of a guerrilla band encamped at Troina. On September 3rd a crowd of over 2,000 marched on Maletto, where the entire population was forced to wear yellow ribands and the mayor was besieged in his house. A report reached the authorities who sent a captain-at-arms, Gregorio Zuccaro, with seventy soldiers to Randazzo. Finding the populace there ignored his cry of 'Long live the King', Zuccaro retreated with his men, capturing a courier near Maniace, who carried papers revealing Brontese efforts to foment rebellion in the neighbouring town. As the troops approached Bronte, they found the hillsides covered with groups of armed men advancing towards them. Zuccaro retired over the Cantara bridge along the Troina road, halting his men on a plateau to fire on their pursuers. A furious fight ensued, which lasted several hours. The Brontesi, more numerous and knowing the ground, suffered a mere two casualties, slightly wounded, but the soldiers, who soon took to headlong flight left behind six injured as prisoners of their adversaries.

Hearing of this disaster, Brigadier Prince della Catena sent out patrols in the woods on Etna, which, lacking the strength to attack Bronte, focused on looting instead. The rebels were not idle either, manning all vantage points. Swollen to 1,200 strong by reinforcements from Troina and Cesaro, and armed with four pieces of artillery, they contemplated an advance on Randazzo. The news of Pepe's landing at Messina however, made the Committee of Public Safety more conciliatory, and they sent della Catena a letter explaining that Zuccaro's force had been mistaken for bandits. The visit of Colonel Palmieri with 500 junta troops enraptured the mob, but after accomplishing little he left three days later and the Committee decided to come to an agreement with the authorities.

The terms offered by della Catena were harsh: all arms must be surrendered forthwith and 24 prominent citizens sent as hostages to

Aderno. Receiving no answer, he marched on Bronte on the morning of September 15th with 2,000 troops. He was met by a procession from the town led by Thovez and several priests, imploring him to refrain from an assault. Della Catena repeated his demands, giving an hour's deadline, although he waited all day for a reply. That evening an army captain was parleying with the rebels, who, seeing him wave a white handkerchief at the royal troops, mistook him for a spy and opened fire. Hostilities commenced and the Brontesi gathered behind the walls, compensating for their paucity in numbers by placing caps on sticks along the parapet which were then fired on by the bewildered soldiers. Field guns began to shell the town, at which the Brontesi undaunted made a sortie and captured one of them.

Night fell and sporadic firing continued. At dawn all the church bells were rung and, led by a shepherd called Vincenzo Cucco, the Brontesi made a mass sortie against the foe. A fierce engagement took place, until della Catena unwisely gave orders to retreat. Leaving their baggage behind, the soldiers fled headlong towards Aderno, while the Brontesi returned in triumph, carrying five of their enemies' heads on poles around the town. Della Catena sent a despatch to the Intendant, exaggerating his opponents' numbers and minimising his own losses, while the Committee also wrote, deploring the bloodshed yet claiming the people had only acted in self-defence and to curb the troops' excesses. The Intendant replied in conciliatory fashion, promising to ask for clemency provided the Brontesi showed real proofs of their loyalty. A deputation headed by Thovez then went to Messina to beg General Pepe to grand a pardon, and on October 29th the town's officials swore their loyalty to the Crown before della Catena at Aderno. As recorded by that thoroughly partial historian, Radice, at a *Te Deum* which everyone attended, a picture of the Virgin Mary could be seen – identical to the lady who, seated on a white mule with a pistol in one hand and a flag in the other, had been seen by both sides in the battle urging the Brontesi on to victory.

In August Thovez had written to England, extolling the new Constitution granted by the King and deploring the formation of the separatist junta at Palermo. He had been elected one of the eight members of the Committee of Public Safety, and had gained popularity by selling them 200 'salme' of the estate's corn. He intended to return to Maniace shortly as, despite an excessively hot summer, all his children were healthy.

But a letter Thovez wrote in October told a very different tale. On August 14th a Warrant for Joseph di Martino's arrest for sedition had arrived from the Intendant at Catania. The Committee of Public Safety had failed to carry it out, claiming they had no military force to subdue the riots that would certainly ensue. Di Martino had donned the yellow riband, and, ignoring Thovez's protests, had distributed others to all the Duchy's staff. Thovez resigned as Deputy, warning the Brontesi to remain neutral like the Duchy. He decided to run the risk of malaria and return to Maniace taking with him his family and the *campieri* to guard the storage barns. Thovez had scant respect for the martial prowess of the rebel troops: panic had ensued and all the church bells at Bronte rung when a distant flock of goats had been mistaken for the royal army! Once his best efforts to mediate had proved unavailing, Thovez had walked to Maniace with his family, with mules carrying their bedding. Fortunately he had taken furniture and possessions from their home at Bronte, for the day after their victory, armed rebels had entered many private houses, demanding money, valuables and drink.

Now that the rebellion was over, Thovez had consented to go to Messina to intercede with the authorities. 'I could not refuse making the attempt in order to encourage the people to go to their work. All the lands were abandoned and had this tumult continued only another month, no corn would have been sown and consequently all the year's rents lost to Your Lordship. I was fortunately able to open a road for an amicable adjustment.' The Brontesi had been fined 1,200 ounces and order had been restored. All in all it had been a wretched episode, and the Duchy had been lucky only to have lost 150 ounces altogether, from a local tax levied by the rebels.

The replies from England praised Thovez's diplomacy and his support for the government. They stressed that Joseph di Martino's revolutionary sentiments rendered it impossible to re-employ him whatever his other merits might be: 'Never again ... deal with someone who has conducted himself in so mutinous and rebellious a manner.'

The rebellion of 1820 had provided a dramatic interlude; all too soon, however, the old familiar problems in the running of the Duchy were resurrected. That autumn Thovez reported the new method of cultivating the vines had failed; ploughing between them had pulled up some and flattened others. The pruning had been injudicious and many of the young plants had died from neglect. Less than half the previous year's vintage had been produced and much replanting was needed. Nevertheless he had sent half a pipe of Duchy wine to the coast for sale on the London market. Should it prove as good as

Woodhouse's Bronte Madeira, 'that alone will be worth as much as the whole estate,' he concluded optimistically.

So convinced was he of this that he decided to employ a winemaker – a local English resident called John Causton. He had had previous experience in producing wines near Messina for the London market, and Thovez felt sure they had hired a real expert. Causton stated that no wine should be sent to England until it had matured for three years, and that the estate vineyards must be extended. He proposed to increase the existing twenty acres by another twenty in May 1822, and twenty more a year later. Within a decade, the Earl was assured, he could expect to receive between £4,000 and £8,000 per annum from wine sales, even if none was exported to England, and allowing for the construction of a store to hold 500 pipes of wine, or four years' vintage.

However, this was not the only point on which Thovez was soon proved to have been over-optimistic. A poor harvest was blamed on the recent troubles; many rents would go unpaid, and he had been obliged 'to furnish our tottering tenants with 120 "salme" more seed corn this year than last'; otherwise they would have abandoned the land. Such misery prevailed at Bronte that he could scarcely imagine how some of the poor could survive the winter. Indeed, in February 1821, 'despite a foot of snow hundreds of the poor walked to Maniace to beg a mouthful of bread.'

Thovez had also turned bookkeeper himself, after discovering the Barretts had never kept a ledger, and that the shepherd had no idea how many sheep or pigs the Duchy owned; but now all was in order. Yet in March 1821 Thovez was still making excuses for sending no remittance to England.

And so life went on. The estate continued to prove a thorn in the side of the Earl and his advisers, and failed to generate any income. Numerous letters, memos and legal papers were exchanged – often crossing each other en route. Estate staff members came and went. The winemaker, Causton, who had been engaged with such optimism, was dismissed at the end of 1821. To compound its problems, Maniace was cut off by snowfalls eight or ten feet deep in February 1822. This prevented both people and mules from getting in or out and also meant that no corn could be sold.

In March 1822 Rosario di Martino died, leaving behind a widow and two boys in desperate straits. When the Earl was informed, he instructed that she be helped with an immediate cash sum – but he was not prepared to give her a pension.

Meanwhile, Smith resigned his post as he found it impossible to work with Thovez. He left the estate for Messina, taking with him the detailed maps of the Duchy, the accounts and 2,000 ounces. He then returned to England in June to explain his reasons for resigning to the Earl and Hutchinson. They agreed that Smith had not been given 'the real and effectual support which was requisite,' nor 'had great provocations from the persons employed under him been repressed,' nor had he been handed the summary of his duties, while he had been relegated by Thovez to a very subordinate position. His employers were convinced of Smith's ability to run the agricultural side of the Duchy on the basis originally envisaged, and had prevailed on him to withdraw his resignation and return to Sicily bearing extended instructions as to his duties, plus a power of attorney to be used in case of Thovez's death or incapacity.

These additional instructions clearly illustrate the power of advocacy of a case made in person rather than by mail. Smith was absolved from all blame for ploughing between the vines, the failure of the vintage was attributed to the general failure throughout Sicily that year, as they had produced adequately the next. Hence he was authorised to repeat the experiment again to give it a fair trial. Similarly with the olives, the contention that planting wild trees naturally better suited to their environment than the less hardy species previously used was agreed, as was further planting of them. Smith had supported the merits of letting direct to the *inquilini* (the direct tenants), hence avoiding the middleman's profit, and of getting tenants from neighbouring communities, so this too was approved; although he had advised against leases of longer than six years. His idea of transporting the wine to the coast, where it would find a ready market, without all the risks run in exporting it, was also to be adopted. He was to be provided with a horse or mule at Duchy expense for his work, and was to be solely answerable for the success of all the farming operations, although the hope of his cordial cooperation with his colleague Thovez was piously expressed.

Meanwhile Hutchinson wrote to Thovez outlining the details of Smith's newly-defined role. He also added that, as the Earl's income was so much reduced, 'in common with all persons of his rank in this Kingdom,' it was proposed to reduce Thovez's salary to 1,000 ounces pa from March 1st, 1823, although Smith's remuneration would remain the same.

On October 18th 1822, Thovez wrote back at interminable length, concluding with a request for a ten to twelve week leave of absence the next spring for a trip to England on family affairs – the true purpose of which would, no doubt, be to attempt to recover his position.

Thovez's receipt of Hutchinson's bombshell at Maniace was quickly followed by the return of the victorious farm manager. For the time being Thovez had little choice but to bow to the inevitable. On November 6th 1822, he wrote to the Earl 'I am anxious that both Smith's duty and mine should be so clearly defined that each should be held responsible for the particular part allotted to him.' Hutchinson, in his reply on the Earl's behalf, expressed amazement that Smith's and Thovez's separate duties had not been clearly defined already – what more could be needed?

The arguments, counter-arguments and letters continued, but Thovez's request for leave of absence was granted. Before leaving for England, Thovez received a letter from Hutchinson in mid-March. This asked Thovez to bring all the remittances, 'which we trust will not fall short of £2,000 sterling,' with him to England, while leaving his colleague full power to act in Duchy affairs.

Until Thovez's departure, both sides continued to bombard London with accusations and counter-charges. And during the next five weeks Smith sent a string of increasingly hysterical letters to London. Finally in summer 1823 Thovez left for England. On August 28th it was recorded that the Earl and Lord Bridport had met the Agent in Hutchinson's Chambers. The discussion had lasted so long that it was adjourned to the Nelson residence in Portman Square. The Earl intimated that he would agree to Smith's dismissal, provided Thovez's own salary was reduced to 1,000 ounces pa as previously proposed. The 200 ounces saved would go with Smith's salary to pay a more efficient assistant. The next morning Thovez demurred at this reduction and was given 24 hours to accept the terms. This he reluctantly did, asking that his salary be restored if he could bring the remittances up to the levels produced by Forcella. The Earl did not consent.

Many other matters were decided as well. The perpetual lease of the house at Bronte was approved at a rent of 30 ounces pa and with the liberty to buy it at any time for 600 ounces. Repairs to the church at Maniace were authorised, 'with as little expense as possible,' plus new vestments for the priest and some candlesticks. A competent local surveyor should be engaged to report on possible improvements to the estate. Various memorials from the Brontesi were examined; all the requests for money being rejected, including Dr. Giuseppe Spedalieri's for a pension after fifty years as bookkeeper at Maniace, except for one minute grant towards establishing a girls' school. In reply to a letter from Joseph di Martino agreeing to drop his other claims if 112 ounces of salary outstanding and the carriage of his furniture to Palermo were paid, Thovez was instructed to make any settlement he could to avoid proceedings being instituted. Again Thovez was enjoined to practise the strictest economy. The largest possible remittances should be made, 'which Their Lordships will consider the best assured test of your ability, diligence and integrity.' Thovez left again for Sicily on September 14th.

Ignorant of these developments, Smith's correspondence continued unabated. His letters crossed with one from Hutchinson of September 2nd which broke the news that the Earl and Bridport 'have with very great reluctance and after considerable discussion and reflection,' concluded that the breach between Smith and Thovez was too great to be healed. Both protagonists had declared so; thus one would have to go. As Smith had previously declared he was unequal to the whole running of the Duchy: 'Their Lordships think it better as the lesser of two evils that you should retire.' They regretted losing his services, which they could not evaluate fairly, and would gladly give him a testimonial. Thovez had been told 'to forbear from anything like exaltation over you'. While Smith's salary would be paid until the end of his current contractual year, mid-April 1824, he could also retain the use of his house. Should he and wife choose to return to England, the Earl would contribute £40 towards their expenses. For the moment Smith had best keep the letter's contents a secret. In a brief note to Barker (the British Vice-Consul at Messina), Hutchinson explained what had happened, repeating that the Earl was in no way displeased with Smith, 'and feels much disappointed at being obliged to make this sacrifice'. Would the Vice-Consul kindly render the couple any help they might need, 'save only pecuniary assistance'.

The problems of the Duchy had not been solved by ending this protracted struggle between its administrators. But from now on its management would proceed along intermittently consistent lines, and even if none of the parties had attained a wholly satisfactory solution, they had all acquired a slightly greater perception of the realities of life at Maniace.

CHAPTER XI

The compromise with reality

'This host of locusts in the persons of Mr. Thovez's father, mother, brother and sisters, relations and friends, has settled on your estate to fatten on the produce of it. No wonder after this if Your Lordship receives but little rent. I shall not be surprised if bye and bye you do not obtain any, and I am truly sorry to foresee this sad consequence'; thus Hutchinson gloomily wrote to the Earl in December 1827. His judgement was exaggerated, if essentially accurate. For Thovez, badly paid and disillusioned by his employers' lack of interest in any schemes for the long-term betterment of the estate, had concluded that his best course was to live off it as comfortably as possible, although he could still act with vigour in defending the Duchy's rights. Meanwhile the Earl and his advisers in England had come to accept the impossibility of managing a property from 2,000 miles distance with communications so appalling, and despite their complaints at the paucity of remittances and periodic threats about changing the administration, to realise the lack of any better alternative.

In summer 1824, Thovez wrote to the Earl saying he wished to employ his own brother, Henry, as a clerk on the same salary Smith had received. The reply from England firmly quashed the idea. He must manage as well as he could without a clerk: 'if the burthen is too great for you, His Grace would prefer your resigning,' of which ample notice would be expected: 'since from the failure of the experiment of keeping an agent at Bronte, His Grace has serious thoughts of letting the estate for a term of years, for which he has had repeated applications.' If not an outright distortion of the facts, this was stretching the truth, for the last such proposal had been made by the Prince of Paterno in mid-1822. Meanwhile, Thovez again wrote lengthy explanations as to why he was unable to send remittances to England.

In summer 1825 a new and serious problem surfaced for the Duchy, one moreover which would take thirty-five years to solve. In April Thovez had casually mentioned that he was off to Catania to consult with the lawyers on the question of the abolition of all 'promiscuous rights': 'a matter of the greatest importance touching His Grace's woods, which the Brontesi have ever considered as their own.' With fresh legislation pending they were trying to recover 'their invaded rights as they see them,' an attempt he wanted to forestall.

By July he told Hutchinson that he had officially applied to the Director-General of Woods and Forests to restrain the Brontesi from cutting timber as proscribed by the Forest Laws. Furthermore he intended to appoint two guards for the woods to arrest transgressors. 'The Brontesi united to a man have left nothing untried to defeat my object'; now the Town Council had proposed also stationing guards in the woods, 'to protect what they call their rights.' A week previously, 'a tumultuous assembly of people' had foregathered in the market-place at Bronte, shouting that Thovez wished them to die of cold. The authorities had done nothing to quell the riot, although luckily violence had not erupted. Fearing for his family's safety he had asked the Intendant of Catania to send some police. Thovez requested permission to seek redress before the courts and employ whatever lawyers might be needed. Granting this, Hutchinson replied that the Earl approved of the measures taken and looked to a definitive settlement of the woods issue that year.

Throughout the autumn the disputes continued unabated. On September 29th 1825, Thovez gleefully reported that his brother had had an audience with Medici. This had resulted in an order to Palermo to see that justice was done to the Duchy. The Council of Intendancy had been browbeaten by the declaration that a direct appeal to the King had been made, and it duly found in the Duchy's favour. However on reaching Bronte two days later, Thovez had found the whole town illuminated as they wrongly believed that they had gained the victory. They too were now taking their case to higher authority; 'the Brontesi are the most determined scoundrels in Sicily.' At least he could now put three more guards in the woods, although the case was giving him endless worry. 'Tomorrow I move with my family to Maniace; the Malaria, I understand, has left it and I must begin preparing for the vintage.'

Congratulations were again proffered by Hutchinson, although it was hoped: 'these contests will not divert your attention from the main object of securing remittances.' Both the congratulations and the hope were premature. The root problem, as Thovez accurately deduced, was that over the centuries the indolence if not outright connivance of most agents of the Grande Ospedale had encouraged the Brontesi's depredations, while Forcella's behaviour in allowing the abuses to multiply was inexcusable.

Other outstanding issues had not been forgotten, although the lawsuit about the woods had assumed primary importance. Thovez had been irritated by the inference of self-interest in the proposal to engage his brother as clerk, pointing out that initially he had had the assistance of both Smith and di Martino, while the lack of someone must infallibly mean that business could not be regularly conducted. The Earl's dissatisfaction aggrieved him; had he not devoted all his time to Duchy affairs? The losses could scarcely be deemed his fault, not if the corn could only be sold at a great sacrifice, while disposing of the livestock would merely obviate the possibility of keeping any land in hand. If indeed the Earl wished to give up having an agent and let the estate, with his inside knowledge he would gladly tender for it himself, paying a year's rent in advance. Should they want to replace him, he would willingly resign provided his family's expenses were paid back to England. In any other circumstances he would stay at his post.

The outburst elicited a soothing reply from Hutchinson. Apparently the Earl had not abandoned the idea of letting the Duchy, on condition that a suitable offer was made. He would prefer doing so to a company, and would not give it to anybody on a first refusal basis; indeed maximum publicity should excite competition. However no such final decision was presently contemplated; it would depend on whether Thovez's exertions led to increased remittances, 'and a more regular and steady succession of them.'

On August 26th 1826, Hutchinson compiled a four-year account of disbursements and receipts from Maniace since June 1822. The receipts totalled a mere £4,343, of which £1,243 should be counted under 1826, as Thovez had just sent a decent remittance that July. After deducting charges of £774 for legal and administrative expenses, it left an average annual income for the period of £594-18-6d.

For the next twelve months, as if to disprove Hutchinson's analysis, the news from Sicily became more cheerful. Further small remittances arrived, the vines were reported flourishing, most of the land was now let at reasonable rents, while the lawsuit with the Brontesi, although entirely unsolved, was conducted on a lower key with appeals pending on both sides. In fact this was the proverbial lull before the storm, for another scandal was about to break over the Duchy. John Causton, whose offer to make wine for the estate had earlier been refused by the Earl, had been carrying on his business at Savoca in the face of increasing difficulties. In 1826, with his funds exhausted, he had applied to his friend, Thovez, for a loan in return for a share of the business.

Blithely disregarding his employer's specific prohibition from engaging in such ventures, Thovez had agreed to advance the money. Even this, however, failed to avert Causton's bankruptcy, which occurred during the summer of 1827. But his new partner found any ties of old friendship secondary to financial considerations, and promptly demanded compensation. On July 5th, Causton's wife, Colette, wrote to Thovez explaining the impossibility of obtaining security for three times the sum originally advanced. After previous assurances of his affection, she could only ascribe his change of attitude to the necessity of providing for his brothers, Henry and Francis. Yet her financial and physical suffering had been less than the emotional pain. 'Having declared my mind to you, to whom I once looked up as a brother . . . I forgive you all the injuries you have done us and intend doing.'

Despite this outburst, Thovez remained unmoved, applying to the courts for an injunction to have the property and wine stock at Savoca sold by public auction. Barker's letter of August 23rd deplored this step, instead suggesting a gradual sale of stock to foreign buyers, which might restore Causton's credit. The alternative was certain ruin for the family and creditors, of whom the Vice-Consul was one himself. Finding Thovez still inexorable, Causton directly addressed the Earl on October 30th. He cited the Agent's oppressions, his wish to gain control 'of an advantageous and profitable business in perpetuity' and to sell off the wine in stock at three times the liquidation valuation. Thovez had even purloined his keys to the cellars and was ignoring all letters sent to him. As to the brother, Henry, who was directing the case, 'there is no subterfuge that can be used but he is guilty of it.' With mounting hysteria, Causton also accused Smith, now returned to England, of common theft, and alleged that his wife Colette had first been invited out to Sicily by the Thovez family and treated as a sister.

Commenting on this bombshell, Hutchinson advised the Earl on December 4th not to get involved in the quarrel, although indicating his wish for a settlement. The incident showed where much of the Duchy income had been going, and how the entire Thovez tribe had battened on the estate. The Earl's letter to Bridport stressed that Causton had gone out to Sicily entirely on his own initiative, and the business at Savoca was nothing whatsoever to do with them. Nevertheless Thovez had disobeyed the clearest orders by advancing the loan, and then once Causton's speculation had failed, 'by carrying it on with my money and at my expense.' In reply Bridport agreed that Causton's complaints could not be overtly supported, but they should find a new Agent as the Duchy revenues were evidently being mis-appropriated. Discretion must however be maintained, so that Thovez got no inkling of this decision.

It seems ironic that, considering all previous crises, this relatively minor affair provided the impetus to drive a member of the family to visit their Sicilian property for the first time. After protracted corre-spondence, the Earl's son-in-law, Bridport, reluctantly agreed to go out to Maniace in autumn 1828, once the heat of the summer had passed. He would make an assessment of the situation on the spot, and engage a replacement for Thovez if necessary. Thovez was not even informed of the impending visit until August.

Bridport arrived in Naples that December, and by March 1829, he decided that the winter storms had abated sufficiently to make his voyage to Sicily bearable. He wrote home from Catania on April 9th that he had had 'a disagreeable passage' from Naples, although he had been very civilly received by the Viceroy, who had made many promises of assistance. Journeying on to Messina he had met Causton, whose character was described as bad. The last part of the journey was the worst; 'the road to Maniace is more horrible than you can imagine, and having to pass rapid torrents in the dark was very dangerous.' Indeed one of the mules carrying the bedding had been washed away and drowned. Bridport wholly endorsed Lord Ossory's description of Bronte made after a recent visit: 'a disappointing place with its pile of rude houses surrounded by lava beds'.

Much more surprisingly, however, Bridport's letter, followed up by two subsequent ones from Naples of April 25th and 27th, not only exonerated but actually supported Thovez. He had formed a gloomy opinion of the estate's potential. It was unsuited to olive growing and, although the vineyards flourished, the costs swallowed up the profits. Wheat seemed a good prospect with an abundant harvest, but prices were still so low, and more money must be spent on building magazines. It was hardly surprising the Duchy did not produce more income; although he was bringing back £250, 'there is no prospect of any great remittance.' Under prevailing conditions they would do well to net £1,000 a year from the estate, although in the long term revenues should improve, provided the outstanding lawsuits were settled. These were 'of the greatest importance,' as he gathered that all the landowners had experienced difficulties over the peasants' customary rights in the woods; indeed some had been almost ruined by them.

In Bridport's view the Duchy's interests would not be served by the removal of Thovez, who was doing his best in a country where the course of law was slow and tortuous. Furthermore he should be kept at his old salary for the present, since he doubted that any reasonable substitute would take on the job for less. After arriving back in Naples, 'rather fatigued by my journey', he reiterated this. It was far more vital to procure some 'strong directives' from the court for the Sicilian Tribunals, otherwise the estate would remain permanently crippled by litigation. The Agent had definitely won his point, merely by being shrewd enough not to try to influence his employer directly. For by staying out of the way (he only appeared for one day at Maniace during the week of the Bridports' stay, on the excuse that the conduct of the lawsuit kept him tied to Catania), he had let him discover an inkling of the realities of life in Sicily for himself. The effect on a middle-aged Englishman, endowed with a mediocre intelligence, limited imagination and not one word of Italian, was as he had expected.

On receipt of the first despatch from Catania, the Earl had replied: 'I think you have done quite right in not dismissing Thovez at this critical moment . . . we can discuss these matters at our leisure when we meet.' As requested he was sending out copies of the estate maps post-haste. Anxious to restore family relations which had been damaged by his remarriage, he also praised Bridport's small son, Alexander, 'who gets on amazingly well with his new grandmama. He has written her a very nice letter since his return to Eton, which she has answered; they are become great correspondents.' And indeed when Bridport did return to London in June 1928, the Earl entirely approved the course of action adopted on the trip to Sicily. Henceforward, despite scanty remittances and recurring problems, Thovez's position as Agent was effectively unchallenged.

For the next eighteen months Thovez, secure in his position, wrote assiduously to England reporting every detail of Duchy affairs. This served not only to convince the Earl and Bridport that they had chosen right in not dismissing him, but also stemmed complaints that they were not being kept informed.

But the honeymoon between the Agent and his employers was all too brief. Remittances from the estate dried up once more. On June 18th 1832, Hutchinson commented sharply 'on your long silence, which induces me once more to address you and I trust I shall receive an early reply; otherwise it will oblige Lord Bridport to send a person out to Bronte to ascertain the state of his affairs.' Sure enough the reminder was timely, for more remittances were dispatched within a fortnight although Thovez scarcely bothered to include any news. On December 1st, the agent wrote describing the new eruption of Etna and the heavy earthquake felt at Nicolosi, which had done little damage to the estate, and merely mentioned the various lawsuits pending.

1833 was to prove hardly more encouraging. On April 24th, Thovez wrote ruefully admitting that his victory over the woods had been illusory. The Brontesi had filed a new suit, claiming all the forests and most of the farmland in addition, citing arguments back to 1651. By mid-September, Thovez had grown still more pessimistic. The Brontesi had advanced a welter of legal precedents and the Forests case was again at a standstill.

In terms of the broader picture of Sicily, the island had remained tranquil for 15 years or so since the riots of 1820–21, in part because of the presence of an Austrian occupying army. For the remainder of Ferdinand's reign all measures of reform were shelved, the constitution was suspended and taxes, albeit fairly moderate, were imposed without summoning Parliament. The law of 1824, which sought to reform the *latifondi* by allowing creditors to take land in settlement of its owners' debts, did little to assist Sicilian agriculture, as the *gabellotti* who benefited were no more interested in improvement than their predecessors; while as the Duchy illustrates, attempts to transform promiscuous rights merely resulted in interminable lawsuits.

The old King died in 1825, to be succeeded by his son, Francis. Weak and intolerant, his reign represented at best an interregnum, when Luigi de Medici ran the country, and the population was described as 'divided into two classes, conspirators and neutrals'. He died in November 1830, leaving his throne to his twenty-year old son, Ferdinand, with the words: 'Be good and just before God, and do not let yourself be seduced by power or pleasure.' The new monarch was intelligent and energetic – if headstrong and stubborn – and determined to introduce the necessary reforms and balance the budget. Born in Sicily, he visited the island in July 1831, receiving a tumultuous welcome when the crowds vied to drag his carriage through the streets. A new census was ordered in 1833, in the hope that an overhauled land tax could reduce the *macinato*, while the peasants were encouraged to assert their rights on the ex-fiefs. Naturally this did not please the nobility, and Ferdinand was accorded a much cooler reception when he revisited Sicily in 1834. The trouble was that the Naples government was still too remote and lacked an effective local bureaucracy to implement its policies. Moreover the crime rate continued to rise. Smuggling flourished, while there were only 150 rural police throughout the island, and the judiciary was so underpaid that it survived principally by taking bribes.

Economic development proceeded little faster than political progress, with the middle class almost as prejudiced against trade as their social superiors. Lack of any interest in developing a merchant marine did not encourage exports. The only major innovation after 1815 was sulphur mining, with a pool of cheap labour and guaranteed demand from Britain, although this did not affect the area round Maniace, and by the 1830s output was outstripping demand. The few new agricultural enterprises, such as the wine-growing round Marsala and the citrus fruit and essential oils business in Messina, were fostered by foreigners like Benjamin Ingham, John Woodhouse and William Sanderson. Otherwise the land was devoted to cereal production, for cattle and sheep farming did not flourish with the lack of shelters and animal foodstuffs. Even here with primitive methods of cultivation, and slow transport by mule over the 250 miles of carriageable roads in all Sicily, little improvement seemed likely. Deforestation was a still worse problem; it being reckoned that between 1815 and 1845 half the island's remaining woodlands were felled, for the need for fuel was accentuated by a charcoal shortage. All the difficulties involved in running the Duchy should be seen against this background, and by the mid-1830s both owners and agent had reluctantly come to the conclusion that any hope of creating a prosperous model estate was limited.

The Hoods and Maniace

CHAPTER XII

A naval family

'This marriage has made me very happy. It is a Union of Names that will not easily be forgotten', wrote Fanny Nelson, the Admiral's widow, in 1810. She had been flattered by the call paid on her by a newly-married couple; her niece Charlotte, who had just wed young Samuel Hood. The comment was apt enough, for a glance at English naval history in the later 18th and early 19th centuries reveal that no other single family of seamen contributed between them more to their country's service. With the death of her brother, Horatio, Charlotte had now inherited the Duchy, which was to pass through her to successive generations of Hoods up until its sale in 1981. It is therefore perhaps worthwhile to examine the background and attainments of a great naval dynasty.

John Hood of South Perrott in Dorset, a prosperous yeoman farmer in the reign of King Henry VIII, is the family's first recorded ancestor. During the 17th century his great-grandson, Tremor Hood of Mosterton, greatly increased the family fortunes, so that his children were regarded as local gentry. One of them, Alexander, had a son, Samuel, in 1689, who went into the church. He held the living in a succession of villages in the neighbourhood, before becoming vicar of Butleigh near Glastonbury, with a numerous family of his own.

In autumn 1740, Captain Thomas Smith RN, on his way from London to Plymouth, was stranded at Butleigh where his carriage broke an axle. He spent the night as the guest of the vicar, and after dinner began extolling the virtues and excitements of a life at sea. His audience listened enthralled, and when Smith offered to take one of the sons of the house to sea with him, 13-year old Alexander Hood jumped at the chance. The following January he started as Captain's servant on HMS *Romney*, and the glowing reports he sent home soon

149

persuaded his 15-year-old brother, Samuel, to join him. It is ironic that their third brother, who stayed behind at Butleigh, drowned shortly afterwards in the River Brue, while both of them lived well into their eighties.

By 1743 both boys were midshipmen, and by 1746 both had been promoted lieutenant. The young men had very different characters: Samuel was tall, large-featured, generous and usually in debt; Alexander was smaller, more handsome, hard-headed and parsimonious. Both distinguished themselves during the Seven Years' War. Samuel had won his spurs in North America and the Levant, while Alexander had been made flag captain to the C. in C. Mediterranean fleet, and had served in the blockade of the French coast and under Hawke at the great victory in Quiberon Bay. Both had also married: Samuel to Susannah Linzee, also of seafaring stock, whose father was nine times Mayor of Portsmouth; Alexander to an heiress 23 years his senior, Maria West, through whose cousins he was now kin to the Pitt/Lyttelton/Grenville connection. In 1767 Samuel, promoted commodore and flying his broad pennant in the *Romney*, where he had begun his career, became C. in C. North America, and for three years while the colonies were in ferment, he conducted the difficult task of patrolling the ports with tact and discretion.

Meanwhile their younger cousins were making their mark, too. No fewer than three Hood brothers had gone to sea. The eldest, Arthur, drowned in the Caribbean in 1777. The youngest, Samuel, joined the Navy in 1776, and saw much action in the West Indies during the American Revolutionary War. The middle brother, Alexander, had gone to sea aged a mere nine-and-a-half and had sailed on Captain Cook's second voyage round the world.

In the 1770s the careers of the older Hood brothers seemed to have stagnated. Samuel, after commanding the guardships at Portsmouth, was made Governor of the Naval Academy and commissioner of the Dockyard there. His life pressganging sailors and fitting out ships for other men to fight must have been rather dull. Alexander had fared little better. He had been appointed the nominal captain of the royal yacht, a reward for his connections by marriage, but not an inspiring job.

Good fortune, however, often smiled on the Hood brothers. Alexander, who was leading a comfortable life between his town and country houses, was recalled to active duty after Admiral Kempenfeldt's flagship had sunk with all hands in August 1782. The Admiralty needed an experienced officer urgently, and Lord Howe had particularly asked for him. Thus Alexander was put in command of the port squadron of the Grand Fleet which sailed to relieve Gibraltar, and was promoted Rear-Admiral of the White. Samuel had been made a Rear-Admiral too, of the Blue. In 1780 he had been appointed second-in-command in the Caribbean to Rodney, who was soon invalided home leaving him in charge. Samuel hoped for the glory of an engagement. His wish was granted in 1782 when the British, with Rodney back in command, gained a splendid victory over De Grasse's Franco-Spanish fleet at the Battle of the Saints. Here the young Hood cousins, Samuel and Alexander, served under him, the latter as his flag-captain.

Peace was signed in 1783 and Samuel was created an Irish baron. In the 1784 elections both admirals were returned to Parliament, and both were promoted Vice-Admiral in 1788: Samuel after a spell as C. in C. Portsmouth was appointed a Member of the Admiralty Board, whereas Alexander had been granted the honorific office of Rear-Admiral of Great Britain and dubbed a Knight of the Bath. It was therefore hardly surprising that when war with Revolutionary France was declared on February 2nd 1793, the services of both admirals were in demand. Moreover, their support of Pitt's ministry made them doubly welcome. Samuel took command of the fleet sent to the Mediterranean. Here, despite the many difficulties involved in the occupation of Toulon by the allied forces, he showed his mettle. Eventually, in August 1794, after a long and exhausting campaign, Samuel, feeling his age, applied to go home on leave. Permission was granted and on October 12th he sailed for home. In trying circumstances he had shown an indomitable spirit, although his younger colleagues were to complain that age had begun to make him obstinate, high-handed and arrogant. His friend Horatio Nelson, however, remained fanatically loyal to him, writing: 'when Lord Hood quits, I shall be truly sorry to remain, he is the greatest sea officer I ever knew, and what can be said against him, I cannot conceive. It must be only envy; better be envied than pitied.'

After his return to England, Hood put his name to several memoranda to the Admiralty effectively criticising the conduct of the war at sea. From a senior serving officer such behaviour was not appreciated. Samuel was never to be employed at sea again, a decision which aroused indignation in many naval hearts as well as Nelson's: 'Oh, miserable Board of Admiralty! They have forced the first officer in the service away from his command. His zeal, his activity for the honour and benefit of his King and Country are not abated.' Hood remained an MP and on friendly terms with Pitt. Recognition of his services came quickly: in March 1796, he was created a Viscount of the United Kingdom and made Governor of Greenwich Hospital, a post he held for the remaining twenty years of his life. When long afterwards he wrote seeking a pension, the Treasurer of the Navy replied: 'I conscientiously believe there was no admiral in British history, with the exception of the late Lord Nelson, who so often and so eminently distinguished himself as Your Lordship, and he took a pride in acknowledging or rather boasting of you as his Master and Instructor.'

The arrival of the body of his prize pupil to lie in state in the Painted Hall at Greenwich in January, 1806, before the funeral, must have been a severe shock for Hood, but he bore up manfully, and at the age of 81 supported the chief mourner. He had written about Trafalgar: 'Never was a more complete victory gained by sea or land, or can ever be.' His death at Bath in 1816 marked the end of the Hood naval tradition for some time, although it was to revive once more in the future.

His brother Alexander in 1793 had been given one of the divisions of the Channel Fleet under Lord Howe, whose duties were largely blockading the French Navy in its Breton harbours. He was closely involved in Howe's victory of 1794, known as 'the Glorious First of June' in recognition of which he was granted an Irish barony, choosing the title of Bridport, a market town in Dorset near his family roots, and the motto 'Steady'. Back at Spithead he was afflicted by 'gouty complaints', yet he was on active service again in June, 1795, escorting an expedition sent to help the Vendée rising in Brittany. After one battle with the French, Captain Mahon praised the Admiral: 'Never on any occasion of service did Lord Bridport's judgment and resolution shine more conspicuously; nor was any commander of a fleet engaged with more vigour and fierceness. Nor should it be omitted to notice that when his ship the *Royal George* was so near the coast that the pilot on board refused to proceed, he took the helm himself.'

Honours were showered upon Alexander. He was offered command of the Mediterranean Fleet in succession to his brother, which he refused. The next year he became Vice-Admiral of Great Britain and a peer of the United Kingdom. Although unfit for active service, Howe remained in nominal command of the Channel Fleet, but it was Bridport who bore the brunt of the work. In 1797, a mutiny broke out at Spithead. Alexander sympathised with the mutineers' petition for better pay and conditions and was appalled when it went unanswered by the Admiralty. He advised Lord Spencer and the Board to grant the men's demands; the sticking-point however was a pardon, which the men wanted signed by the King himself. The mutineers trusted Bridport: 'They consider the whole fleet as zealously attached to him as their father, their friend and a nobleman willing to assist their honest endeavours.' Howe finally arrived with the pardon and order was restored.

For seven years running Alexander kept station off Brittany, often in foul weather and lacking the frigates which could have ensured proper reconnaissance. Eventually, Bridport requested from the Admiralty 'proper leave to retire from my public station . . . humbly trusting that after eight years' faithful service my request will soon be complied with.' In 1800, he received orders to strike his flag. A long and distinguished career was over, and in recognition he was elevated to Viscount.

No sooner had he retired than Bridport was busy with a new project. In 1757, just after his first marriage, he had bought an estate, Cricket St Thomas, between Chard and Crewkerne in Somerset, and next to the main road from Salisbury. Suitably enough, it was also extremely near to the villages from which his family had originally sprung. Records of the place antedate the Domesday Book, and it had passed through a variety of hands, including in the 14th century those of Sir Walter de Rodney, one of the Admiral's ancestors. Its church, also dating from the early 14th century, had been associated with a neighbouring one at Whitedown, where couples could marry quietly without the banns being published. This curious practice had been stopped by the Marriage Act of 1754.

At first Alexander had done little to Cricket Lodge, the modest house on the property, which stood on the site of the present kitchen garden. This was, however, largely destroyed by fire, and Bridport, who after his first wife's death in 1786 had remarried Mary Bray, an heiress many years his junior, was determined to build himself a worthy residence. Therefore in 1801 he commissioned Sir John Soane, the renowned architect who had designed the Bank of England, to rebuild and enlarge the site of Cricket Lodge. The new house was built from Ham Hill stone, quarried locally, and was completed by 1804; plans for it can still be seen at the Soane Museum. A delightful letter to Lady Bridport from Mrs Soane also survives: 'Indeed I do not wonder at Lord Bridport and yourself preferring your charming retreat to the noise, dirt and bustle of this filthy town (London). At Cricket all nature is at peace, and every countenance grateful for the blessing it enjoys.'

It was here that Bridport spent much of his old age. He continued to take a keen interest in naval affairs, often speaking on them in the House of Lords, although ill-health made him decline the invitation to be a pall-bearer at Nelson's funeral. He died at 87 in 1814. His epitaph reads 'to give the character of Lord Bridport in the most concise form possible, can be done in the one word, which he adopted for his motto, "Steady".' At his express wish, the Irish peerage descended to his great-nephew, Samuel, who had married Charlotte Nelson. On the death of his widow they also inherited the estate of Cricket St Thomas.

And what of the younger Hood cousins? Captain Alexander Hood had been given command of the frigate *Hebe* at the outbreak of war, soon transferring to HMS *Audacious*. On April 21st 1798, as part of the Channel Fleet, he was cruising close inshore when the *Hercule*, a French 74-gun man-of-war was sighted under full sail making for the safety of port. Several vessels gave chase, but Hood's ship, the *Mars* alone closed with the enemy, and a titanic duel ensued. The two ships were so closely entangled that the guns could not even be run out. After an hour of fierce fighting, the *Hercule* struck, with 313 dead and wounded, her hull in shreds and her guns dismounted. The chaplain took the sword of the dying French captain, L'Héritier, and put it in Hood's hand, for the latter was lying in agony in the cockpit, his legs shattered by shot. At this, 'he smiled, thanked God, blessed his wife and expired.' Bridport, his commanding officer, lamented: 'An honour to the service and one universally beloved. He has fallen gloriously.'

Captain Samuel Hood was appointed captain of HMS *Juno* in 1793 and sent to the Mediterranean. There he had made his name by inadvertently taking his ship into Toulon harbour, unaware that the allies had just evacuated it. The *Juno* was boarded by French Revolutionary soldiers, and only prompt and decisive action by its commander prevented the vessel's capture. Later he had taken part in Nelson's bloodily-repulsed assault on Tenerife, behaving with conspicuous gallantry. When Nelson departed for Naples, he left Samuel with a squadron to blockade Alexandria. Hood took a major part in subsequent operations, helping evict the French from Naples and holding Salerno with 40 marines against a counter-attack by 3,000 men. Only after a bad bout of fever was he invalided home.

Promoted Commodore after war had resumed in 1803, he was posted to the West Indies station, where he blockaded Martinique so effectively as to earn a KCB. Sir Samuel returned to European waters in 1805, and commanding his squadron off Rochefort he lost his right arm in action. Reputedly George III wept on being told the news, exclaiming: 'Would to God the French had their frigates again and Hood his arm!' While he was recovering from his wound, the Battle of Trafalgar was fought, and it became Sir Samuel's lifelong regret that he had not been present. There were other opportunities for active service, however. Now Rear-Admiral, he was made second-in-command of the British fleet sent to the Baltic in 1808 to help the Swedes against Russia. At the Battle of Oro Sound he showed unrivalled coverage by saving his ship, the *Centaur,* from capture by the enemy after it had run aground. In the words of the official despatch: 'By almost superhuman exertions both ships were towed into deep water by their remaining boats and moored. The sight of the two British ships free to bring their broadsides to bear caused Admiral Haikoff to recall his ships, although his fleet numbered twenty.' Although made Vice-Admiral and a Baronet, he declined a seat on the Admiralty Board, having always preferred life in the front line. So in 1811 he was appointed commander-in-chief East Indies, where his patrolling of the coasts and rigorous suppression of smuggling saved the Company much money. Tragically he caught a terrible fever at Madras in 1814, and after three days in delirium died aged only 52. As the Naval Biography put it: 'He stood so high in public estimation by the number and importance of the actions and the benefit of his services . . . that his loss was considered a great and severe misfortune to the country.' His portrait by Hoppner has quite a resemblance to Nelson, whom he had worshipped. The baronetcy went to his nephew, from whom descend the Somerset family of Acland-Hoods.

These, then, were the Hoods from whom sprang Samuel Hood, 2nd Baron Bridport and husband of the new owner of the Duchy of Bronte. In little more than half-a-century the Hoods had established themselves as a part of the great English naval tradition. One panegyrist even claimed: 'The Hood family appears to merit a distinction above the many that have immortalised the annals of the British Navy. I know of no family to compare with them in gallant deeds, but that of the Dukes of Brunswick, sixteen of them whom lie in the Ducal vaults having fallen on the field of glory.' Of course not all the descendants of Alexander Hood of Mosterton would so distinguish themselves, while even among those directly connected with Maniace, the naval heritage would lie dormant for nearly a century. But it did not die. One relation became First Sea Lord and died Lord Hood of Avalon, while another, Charles Acland-Hood, a midshipman, went down with his ship, HMS

Invincible, at Jutland in 1916, alongside his kinsman, Rear-Admiral Horace Hood. And last, but not least, Lieutenant Maurice Nelson Hood of the Royal Naval Division, and father of a future Duke of Bronte, died in the trenches at Gallipoli.

CHAPTER XIII

The absentee proprietor

'I shall never come back here, unless there is a revolution in England, and even then I should probably go elsewhere,' wrote Charlotte Bridport in 1836, just after returning from the first and only visit she ever made to her Duchy. The year after her father's death, she had persuaded her reluctant husband to make the journey to Sicily once again. On arriving at Messina she had been amazed to discover that there was no road to Bronte, and the only way for a lady traveller to get there was in a *lettiga*, a litter slung between two mules. The trip proved even rougher than she had expected, so she reached Maniace in a state of complete exhaustion. Within a few days, horrified by the squalor and the primitive conditions of life, and after only a cursory inspection of the estate, she had departed. Although she lived until 1873, Charlotte never went back and seldom referred to the Duchy; indeed it was to be another twenty-eight years before any member of the Hood family again set foot on the property.

This indifference meant that Samuel Bridport continued to deal with the correspondence and decisions about running the estate. Weak character that he was, after the Earl's death things began to drift. He showed no inclination to hand over control to his own son Alexander, who had to wait until after his father's death in 1868 to be given any real say in the management of the Duchy. Bridport's failure to grasp the realities of life in Sicily would persist until the end.

Another irritant was the dispute over Charlotte's succession to the Duchy. Ever since his son's death, the Earl had been determined that, while he could not alter the succession to the title, he could make sure that as much of his property as possible should descend to his daughter and her children rather than to the Boltons. Having been forced to concede that Trafalgar must belong to whoever happened to be Earl Nelson at the time, he fought twice as hard to leave his Sicilian estate to his own direct heirs.

The Earl's remarriage destroyed the elaborately reconstructed façade of family unity, and the Boltons began to worry whether they might be excluded from the succession altogether. Tom, whose amiable disposition made him universally beloved, certainly wished to live at Trafalgar, but his interest in the Duchy was at best putative. He was probably advised, however, that it would form a useful bargaining tool in negotiations with his uncle. Unfortunately, the family became embroiled in a drawn out legal dispute over the inheritance. The Sicilian lawyers decisively ruled in Charlotte's favour.

But everything was soon to change, because not long after the Earl's death in February 1835, Tom Bolton fell ill. He had been shocked to learn that his uncle's will had appointed Charlotte as his absolute heiress – thus making some sort of family legal fight inevitable. By November 1835, the situation had become clearer, Tom Bolton himself, or 2nd Earl Nelson as he had just become, had died aged just forty-nine, leaving a twelve-year-old son, Horatio. The boy's guardians now felt they had a case, and in 1838, a Bill in Chancery was filed on behalf of Horatio, 3rd Earl Nelson claiming him to be the rightful heir to his great-uncle's Sicilian property. The Bridports filed a counter-suit and in 1841, the Chancery lawyer found in favour of Charlotte's claim to the Duchy. The Nelson trustees objected to the finding, so the case had to be referred to a higher court, and in November 1846, the Master of the Rolls also found in Charlotte's favour, overruling all the objections raised, and by a subsequent Bill dated March 12th 1847, he dismissed the Nelson claim to the Duchy. A final settlement was reached agreeing the Nelsons' absolute right to the Earl's English and the Bridports' absolute right to the Earl's Sicilian estates. Charlotte also agreed to pay Horatio's legal costs, and there the matter rested, although good relations were not restored for many years.

These disputes meant, in effect, that no one knew for more than a decade after the Earl's death who would inherit the Duchy. Furthermore, Thovez was unwell. Exhausted by the battles of the 1820s and demoralised by the mistrust with which he felt he was regarded by his employers, Thovez had prematurely aged. In 1834 he was complaining of influenza, measles and a nervous affliction, which had affected his right hand. Throughout the later 1830s his correspondence markedly declined both in frequency and volume, as his health deteriorated. On October 2nd 1839, Philip Thovez died, and was buried in the church at

Maniace. He was succeeded as Agent-General to the Duchy by his nephew, William, son of Henry Thovez, who had already been working as his assistant since 1837, and therefore had some experience in running the estate. William had previously worked in the wine trade at Marsala and was married to a Sicilian, Rosaria Fragalà. The Bridports, subscribing perhaps to belief in the devil you knew, approved his appointment.

Aware of all the disappointments and the frustrations endured by his uncle, William Thovez adopted a policy of inactivity. He opted for as quiet a life as he could get, introducing no more reforms or improvements on the estate, and merely concentrating on producing sufficient revenue to assuage the stream of demands from England.

On the wider historical stage too, little had changed. In 1837 a terrible cholera epidemic had started in Palermo and quickly spread throughout the island. It was used as a pretext for risings in Syracuse and Catania, where the yellow flag of Sicilian independence was raised. The unrest spread to Bronte and Maletto, although without the violence which had marked the revolt of 1820. The Duchy itself was not directly affected, and these disturbances led the King to abolish the island's remaining separate rights; henceforward Sicilians were to be eligible for all offices on the mainland and vice versa. The problems could not, however, be solved so easily, and Pietro Ulloa, who was sent to reform the magistrature, reported: 'there is scarcely one official who is not prostrate at the sign of a grandee, or who does not intend to reap some profit from his post.' Appalled by the endemic corruption, he advocated a far-reaching overhaul of the government.

In September 1838, Ferdinand visited the island and for three months he worked hard promulgating a mass of reforms. His stay convinced him of the need to eradicate the causes of discontent by more land reform, by the re-establishment of Messina University to provide more educated administrators, by completing the *catasto* (land registry) and by reducing the *macinato* (tax on grinding corn). One direct result of his reforming zeal saw 1,305 miles of new roads completed in the next few years. Yet some of the consequences were less fortunate in particular that peasants were encouraged to continue to assert their now illegal promiscuous rights and thus hamper proper cultivation of the land.

The Duchy was, of course, affected by these reforms and the Brontesi now prosecuted their lawsuits with renewed vigour. Indeed judgment was given against the Duchy in several cases, although as these were mostly overturned by a higher court, nothing very much happened.

The early 1840s were a time of economic prosperity, with agricultural prices fairly stable and the estate running relatively smoothly. But the lid was still bubbling on the pot; and 1848 would show just how volatile Sicily really was.

The revolution that took place in Sicily began in the New Year against a backdrop of an unusual degree of unrest in Palermo: the University was closed because of student riots and eleven prominent liberals were arrested. Ferdinand's birthday celebrations on January 12th marked the start of the revolt, and the agitators ensured it spread like wildfire. Within three days the garrison had lost control of the city. Emboldened, the rebels rejected all concessions, and the feeble Neapolitan generals tamely agreed a cease fire and the evacuation of Palermo. The royal palace was ransacked, and by February 1st the Bourbon troops had withdrawn from almost the entire island.

A new Parliament was set up, and a coalition government formed under the septuagenarian Ruggero Settimo, who grandiloquently declared: 'The evils of war have ceased and from this moment an era of happiness has begun for Sicily.' The rhetoric scarcely matched the facts. Disorder reigned throughout the island; there were bread riots and attacks on landlords' houses; government officials fled for their lives and property title deeds were symbolically burned. Many gangs were composed purely of criminals, in the pay of various factions. The Junta was forced to recruit a National Guard, which was primarily an unpaid militia designed to protect property. Within a few weeks virtual civil war was threatening.

It seems likely that awareness of the debt of gratitude the Sicilians owed to England for moral support in the rebellion had so far saved the Duchy from molestation. Thovez and his family kept a low profile at Maniace. In April, however, Parliament deposed the King, and when this news reached Bronte, a mob from the town, urged on by two brothers, Carmelo and Silvestro Minissale (who were both currently engaged in lawsuits with the estate), stormed towards Maniace. Hearing of their approach, Thovez and his family fled to Catania, and sought the protection of the British vice-consul. The mob divided up the Boschetto vineyards, then the farmland. The Minissale brothers, having secured a large portion of it for themselves, returned to Bronte in triumph, while all the church bells were rung.

The vice-consul sent a sharp protest to the Central Committee. The Minissales were named as instigators of the affair and prompt compensation was demanded for any damage done. The Central Committee ordered the Minissales' arrest, and declared its Brontese

35. Obelisk at Serraspina.

36. View of the Saraceno valley.

37. View of Maniace under snow (courtesy of Speer Ogle).

38. View of the old Duchy Palazzo in Bronte.

39. View of drawing room at Maniace looking towards the hall and study in the early twentieth-century (author's collection).

40. La Falconara, Alec Nelson Hood's villa in Taormina, seen from below.

41. King George V and Alec Nelson Hood at La Falconara during the King's visit to Sicily in 1923.

42 & 43. Two of the famous photographs of Taormina youths, as taken by the German *"barone"* (author's collection).

44. Interior of Casa Campobello, Percival Campbell and Miles Wood's villa in Taormina.

45. Culver Sherrill (right), one of Taormina's last American residents, in his villa.

46. Casa Cuseni, Robert Kitson's villa in Taormina.

47. View of Taormina from Castelmola.

48. Miles Wood and Percival Campbell on the beach at Taormina.

49. Alec Nelson Hood's seat in his garden at La Falconara.

50. View of Villa Sant'Andrea, the Manleys' house on the beach at Mazzarò, below Taormina.

51. View of the library at the Villa Sant'Andrea.

52. Feast day of St Sebastian, patron saint of Maniace (courtesy of Linda Suffolk).

53. Lunch party at Maniace in the 1970s, with Princess Margaret (courtesy of Linda Suffolk).

54. Alexander Bridport in front of his old family home, Cricket St Thomas in Somerset (courtesy of Linda Suffolk).

55. Peregrine Hood's first birthday party. Behind, Bastiano, the butler at Maniace, with Salvino, one of the footmen; in front: Henrietta Manley, Linda Bridport, Antonia Manley (courtesy of Linda Suffolk).

56. The Duchy's long-serving agent, Frank King (courtesy of Linda Suffolk).

57. View of the Celtic cross in the courtyard from the castle roof.

58. Linda Bridport with her horse and dogs in the courtyard of Maniace.

59. Arches in the courtyard at Maniace.

60. Alexander Bridport with a local farmer.

61. Wine barrels in the castle cellar.

62. Drawing room of the Castello.

63. Upstairs corridor at Maniace.

64. Alexander and Linda Bridport with the Duchy staff in the courtyard of the castle.

65. Portrait of Peter Bridport with his wife and son (courtesy of Alexander Bridport).

colleagues liable for all damage done to Duchy property. However, a few months later all charges were dropped and no civil suits were instigated.

Meanwhile in Naples, Ferdinand had regained his authority. Now, convinced that British and French support for Sicily would be solely verbal, he was ready to launch his counter-attack. On August 30th a Neapolitan army under General Carlo Filangieri, 24,000 strong, crossed the Straits and began a savage five-day bombardment of Messina, which earned Ferdinand the opprobrious nickname of *Bomba* throughout Europe, but it had the desired result. Under pressure from France and England the King agreed to a six-month armistice; his troops occupied the north-east corner of the island as far as a line from Taormina to Tindari, leaving the rebels in control of the rest.

Bronte was squarely in the rebel zone, and had sent men for the defence of Messina. In this interim period virtual anarchy prevailed, army deserters and bandits roamed the countryside and the committee appeared incapable of maintaining order. Fortunately they nominated Antonio Cimbali, an ex-regular soldier, as captain-at-arms in October. He cleverly recruited twenty-four men, all ruffians, as guardians of the peace, who, once they were properly paid and disciplined, became an extremely effective force.

In March the armistice expired. Incredibly the Palermo Junta had combined a total unwillingness to negotiate with an almost equal unwillingness to look to their defences. On April 13th 12,000 Neapolitan troops were landed at Riposto and advanced on Catania, which fell after some fierce fighting. The rebels' resistance collapsed like a house of cards, although they continued to put out absurd propaganda. The moderates in their turn had had enough; when the radicals raised the red flag and began looting, some of the ex-ministers and leaders of the *squadre* (gangs) quietly met with Filangieri, whose army entered Palermo entirely unopposed on May 15th. The revolution was over.

Peace was restored in Sicily by midsummer 1849. The King had appointed Filangieri as Viceroy, creating him Duke of Taormina among his other honours. Too politic to institute wholesale pro-scriptions, the new Viceroy finally excluded only 43 names from the general amnesty he granted, and of these most had already fled the country. As one English observer noted: 'all the liberated convicts, murderers and robbers are freely pardoned.'

Filangieri restored order with a mixture of tact and firmness, so that even such trouble spots as Bronte seemed pacified. The Sicilian nobility flocked to the splendid receptions he gave, and it was on his advice that Ferdinand revisited the island in October 1852, receiving a tumultuous welcome at Messina and Catania, although he avoided rebellious Palermo. The conviction grew that the Sicilians might hate the Neapolitans but not their King, while the Mazzinian idea of a united Italy solely appealed to a few hot-headed intellectuals. Sadly, Filangieri resigned his post in 1853, exasperated by seeing his schemes for reform nullified by the small-minded ministers at Naples. Yet the island stayed quiet throughout the decade; two petty insurrections in 1856 were easily quashed and many Sicilians vied with their com-patriots on the mainland at rejoicing when Ferdinand escaped assassination by a deranged soldier at a military review.

Nevertheless the 1850s saw no solution to the fundamental problems besetting the country. Trade and agriculture largely flourished, but the infrastructure was still lacking to promote an industrial revolution. The peasants resented the reimposition of the *macinato* and in the countryside a new class of property owners emerged: the so-called *gallant-uomini*, who controlled many of the ex-feudal estates and by purchase or fraud much of the village common lands as well. Chiefly concerned with power and respect, the *cappelli* (hats) were not above inciting the *beretti* (caps) to mob violence for their own ends, while they aped their betters by refusing to improve the land and farm it directly themselves.

The Duchy mirrored these developments. Once order had been restored, William Thovez returned from Catania and resumed his duties. Correspondence with England had grown relatively infrequent while the Bridports were both ageing and disinclined to consider improvements. As the decade was generally one of reasonable harvests and stable prices, remittances were regularly sent to England, although seldom for large sums. In April 1856, Thovez reported to the new London lawyers Delmar & Wynne on one change; he had completed the arrangements for transferring the Duchy into a hereditary Majorate (ie it could be left to one son, normally the eldest, and did not have to be divided up among all the children).

In May 1859, Ferdinand had died at Caserta aged a mere 49, only briefing his heir on affairs of state on his deathbed. The succession of a weak and inexperienced new King, Francis II, gave a fresh impetus to revolt. For the time being, Sicily appeared quiet, albeit mainly thanks to Salvatore Maniscalco, the ruthlessly efficient chief of police, but not for long.

In 1860 secret messages from the north, urged rebellious factions within Sicily to prove themselves worthy of outside help by starting a rising on their own. On April 4th the two Risos, the Baron and the plumber, began the revolt at La Gancia convent in Palermo, and although Maniscalco arrested many of the activists, including young nobles like Corrado Valguarnera (the model for Tancredi in Lampedusa's *The Leopard*), he could not quell the storm. On May 11th Garibaldi's Thousand landed at Marsala. Good fortune smiled on Garibaldi for the Neapolitan frigates at Marsala dared not open fire on his disembarking men for fear of hitting the two English warships in the harbour, which they wrongly assumed were aiding the invaders.

In little over a fortnight, after a bloody engagement at Calatafimi, Garibaldi had entered Palermo, benefiting from the staggering ineptitude of the aged Bourbon generals, whose chief, Ferdinando Lanza, could only propose falling back on Messina as in 1848. By June 6th a capitulation was signed, whereby 20,000 of Francis' troops tamely evacuated the city, and although General Tomaso Clary's vigorous defence of Catania saved it from the Garibaldini, he too was ordered to retire on Messina with his 15,000 men. The Neapolitan soldiers fought bravely at the Battle of Milazzo, but on July 28th Clary surrendered Messina without firing another shot. The whole island had fallen to the insurgents and Bourbon rule in Sicily was at an end.

During these momentous events, Bronte had been in a state of revolutionary ferment. The town had sent Garibaldi an enthusiastic address, and a number of young men left to enrol under his banner. The trouble was that the Brontesi saw in Garibaldi not merely their deliverer from the supposed tyranny of the Bourbons, but a panacea for all their ills. They believed that he would finally abolish the *macinato* and divide up the Common lands as his Decree of June 2nd seemed to have promised. However, during the five months he was Dictator of Sicily, Garibaldi was far too preoccupied with pressing his attack on Naples to devote proper attention to governing the island, and his programme of reforms was hopelessly over-optimistic. Added to this, the provisional administration of Palermo had failed to curb the *squadre*, and anarchy threatened in much of the countryside. This background explains the horrors that were to follow, adding to the widespread misapprehension that, with the fall of the Bourbons the gift of the Duchy to Nelson's heirs must also lapse, on the curious grounds that the 75,000 ducats paid as compensation to the Hospital had come from public moneys voted by Parliament and not from the royal purse. What was forgotten, or simply not realised, was that the owners of the estate were the nationals of Great Britain, a power which the new regime had absolutely no wish to offend.

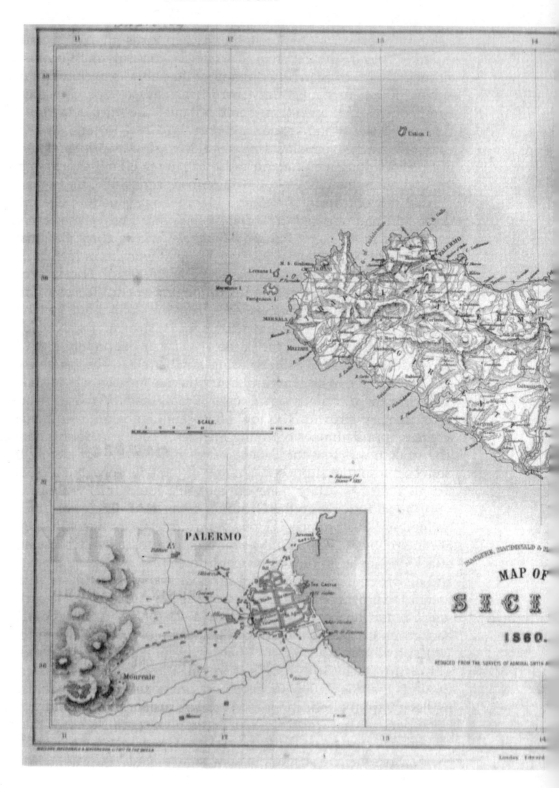

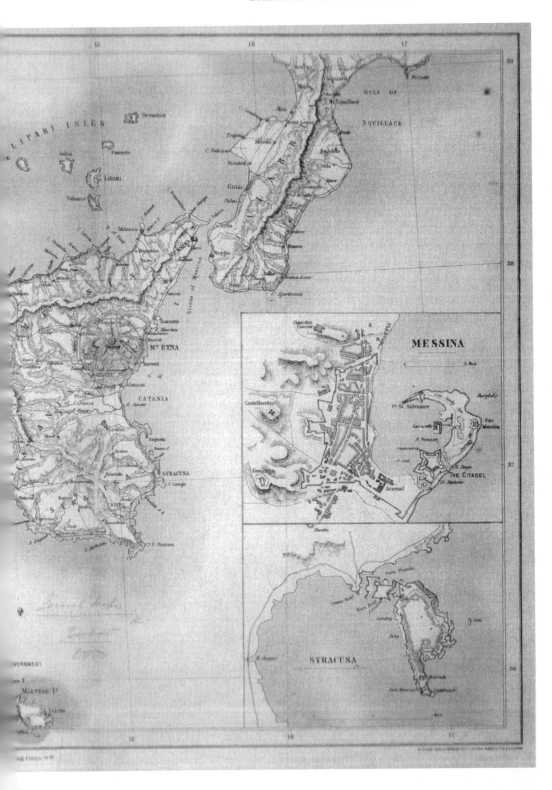

CHAPTER XIV
Riot and revolution

By mid-summer 1860 the town was more deeply divided than ever. At the head of the populist party stood the Lombardo brothers, Placido and Nicolo, the Minissale brothers of 1848 fame, and Luigi Saitta. The Duchy supporters included the lawyers, Giuseppe Liuzzo and Nunzio Cesare, the mayor, Antonino Leanza, and ex-Bourbon adherents such as Bernardo Meli. Fresh municipal elections had been held in May, in which, surprisingly, the populist candidates, Saitta and Nicolo Lombardo had been defeated, while Cesare and Meli had been elected in their stead. Those defeated bitterly complained they had been mis-represented as Bourbon stooges, and that their successful opponents would not carry out the policies promulgated by Garibaldi. As the authorities in Catania paid no heed to them, this fanned the popular discontent. Vocal demonstrations demanded the division of the common lands, as had already been done in towns like Aderno. A proclamation then arrived from Catania admonishing the Brontesi to respect Duchy property.

Four companies of the National Guard had now been formed, three of which were composed of Duchy supporters, while the fourth, led by the Lombardos, was largely recruited from the peasants. Relations between them rapidly deteriorated. In retaliation for destroying their adversaries'; billiard table, Lombardo's men were spat on and punched in the street. This rivalry within the National Guard mattered particularly as the services of all law-abiding citizens were badly needed. Garibaldi's victory had opened the prisons, releasing a flood of malefactors on to the countryside with a vested interest in disorder, who encouraged others to believe that what they could not get in ordinary times by means of the law could then be seized in a revolution, which always recognised a fait accompli. Among them were several notorious thieves and murderers, such as Arcangelo Attina and Francesco Gorgone. It was decided that they must be arrested which they duly were on July 8th by Frank Thovez (the agent's brother) and his company of National Guardsmen. Attina was captured in the Capuchin church, where he claimed he had gone to pray, although an outsize knife was discovered in his pocket. Nicolo Lombardo travelled to Catania to protest about the arrests, and, finding scant satisfaction there, suborned a guard, who let the prisoners escape before they could be transferred to a safe gaol. The temper of the mob worsened; its ringleaders plotted to foment an uprising on Sunday, August 5th, the feast of Santa Maria della Catena, when all the peasants would anyway be in Bronte. Faced with this prospect, Lombardo turned to one of the ringleaders, Rosario Aidala, a mason, for assurances that life, property and the municipality's chest, then containing over 100,000 lire, would be respected. Aidala professed amazement that anyone could doubt his intentions.

A macabre ceremony took place on the evening of July 29th. A crowd of urchins paraded through the streets, singing the *Miserere* and *De Profundis* underneath the windows of Duchy supporters. Several National Guardsmen wanted to open fire, but were restrained by the vacillating Bernado Meli. Instead a despatch was sent to Catania asking that soldiers be sent to Bronte. The Intendant wrote back to Lombardo personally reminding him of his responsibilities as a Captain of the National Guard; otherwise nothing was done. On the evening of Wednesday, August 1st it was the turn of Lombardo's company to stand guard. At around 5 pm the church bells started ringing and wild cries were heard. Throughout the night men wandered through the streets, and rumours abounded against the incongruous background noise of shepherds playing their bagpipes. Terrified, some of the National Guardsmen attempted to flee the town, mostly in disguise.

By the following morning, Bronte was totally blockaded, every exit was sealed and anyone trying to leave was turned back. At midday the main square was a boiling mass of people yelling: 'Our blood has been sucked! We want the division of the land!' Suffering from gout, Meli was carried in a chair to confront the mob and solemnly promised all their grievances would be settled. The ringleaders shouted back that as soon as everything had calmed down these promises would be retracted. Armed men began to go from house to house, menacingly demanding money, food and wine. Not one National Guardsman was to be seen.

Sensing the growing chaos, Cimbali, a prominent councillor sadly exclaimed that it was a case of *'sauve qui peut.'* The bells sounded the alarm at 11 pm that night, but it was too late. Preceded by a crowd of urchins screaming: 'Long live Italy! Death to the Rats!' a mob swarmed through the town. Stones were thrown at the windows of houses belonging to known Bourbon or Duchy supporters. Several were set alight, the furniture was thrown out of the windows and systematic looting commenced. Even the women joined in, fetching mules to carry away their plunder, while the whole time drums and trumpets sounded above the din. Many householders voluntarily opened their doors to avoid trouble, yet the mob, mostly drunk by now, grew ever more violent. Soon the theatre, the archives building and the barracks were in flames and fires burned in every corner of Bronte. Abandoning their homes, many fled to take shelter in some friend's cellar.

The sun rose on Friday, August 3rd, its brilliance partially obscured by smoke from the still burning buildings. A mob rushed off to Nicolo Lombardo's then to Saitta's house, acclaiming them as the new Mayor and President of the Town Council. Any ideas either might have had of restraining the mob's fury were shortly to be dispelled. Ignazio Cannata (a Duchy lawyer) was found cowering under a pile of manure in a stable. To cries of: 'Now we'll wash that dirty piece of cloth in your thieving blood,' he was dragged bleeding through the streets to a spot outside his son, Antonio's house. Here, just alive, he was thrown on to a hastily contrived pyre. As the flames rose, they continued stabbing Cannata's corpse; a man from Maletto named Bonino was alleged to have licked the blood from his knife, then cut out the liver and eaten it.

Another band of rioters dragged Nunzio Radice Spedalieri, the father of the Brontese historian, from the cesspit where he had been hiding for the past two days. At that moment Antonio Cannata, son of the murdered lawyer, came out of his house bearing a flag of truce. The mob fell on both men, in the struggle Radice escaped and was pushed into a nearby porch, although the innocent Cannata was killed and tossed onto his father's pyre. A group of Duchy supporters, thinking the riot had subsided, left the Church of the Annunciation and were immediately surrounded by an enraged mob. Terrified, they walked on, shouting: 'Viva L'Italia!' – alas, to no avail. Lombardo and Saitta watched helplessly as eight more men were pulled down and butchered. The remainder fled in all directions, and, disguised as women or peasants, again tried to escape from the town. Cimbali, fearing that his hour too had come, told his assailants: 'I am ready, but I beg you to kill me quickly, for I could not live in such agony.'

Actually he was too popular to be harmed, and accompanied by various friends and relations he made off under cover of darkness to Catania.

The atrocities continued all that night, while looting and arson went unchecked. Some of the richer citizens were forced to sign over titles to land which they were accused of having bought too cheaply. However the Duchy palazzo, which stood in the middle of Bronte, remained unscathed. The British flag flew there and at Maniace; perhaps the memories of 1848 were too vivid to permit a frontal attack. In fact it was virtually deserted, while a few frightened servants skulked at Maniace, for the entire Thovez clan had escaped to Catania before the start of the riots. At about 1am the town crier proclaimed through the streets that any person still harbouring *sorci* (rats) in their house, had better expel them on pain of death or burning. Many promptly followed his advice, and more wretched fugitives were hounded through the town.

At last during the morning of Saturday, August 4th, a company of National Guardsmen from Catania arrived outside Bronte. Their Commander, de Angelis, was welcomed by all the responsible citizens, although he was too afraid of provoking further disorders to take the necessary measures. He ordered his men to disarm before advancing, and the mob, finding itself still unrestrained, went on with a house to house search for fresh victims. That afternoon a group including Rosario Leotta, secretary to the Duchy, his ten-year-old son and half a dozen more were arraigned before the mob. Attina, one of the ringleaders, declared: 'People of Bronte, you must be the judge to acquit the innocent and condemn the guilty.' Leotta was duly condemned along with three others. Although de Angelis and Lombardo begged to have them taken to Catania, the mob demanded the sentences should be carried out on the spot. The four were murdered forthwith, while the authorities and National Guardsmen stood by impotently.

On August 5th, realising that troops might be on the way, the rioters began to plan a defence of the town. Sentinels were posted on the campaniles and on the Aderno road to give warning of approaching soldiers. Under the command of Rosario Aidala, the mob appeared resolute. Several prominent Brontesi, horrified by the prospect of more massacres, now plucked up courage and suggested that a deputation be sent to Catania to explain the reasons for the riots and to request an amnesty. Just as it was setting out and the priests had re-established some semblance of order by forming a ragged procession behind images of the Virgin, the cry went up that troops were indeed approaching. Colonel Giuseppe Poulet with 400 soldiers from Catania halted on the edge of the town and both sides eyed each other nervously. The clergy seized the opportunity to welcome Poulet, inviting him to enter Bronte in peace. The ruse worked. Aidala ordered his men to disperse; hostilities had been narrowly averted. The ringleaders marched alongside the colonel volubly recounting their grievances, with which he diplomatically pretended to agree.

The entry of the troops turned into a triumph as all the church bells pealed out again. Poulet entrusted Lombardo and Saitta with maintaining order. That night there was indeed only one murder, in a neighbouring hamlet at that, and when the order to disarm was posted at dawn on the 6th, most of the rioters vanished into the countryside.

On the morning of August 6th, General Nino Bixio marched into Bronte with two battalions of *bersaglieri*. One of Garibaldi's most famous lieutenants, who had taken a major part in the campaign since the landing at Marsala, he had been on the coast at Giardini recruiting soldiers for the invasion of the mainland. Urged on by Thovez, the British vice-consul in Catania, John Jeans, had sent the Dictator numerous telegrams urging intervention to protect the Duchy's property and employees. Thus, on hearing reports of the atrocities, Garibaldi acted swiftly: 'to suppress this small dash of communism'.

Bixio's men had set out on the night of August 4th and by forced marches had reached their destination within 36 hours. The General was the very man for the job. In G M Trevelyan's words: 'Between the working of one great action and the next he was chiefly heard of through the deeds of insane violence.' Already celebrated for horsewhipping some of his volunteers who were late getting out of bed, he had struck his comrade-at-arms, Agnetta, in the face for some imaginary insult. When they fought a duel in Switzerland the following year, he was to be shot in the hand and crippled for life.

Bixio was ceremoniously welcomed by the Brontesi. However, seeing the gutted and looted buildings, his volcanic temper rapidly rose. He peremptorily ordered Poulet to seal all exits from the town and to arrest the malefactors. Lombardo, who had ignored warnings to flee, was brought before him and greeted thus: 'Ah! so you are the leader of this rabble!' On the same day Bixio commanded a special military tribunal to assemble at Bronte and summoned four more battalions to occupy Randazzo and other neighbouring towns. He proclaimed that: 'The town of Bronte, guilty of crimes against humanity, is declared to be in a state of siege.' Its inhabitants were given three hours to surrender their arms, while a war tax of ten ounces per hour was imposed.

When the military tribunal convened on the 7th, Lombardo, Saitta, and the Minissale brothers and many others were brought before it. A provisional town council was set up with Sebastiano de Luca as Mayor, and Cimbali as one of its members. Bixio had left for Randazzo, whence he issued a stream of directives, while Poulet, who had been rash enough to urge clemency, was sent back to Catania with his men. A pall of gloom hung over Bronte, for the General's latest proclamation had struck fear into every heart: 'The Court of Naples has educated you for Crime, and today drives you to commit it. A devilish hand has directed you to murder, larceny and arson . . . either you will remain quiet, or we as good patriots will destroy you as the enemies of humanity.'

Formal hearings of the Tribunal began on the 8th, and the proceedings lasted four hours. At midday the accused were told they had one hour to prepare their defence. After listening to it, the Tribunal rejected all their pleas. Saitta, Lombardo and the rest had been secretly denounced as Bourbon agents, who had promised to reward the thieves and had also helped themselves to part of the booty. Lombardo spoke briefly, reiterating his innocence. The Tribunal reconvened at 8pm condemning Lombardo and four others, one of whom was the village idiot, to execution. The rest were to be sent for trial before a court-martial at Messina. Early on the 9th the five were led out to face a firing squad, while Bixio watched impassively from his horse. The shots rang out with Lombardo still exclaiming he was as innocent as Christ himself; and the corpses were left lying there in their own blood until dusk as a public spectacle.

On the 10th the General departed from Bronte for good, taking with him nearly a hundred prisoners and leaving behind a battalion of troops. The National Guard had been reconstituted under Cesare's command and held answerable for keeping the peace until a Committee of Public Safety had been created. Bixio's parting comments showed his contempt for everyone concerned: 'Those in Sicily who are called brave gentlemen, we would call miserable cowards. Why did they not defend themselves? Everyone deserted their posts crying for help and the ignorant rabble made itself master of the town. Men of honour do not behave in such a fashion.'

So ended one of the most notorious episodes of the Risorgimento. In a fever of anxiety not to miss the invasion of the mainland, the general had done what he felt to be expedient, and his actions were explicitly approved by Garibaldi. Yet accounts of his fiery and impetuous temperament were anyway exaggerated. Certainly his conduct had been arbitrary; equally certainly the worst criminals, the ringleaders of the mob, had largely escaped retribution like Saitta, the Minissales and Lombardo's brother, Placido, who were pardoned by the Messina Court-Martial. For Bixio's letters show him not unsympathetic in principle to the division of common land; indeed he considered the question needed investigation, for who would wish to govern a country composed half of beasts and half of cowards? As he wrote to his wife: 'The Dictator sent me to that place with part of my brigade, an accursed mission for which a man like myself was never destined.'

The final reckoning was put at 26 people murdered, 36 houses burned and more than 200,000 lire's worth of damage done to the town. Such was the balance sheet of Bronte's three-day long nightmare, where terrible excesses had exacted a no less terrible revenge.

Meanwhile the Risorgimento pursued its inexorable course. On August 18th Garibaldi crossed the Straits from Gardini below Taormina, a considerable military feat, and Reggio quickly fell after a perfunctory defence. On September 5th poor Francis, abandoned by almost all his subjects, announced his decision to defend his kingdom from Gaeta, thus sparing his capital from further bloodshed. Two days later Garibaldi entered Naples in triumph; his clever tactics had ensured he would be universally welcomed as a liberator. United Italy had advanced a step further, while Piedmontese law, its currency, the lira, and its institutions including the very different Parliamentary system were gradually introduced into Sicily. Those who had imagined that freedom from the Bourbons under some distant northern sovereign meant effective self-government were to be speedily disillusioned.

Perhaps the best consequence of the traumas of 1860 was that both the Duchy and the Brontesi realised it was to their mutual advantage to agree to the settlement of their interminable litigation. The new Italian government recognised the donation to Nelson and assumed the original obligation of paying the Hospital its 5,600 ounces per annum, so dispelling the hopes of the hotheads that the grant of the Duchy might be entirely revoked. Faced with this reality the Brontesi led by their Mayor, Bernardo Meli, signed what became known as 'The Transaction' on June 1st 1861, as did William Thovez on behalf of the Bridports.

The Transaction was not totally satisfactory to anybody. Running to 107 pages and citing the precedents from three centuries of litigation, it was an exceedingly complex document. In essence the Duchy had ceded about half its forests, a large part of its lava and some of its arable lands, being roughly halved in size to 6,592 hectares, at which figure it would remain until after the Second World War. The ancient boundaries still existed only along parts of the northern, eastern and north-western limits of the estate. Yet from the Duchy's point of view it was not all bad. Much of the land ceded had already been let in perpetuity for ridiculously small sums and was of little benefit to the estate. The compromise with Bronte clearly defined the rights of each party. Henceforward the townspeople could not legally claim any land, privileges and rights except those defined and set out in the Transaction. It was conclusively established that the Duchy was the absolute owner of its remaining territory, to which the Brontesi renounced all further claims. This was, at any rate, the intention.

Thovez had certainly recovered his composure by 1861. He reported to Bridport that the new overseer of vines had improved them enormously and the wine was now the best in Bronte while the magazine was permanently crowded with buyers. 'So much for the bright side of the picture, which I am sorry to say has its dark side too.' Repairs on 'that great eyesore of a house in Bronte misnamed "Palazzo Ducale" are urgently needed, if the roof is not to collapse.' A protracted lawsuit with the Minissales had just been decided for the latter. He was, however, cheered by the prospect of the Transaction.

One problem as yet unsolved was the transformation of the Duchy into a hereditary Majorate, which Thovez thought he had successfully accomplished five years earlier. Since the Brontesi had lodged objection to the change in the Entail, a memo had been addressed to the King of Naples in the Duchess's name in July 1859, requesting him to authorise its alteration. Now with a change of sovereign, the process had to be gone through again. The issue was successfully resolved this time and now that the continued existence of the Duchy, with its rights, property and the succession to it were at last assured. What was needed was a greater commitment by the family itself.

CHAPTER XV

The consolidation of the Duchy

On November 4th 1872, William Thovez indignantly addressed Charlotte Bridport: 'I regret to have to bring before Your Ladyship's attention the fact that I have been very ungratefully treated during the last few years, after having saved the Duchy and wonderfully improved it. A week ago, driven to despair, I threw up my post, but Viscount Bridport has come to a compromise with me which, I fear, may not last.' The future fourth Duke of Bronte (Alexander Hood) had paid no fewer than three visits to Sicily within the preceding eight years; he had taken far more interest than his parents had ever done in the running of the estate, and, hardly surprising, had found much to criticise. To demonstrate his family's ongoing involvement with their Sicilian estate, he was now to leave his nineteen-year old son, Alec, to live at Maniace on a semi-permanent basis.

Alexander's first visit to the Duchy had been back in April 1864, with his wife and two elder sons, Arthur and William. Their stay had only been short, but it was evidently a success, as within four years the Bridports – as they became when Alexander's father, Samuel, died in January 1868 – were to return. That autumn they travelled to Maniace bringing Alec, then aged fourteen, and his older sister, Adelaide, and stayed for several weeks.

Alexander Hood was above all else a courtier. Born on December 23rd 1814, he had been sent into the army at a young age, an unusual choice considering the family's strong naval traditions. He had been an officer in the Royal Scots Fusiliers, and in 1838 had married Lady Mary Hill from a distinguished military family and descendant of one of Wellington's generals. She was a friend and contemporary of the young Queen Victoria, while her husband was made a Groom-in-Waiting at the age of 26. He must have been well liked at court, for in

January 1853 Prince Albert wrote to the Commander-in-Chief requesting that Colonel Hood be allowed to exchange on half-pay as he was needed to manage the royal farms at Windsor and become his personal Clerk-Marshal. Gradually he took on more duties, for instance sifting possible sites for the Great Exhibition, vetoeing Battersea Park, and dealing with complaints from the Captain of the Royal Yacht. Very fond of his master, Hood was devastated by Albert's death in 1861. Lady Mary wrote from Cricket St Thomas on behalf of them all to express 'humble and heartfelt condolences on this most sorrowful occasion'; even a year later the Queen recorded in her Journal: 'Colonel Hood has come into waiting and I saw him before I drove out. He was much moved in talking to me.' On being given a tiepin as a memento of Albert, he responded effusively: 'thanking Your Majesty for your ever to be valued present in memory of my good Prince and Master. Whilst during the Prince's life it was my highest desire to carry out His Royal Highness' wishes, so it will now be my constant object to perform faithfully those duties you may entrust to my direction.'

Promoted to Equerry in 1858, Hood seems to have also remained on the Army List, for he progressed steadily upwards, eventually attaining the rank of Major-General. On his father's death he began to hint fairly broadly that he would like the United Kingdom Viscountcy, bestowed on his great-great uncle, revived in his favour. At first the Queen was reluctant, aware that there were no obstacles to his staying in her service as a mere Irish baron, but anxious that, if granted an English title, he might engage in politics, being already well-known as a rigid Tory. She therefore stipulated to Alexander that she would put his name forward to Disraeli only if he agreed to abstain from politics, because she could not afford to lose the services of one of her favourite equerries. Alexander agreed, the Liberal opposition raised no objections and he got his Viscountcy that July.

Once assured both of his undisputed succession to the Duchy and of its new-found territorial integrity, Hood seems to have taken an increasing interest in his future property. Two visits had apparently been enough to convince him that a member of his family must live in Sicily for most of the year, if the best was ever to be made out of the estate. After nearly thirty years in control, it appeared to Alexander that Thovez was not the ideal agent. Following the Transaction, no agricultural land had been kept in hand, the entire estate, barring the small amount retained for the cultivation of vines and olives, being let out to thirteen 'gabellotti' or middlemen, who in turn subdivided their holdings, renting them out to some 300 sharecroppers on terms extremely advantageous to themselves rather than to the Duchy.

In fairness Thovez cannot have had an easy time, for the 1860s were a difficult moment in Sicily. Once the euphoria accompanying the Risorgimento had worn off, disillusion with the deliverers from the north, who ignored autonomist sentiment, was only matched by the Piedmontese officials' horror at southern indolence and corruption. The land reform so blithely promised by Garibaldi had been quietly shelved, while, although the hated *macinato* had been abolished, the tax burden was heavier for everyone. The Piedmontese, ignorant of Sicilian needs, had fostered a free-market economy, which had sent up the cost of food, while industry, faced with more advanced outside competitors, had declined.

Nevertheless, despite this unpropitious background, Alexander believed that the management of the Duchy could be improved. After his third visit in spring 1870, he wrote a detailed report, noting 'my visit to Maniace has given me a clearer insight into the management of the Duchy than I had before obtained and into the character of the Agent.' He had discovered that Thovez had delegated most of his responsibilities to Samuel Grisley, whether in terms of the sale of estate produce or the maintenance of Duchy vineyards and forestry. 'I am informed that Mr. Thovez never makes enquiries of Mr. Grisley as to the actual balances, except when remittances are made; and he gives himself no trouble or concern as to the accounts until the termination of the year.' As for the main house at Maniace, much of the roof was in a deplorable state, while the building urgently required more servants' rooms and closets to convert it into anything resembling a comfortable residence.

There were a few rays of light in the gloom. Writing over fifty years later, Alec Hood recalled how on his first visit to Sicily in 1868, there had been no carriage road at all from Bronte to Maniace. 'We slept at the Palazzo in the town (the first and only time I have slept there); and then our four selves with my mother's maid, Tickel, and a courier, riding on muleback arrived at the Castello by the lower road, escorted by the Duchy guards or *campieri*. The numerous pieces of luggage were strapped to and carried by other mules, altogether forming an imposing procession. The vintage was in full swing, and I remember well meeting the strings of mules with the must in bulging goatskins, the muleteers blowing their horns to advise their arrival at the cellars from the winepress.' Work soon began on building at least the rudiments of a proper carriage road and the stretch from Maniace to

Rocca Calanna having been completed at a total cost to the estate of almost 2,000 ounces, although an additional outlay would be required for widening stretches and erecting supporting walls and pillars. Furthermore the government announced its intention of building a road from Randazzo to Nicosia in the interior of the island at national expense; this would pass straight through parts of the Duchy and further improve communications. But these encouraging developments seemed to be the exceptions rather than the rule, and Alexander Bridport continued to ponder what he ought to do.

In autumn 1872 both the Bridports were back in Sicily, determined to make the necessary changes at Maniace. There were several rows with Thovez, which resulted in the Agent tendering his resignation. This was accepted, although a face-saving compromise was devised whereby he could keep his post in the short term. Thovez sent an anguished appeal to the aged Duchess Charlotte with a string of complaints about her son's and daughter-in-law's behaviour.

However, she replied to Thovez that she had already handed over total control of the Duchy to Alexander. She pointed out that her late husband had left Thovez a legacy of £1,000, and that he had just been given another £100 to cover the costs of his recent trip to London. Dismissively she concluded: 'My son will inform you of the decision he has arrived at with regard to your continuing to be Agent to the Duchy, with which I shall entirely concur.'

Of course matters were not solved so painlessly. Both Samuel Grisley and his son William wrote from Maniace in December with disturbing tidings. William Grisley's letter mentioned: 'the confidence with which Your Lordship honoured my father aroused in the minds of both Thovezs an immense jealousy against him. For this reason they have watched him with ill-feeling and spied on all his movements.' Even after the formal letter of dismissal had come, and had been passed on to all the estate employees, Thovez had continued to behave exactly as before. The Grisleys needed power of attorney forthwith. Meanwhile Samuel Grisley asked Bridport to instruct Thovez to hand over the past accounts and moneys currently to hand.

Actually Bridport was wasting no time. On December 16th he had already ordered his solicitors, Delmar & Wynne, to send out a power of attorney to Grisley. A stern missive was also addressed to Thovez although he was permitted as much time as he wanted to remove his family and furniture. Finally Samuel Grisley had to be reassured: 'Your present position must be delicate. If any in the service of the Duchy act in a manner hostile to you, you have my permission to dismiss them . . . My mind is quite made up as to Mr Thovez; he can no longer be my agent after all that has occurred.'

Just after the New Year, Bridport wrote to Grisley to say that he had received the accounts and was sending out seeds for the garden and some saplings to improve the woods. He also pointed out that on Thovez's departure it would be necessary to buy some more furniture for the house from Catania, as almost all the contents of Maniace belonged to the former agent. Machinery for cultivating the vines was being purchased as well at the request of the newly-engaged supervisor, Monsieur Louis Fabre. The latter, a wine expert from Carpentras near Avignon, had been engaged to improve the Duchy's vineyards and had only just arrived in Sicily. Evidently he too found his position delicate, for a few days later Bridport felt obliged to state in another letter to Grisley: 'Monsieur Fabre was brought to Maniace with the highest possible testimonials as to his ability to attend to the management of the vineyards and the manufacture of the wine. He is to have complete control over the work force on the farm and in the vineyards, as well as over the wine magazines at Bronte. I intend to give him all the support I can.' The following autumn, Bridport visited Sicily, bringing his fourth son, Alec, with him. The boy had just left Wellington, so, unlike his elder brothers who were already settled in some occupation, he was the ideal age to begin the career his father had mapped out for him as the family member resident in Sicily and in charge of the Duchy. After a stay of several weeks, during which he felt he had succeeded in tidying up the estate's affairs, Bridport returned to England. Alec stayed at Maniace, where it was decided that he should live for nine months of every year, with Miss Jane Thomson as companion and housekeeper. She had been governess to the Hood children, and was a faithful friend and servant, who would live at Maniace for the next twenty years. The Grisleys, father and son, made every effort to show him everything connected with the running of the Duchy while Louis Fabre looked after the wine-making. Alec was a ready pupil, quick to learn and full of energy and enthusiasm. His first major project was the restoration and extension of the house at Maniace itself.

Work began in 1875 using exclusively local labour, and lasted for several years. The corridor on the upper storey was extended almost sixty feet, giving the house three more bedrooms and two smaller rooms. It now stretched some 150 feet in length, its walls being gradually covered with prints and paintings, nearly all of which were sent out from England and related to Nelson or the naval Hoods.

Similarly the ground floor of the Castello, as it was now generally known was rationalised, and the staircase leading up from the middle of it to the upper storey was scrapped in favour of the flight of steps constructed by Graeffer towards the southern end of the house. There had formerly been seven or eight small rooms, probably the former monks' cells facing on to the courtyard, plus the kitchen with an enormous fireplace. These were repartitioned to make rooms of a more uniform size, while the kitchen was moved to the middle of the south wing over the main gate.

'I found the church badly kept and used partly as a store, a defect which I remedied. Mass has always been said, on Sundays and feast days, the chaplain being appointed and paid by the Duchy, and it is a point of honour and righteousness to continue with this pious duty,' Alec Hood rather sententiously recorded. Much of the church had remained intact from monastic times, in particular the magnificent Norman west doorway while the capitals of its columns rose from acanthus leaves, those on the right depicting the story of Adam and Eve, those on the left mythological figures symbolic of the Creation. Inside, the nave still had its high Norman pointed arches resting on lava columns alternately round and hexagonal, and lancet windows. Hood had the ugly plaster coating stripped from the columns, while the roof was repaired and the east end of the church rebuilt. The altar, reputedly of Phrygian marble, was cleaned, and the holy icon of the Virgin was restored and stood upon it in a glass case. For the first time in over two centuries, the Abbey Church was again in regular use.

In 1870 Bridport had noted various improvements which could be made to the buildings round the courtyard; part of the mules' stable to be converted into a forge, the existing seed magazine to be turned into a wine cellar with three windows cut under the roof to allow ventilation, and the buttress supporting the aqueduct that carried water to the garden to be rebuilt. All this was now done, and the south wing over the main gate was extended to provide more rooms for estate office staff. No trace of the cloisters which had once occupied the northern end of the large courtyard survived; on their site Hood built another wing with upstairs rooms to house the Abbey and Duchy archives, and store rooms below.

The well in the smaller courtyard dated from antiquity, but the newer buildings surrounding it needed repairs. The big granary, over 200 feet long, with the other stables, magazines and cellars, was made shipshape and entirely reroofed. At the north-western corner of the Castello facing the river, the bastion with its turret and small outhouses was reconstructed to support the enlarged building. Finally in the centre of the large courtyard a Celtic cross of lava stone was erected in 1883, at the instigation and expense of Alec's aunt, Lady Hotham, who had objected that no monument to Nelson existed at Maniace. It bore the vaunting inscription: *Heroi Immortali Nili*.

Most of the garden in 1873 was devoted to cabbages and onions. Hood laid out the eastern end along the façade of the Castello from 1876, adding on the western portion and a further part known as the Palm Garden in 1912–13. In 1901 he redesigned the grounds in front of the main entrance, draining the swampy waste to form areas of grass. A dearth of trees around the house was redeemed by planting four large cypresses and an immense mulberry, brought from Palermo; many others followed. Indeed Alec was continually extending the garden. A lower area, previously a mass of tangled thorns and rocks, was reclaimed and christened 'The Wilderness', being planted with conifers, shrubs and bulbs. Near the gates at the top of the steps leading to the upper garden, he placed on top of a sandstone pillar 'the agate stone capital', all that remained of an eccentric scheme in 1811 to build a monument to Nelson on top of Mount Etna. Gradually the Castello's gardens became a riot of colour. To quote from Hood's writings: 'At no other place have I seen such a wonderful growth of roses both inside and outside the garden limits. Some of the bushes grow high and have hundreds of flowers – the La France and Paul Neyron varieties being the best. The walls are covered with Maréchal Niel and Fortune's yellow roses, which hang in cascades from them, as also from the trees, with masses of wisteria. The violets in early spring are remarkable for their size and perfume.'

This enthusiasm to improve the house, church and grounds was also shown throughout the estate. The vineyards in 1873 were restricted to Maniace itself and the Beviere lands on the south side of the Saraceno river. Nearly all the plants were past their prime and had to be uprooted. Under Fabre's supervision new vines were planted at Boschetto, and the area was gradually extended both to east and west. A grape variety called Pedro Ximenes, which flourished in Sicily, was planted, while Fabre introduced the Grenache grape and vines from Hermitage and Bordeaux. As a result the Duchy wine improved enormously in quality. Large cellars and modern wine presses were built at Boschetto, where the house was enlarged for Fabre to live there. Hood later recalled: 'during the vintages I was in the presses most of the day, up to my knees in must or grape juice superintending the work. Big casks of oak – chestnut staves colour white wine unduly and were discarded – were made from our timber or bought in France; the smaller casks came from Riposto, and a huge stock of wine for blending was kept in them. . . The produce of the vineyards rose to some 60,000 gallons.' In fact Alec began to harbour dreams of launching the Duchy wine on to the English market just as Philip Thovez had dreamed fifty years before.

It soon became Hood's settled conviction that the estate should not farm its land itself. Thus, although he might grumble at the primitive methods of agriculture, nothing was done to disturb the arrangements made just after the Transaction by which the *gabellotti* rented and sub-let the Duchy's thirteen farms, or fiefs as they were still described. They in turn let to some 300 sharecroppers. However, over the years Alec built five new farmhouses and added to others, cheerfully admitting in hindsight that: 'luckily for the Duchy, tenants did not want the luxurious accommodation of their English brothers. Here the sons do not hunt, nor the daughters play the piano, although if the Sicilian womenfolk interested themselves more in things of the farm, eggs and poultry would be more plentiful and therefore less expensive. I tried an experiment once at Balzi Soprani hoping to induce the farmer's family to leave the town and dwell there. A year after I visited the house, but instead of seeing the family comfortably installed in the rooms I had built, I found pigs, goats and chickens closely herded into them, leaving everything in a filthy state. After that I made no further experiments of the sort. The mediaeval custom of gathering in the towns holds today, to the detriment of agriculture.'

The gloomy description of the forestry, which Bridport had compiled in 1870, obviously called for urgent action. Hood planted trees both up in the high forests and along the river which sensibly diminished the risks of malaria. Decayed trees were felled and sold. The principal problem had always been the lack of roads on the Duchy, for the rough *trazzere*, or mule tracks, scarcely facilitated forestry operations. But over the next two decades twenty miles of road were to be constructed on the estate, permitting access by carriage to a summer residence, named Otaiti, 'because it is surrounded by peasants' wigwams', built by William Thovez high on the hillside out of reach of malaria, and on up to the forests. Sawmills nearby were erected about 1880 to house the ten horse-power engine sent out by Clayton and Shuttleworth, which was still functioning in the 1920s. In Hood's words: 'Its advent was a great event in the country. Landed at Messina and forwarded by rail to Piedimonte Etneo, it steamed the rest of the way. I accompanied it on its road journey of three days with the traction engine full of machinery and stone breaker attached. We slept anyhow and anywhere en route; one night in a *fondaco* among mules, pigs and poultry, so at the end of the three days I was unrecognisable. At Randazzo the Mayor and Town Council – the former wearing his sash of office – presented me with an address of welcome saying we had begun a new era of progress, and I had to reply from the engine, keeping one eye on the furnace all the time as the pressure was extremely high.' They proceeded to Maniace followed by a vast crowd, having had to remove the west gate of the town to let the engine through.

During these years Bridport frequently came out to Sicily to inspect the progress. His local Somerset newspaper, the *Chard & Ilminster News*, reported that in October 1875 he was accompanied by Mr Hodder, the head carpenter at Cricket St. Thomas, who was escorting machinery ordered for the estate, and that the c.2,000 mile journey was completed in five days. Maniace was described as: 'built on a site, on which once stood a town, but is now only occupied by a convent, currently being transformed into a spacious and comfortable mansion, the residence of the Hon. Alexander Nelson Hood, who with Miss Thomson has won the confidence and regard of the people.' Both Alec's parents spent the winter of 1877–78 in Sicily along with his two sisters, while his two other brothers, Alfred and Victor, came for the first time in 1883; Victor who was eight years younger than Alec, came out on several more occasions. On July 15th 1884, Lady Mary died in London, and that December Bridport, granted three months' leave of absence by the Queen, travelled to Sicily with his younger daughter, Rosa, and stayed until the following March.

His career at court, however, remained Bridport's chief pre-occupation. He rose ever further in the Queen's favour, attending Disraeli's funeral as her representative; escorting the Crown Prince of Germany and the Princess Royal on their visit to England in 1878; and attending Napoleon III's lying in state and funeral, when he reported: 'they walked bare-headed for a mile, which took half-an-hour. Only the poor little Prince Imperial, wearing a cloak, followed immediately behind the hearse as chief mourner.' In 1883 he informed the Queen from Balmoral: 'I have just been to see the last resting-place of Your Majesty's faithful and attached attendant, Brown . . . and thought both the tombstone and iron railing were most suitable in every way.' Not long after he wrote thanking her for: 'the striking and beautiful likeness of your faithful and devoted friend, which I will always value knowing how greatly the services of poor John Brown added to Your Majesty's happiness.'

In June 1884 Victoria made him a permanent Lord-in-Waiting, an appointment which aroused the ire of the radical press. *Truth*, which Hood subsequently described as 'a rampant society journal', castigated the Queen's choice: '. . . the Ministers very naturally wish to nominate a peer of their own party. Lord Torrington's connection with the court dated from the reign of William IV and he has retained his post for twenty-five years, remaining in under all ministries. It is desired to put an end to arrangements of this kind, which for many reasons are inconvenient. How, indeed, is the business of the country to be carried on, if Ministers are deprived of the right to nominate Peers to the salaries by which these dignified legislators are bribed?' Victoria managed nevertheless to carry the point and Bridport was appointed on the same basis as his predecessor after Sir Henry Ponsonby was sent to beard the Prime Minister. 'Mr. Gladstone, with his usual kindly consideration for the Queen's personal feelings has consented, although Lord Bridport is a strong Conservative. . . It is stipulated, however, that he is not to vote against the Government in the House of Lords, so he was absent from the great division last Tuesday. The Prime Minister would at once have consented to the proposal, if it had not been for the strong resistance of Lord Sydney, who has a truly Whig-like aversion to seeing any of the official loaves and fishes transferred to members of the Opposition.' And there the matter rested.

In the 1840s the Queen had given Cumberland Lodge to the Bridports as their residence. Situated four miles from Windsor Castle in the Great Park, it had been rebuilt for the Duke of Cumberland, 'the Butcher of Culloden', who had defeated the Jacobite Rising in 1745, and who lived there for fifteen years until his death. A passionate huntsman, he had also owned in Eclipse and King Herod two of the greatest racehorses in the history of English racing, while his studgroom, Bernard Smith, gave his name to nearby Smith's Lawn. It had been a convenient base, enabling Bridport to fulfil his duties at Court. The children were born and brought up there, for Alexander's parents had no wish to move out of Cricket St Thomas, and, until they were both dead, he never looked upon it as home. Even then, he found it inconveniently situated for the life he liked to lead, and once the Bridports had moved out of Cumberland Lodge, they acquired a house in London at 12 Wimpole Street where they spent much of the time.

The Queen's affection for him was undiminished. On August 4th 1885, she confided to her Journal: 'Just before dinner I invested Lord

Bridport with the KCB in honour of Beatrice's marriage and in recognition of his forty-four years' service in my Household.' He had accompanied her on her trip to the South of France in 1882, and on the last evening before her sixty-sixth birthday she noted: 'Saw good old Lord Bridport for the first time since the loss of his wife . . . he stayed to dinner.' Victoria appointed him one of the three trustees of the annuity granted by Parliament to the Princess Royal; while despite his age she still expected him to superintend such minutiae as the behaviour of the Court band.

In September 1891 she wrote from Balmoral promising to give him her portrait; at the same time she asked Lord Salisbury to agree to Bridport being awarded the GCB for fifty years in her service, 'the only one of my gentlemen who has been with me so long.' Back in 1886, she had invited Rosa Hood to become one of her Maids of Honour, and was humbly thanked for 'the great distinction which Your Majesty has bestowed upon me.' Soon Rosa too was enjoying life at Court, assuring the Queen: 'We are so much looking forward to our waiting at beautiful Balmoral.' It was perhaps a pity that royal service absorbed so much of the Bridport family's attention; as this was to have its effect both on the Hood estates and on the future career of young Alec.

Since Maniace had become a real home, it began welcoming guests from abroad. The Visitors' Book was started in 1874, and, writing fifty years later, Hood noted that over 500 people had been entertained there over this period; 'some of whom,' he added proudly, 'have been well-known personalities.' One of the first was Frances Elliot, authoress of numerous travel books, and a childhood friend of his mother's, who stayed at Maniace in early 1878, when Alec's parents and sisters were there as well. Her two volume *Diary of an Idle Woman in Sicily* was published in London in 1881. Her prose is fluent and the comments frequently acerbic. It was dedicated 'To my friends at Maniace' and below are some of her observations.

Of Reggio di Calabria, whence she got her first glimpse of Sicily, Mrs Elliot wrote: 'a flat, uninteresting, dirty little town without a vestige of its great antiquity . . . the dust is intolerable, the people are half-naked, insolent and ugly.' Once ensconced on the other side of the Straits; 'the Vittoria is the only bearable hotel in Messina, and that is not saying much.' She took the train to Piedimonte Etnea, where the *vetturino* which was supposed to meet her at the station and take her up to Maniace was extremely late, for which Antonio, the coachman, had a pack of excuses ready. 'All this I knew to be lies; but *cui bono*? When a whole population lies one cannot reproach an individual.' As the roads were freshly mended with lava, progress was at a walking-pace. Everything struck her as black: the earth, the rocks, even the vines which she espied everywhere. The people looked quite different from those on the coast: 'thin, hard-featured, leather-skinned peasants.' After Linguaglossa the vineyards fell away to be succeeded by small hazel woods, 'as green and nutty-looking as Berkshire copses.'

After her nightmare journey, she arrived at Maniace in the dark to find all the Hoods waiting to welcome her. 'In the *cortile* stand the ducal family as in a picture, backed by their *campieri* in a kind of Tyrolese uniform, with servants male and female a score.' She admired 'the old refectory', by which she presumably meant the room at the top of the new staircase; 'half-hall and half-parlour, large, full of colour and filled with the scent of flowers.' The passage was 'a long vista of convent corridors, lightened by ranges of lamps and leading to the bedrooms.' The next morning the view took her breath away: 'I have seen Etna all round . . . but nowhere is it so stupendous as at Maniace.' The house seen from outside was: 'Long, low and many-windowed,' while: 'behind is the old convent garden, where tulips and hyacinths, violets and daffodils, snowdrops and Turk's head lilies crowd into beds of antique patterns. The trees, mulberry and walnut with big bare limbs are much exercised by the wind' – all in all quite a compliment to Alec's horticultural efforts. She also found the dogs charming: 'Gru and Bino of the lion's head, Alec's especial pet', although when a black horse named Baleno (lightning) appeared, harnessed to a basket-carriage, she vehemently declared that she preferred walking.

Everything of course was unlikely to have been quite perfect to such a sharp-tongued observer. 'The only discord was caused by Alec's French wine-grower [Fabre], who through the kindness of Her Grace is admitted to dinner. The man is coarse, contradictory and ill-dressed.' Life at Maniace showed its ridiculous side to Mrs Elliot too: 'We all walked to Boschetto, I laden like a pack-horse and wretched. When we reached there the Duca, with the courier, Mr Curzon, in a mixed theatrical costume of a Highland character, took off their jackets and started to help the six old men, who were breaking stones to form a new road.' She certainly did not appreciate the picnic organised in her honour. 'Dramatis personae present at the start: Etna, four mules with several stray donkeys, a *campiere* armed to the teeth and a basket of provisions.'

They rode in single file, each mule being led up the Duchy road, recently completed to bring timber down from the mountains. Along its four-mile length towards the oak forests fringing the heights, they passed 'a disabled stone-crusher, which had lost a wheel and stood useless by the roadside, as an iron tyre had flown off striking a stone cutter dead, the Sicilians would never work at it again.' Eventually they drew in to Otaiti: 'a brick hut so-called because the men from Maletto, who work there, live in round mud wigwams with smoke pouring through the doors.' The picnic on the nearby hillside was not exactly 'the sheltered nook within friendly walls' she had imagined, but rather eaten at '3,000 feet perched above Maniace, not a coign of shelter, with Etna for a background and all the winds of Aeolus for neighbours.' All in all, however, she had enjoyed her visit and liked Alec: 'I cannot tell you how nice he is; he is his father's alter ego and permanent agent.'

More visitors soon followed. In 1881 Lady Ely, a Lady-in-Waiting and confidante of the Queen, came to stay at Maniace; reports of one of her mistress's favourite courtier's Sicilian estate were doubtless relayed to Windsor. Another literary figure, Mrs Lynn Linton, 'the well-known essayist, critic and novelist' in Hood's phrase, appeared in 1883. The long article she wrote, entitled 'Bronte on Mount Etna', was published in the *Temple Bar Magazine* in 1885, and although her cumbrous, flowery prose is far less amusing than Mrs Elliot's, she gives a good description of the vintage 'When the gangs walk to and from the vineyard to the treading-vats they are preceded by bagpipes, to the sound of which they march in time, and sometimes break into a dancing-step as they go. They get up an impromptu dance in the yard, while the foremost of the file, whose baskets are already empty, are waiting for the last who have yet to cast theirs into the mass . . . When we meet them filing to and fro along the narrow paths, the bright-eyed boys pull off their caps, while the girls put their hands together in an attitude of supplication, as they say *'Cenza benedic'*, which means in full, *'Eccellenza, benedica'*. *'Benedicite'*, replies the Duchino, the sovereign and lord of this little kingdom – or rather the Viceroy, the Duca proper being his father.' Of the pressing, she writes: 'The grape-treading is done by men only. Here, at Maniace, where wine-making is conducted with scrupulous care, the treaders wear soft leather moccasins kept only for the press-room, for to tread the grapes is a better way than to crush them by machinery.' As for the product: 'Bronte wine is already famous throughout Sicily, but the Maniace wine is Bronte in excelsis . . . No man who has once drunk it would wish to change it for any other, and by contrast our Maniace brands make French claret taste thin, and French burgundy coarse. There

187

seems to be something in the fiery heart of volcanic soil which gives a special value to grapes.

Mrs Linton also gives some fascinating information on Sicilian folklore, which she had gleaned from Miss Thomson, who had been assiduously collating it. Here are some examples:

> 'On the Feast of the Epiphany (January 5th–6th) a fight takes place among the winds, and whichever gains the victory will be the prevailing wind for the year.'

> 'Two tenants appeared at the Castello to discuss business, and as it was a cold day, the Duchino shut the door of his office. One of the men turned pale and fell silent. On being asked what was the matter, his companion replied that they were afraid that the wind had been excluded, and, if anything happened, would prevent them from running away. The door was reopened, their spirits revived and the discussion recommenced.'

> 'In August 1881, a rich and wicked priest had died at Bronte in the middle of a terrific storm. Just as his corpse was being carried into the Church, a young woman, the respected mother of three, was receiving the Sacrament. When she opened her mouth, the priest's spirit passed into her, and ever since she had been prone to fits of madness, in which she spoke with his voice, confessing to many of his crimes. All attempts to exorcise her had failed, for the demon threatened, if driven out, to possess some other young woman.'

> 'To cure a dog of biting, a long bramble should be dug up by its roots and tied between two trees; then the dog must be made to pass under it three times. Thereafter he would only bark at strangers instead of biting them.'

> 'For earache a narrow linen strip must be folded into a conical shaped, soaked in melted wax, placed in the ear when cold and then ignited; while for headaches a dog or fowl has to be killed, dissected and pressed still warm against the sufferer's head.'

These early visitors to Maniace must have found the place strange, if not a little sinister. Then, as today and as so often in previous centuries, Sicily was a country where insecurity and lawlessness were an accepted feature of ordinary life. In his diaries, Hood describes numerous instances of brigandage, several of which attracted considerable notoriety. One such incident occurred on November 10th 1881. Three armed men were spotted close to the Castello by

Giuseppe Meli, one of the *campieri* who raised the hue and cry. Alec started in pursuit with several Duchy employees, in heavy going after rain. They were gaining on the fugitives, when one of the latter raised his gun and took aim. At this Hood fired his rifle, and as the bullet splintered a rock at the brigands' feet, two of them surrendered forthwith, while the third jumped through some bushes into the river. A subsequent search proved fruitless, so it was presumed he had been washed away by the current. The incident was reported in the British press, while *Punch* provided a witty postscript. Under a heading, 'The Dignity of Constables', it suggested: 'Let the Honourable Alexander come over here. Plenty of work for him and his policemen. We know that in the Middle Ages, the Lord High Constable was a dignified officer of the Crown; the Constable of the Tower was a tremendous swell. So also could be the Constable of Brompton Boilers, the Constable of Cromwell Road and so forth. Hang the Brigands! Let Greeks catch Greeks, and do you, Alexander with your Staff come and help our Bungling Bobbies to catch the Brutal Burglars in the act of burgling.'

Brigandage was not, however, Alec's main preoccupation in Sicily during the 1880s and 1890s. His dream of finding an English market for the Duchy's wine was coming to fruition. Fabre had been an efficient overseer in extending the vineyards, which now produced about 60,000 gallons pa. He had also skilfully blended the Hermitage and Bordeaux grapes, the result of which was a somewhat heavy claret-style wine. But Hood did not feel this would be suitable for the English market, as it would have to compete with the far better known French vintages. He therefore sought the advice of P. E. Rainford, the British Vice-Consul at Messina, 'and under his wise direction and my personal superintendence a very fine Duchy of Bronte wine, much appreciated to this day (1924) was the outcome. It has the character of a Madeira and a Marsala, but with a flavour and bouquet peculiar to itself and superior to the latter.'

This was a drink designed to appeal to late Victorian palates. In autumn 1889 Alec prepared some brochures which were distributed to various wine merchants, hotels and inns around England, as well as to naval messes. In them he described the wine as 'light in colour, absolutely pure in quality, well matured and it possesses great aroma and natural body. It is solely the produce of the Duke's vineyards, and is made with the most scrupulous care and attention. It is equally good for dinner, or after-dinner drinking; and it has been found an exceedingly healthy wine for invalids. It will keep any length of time and improve greatly in bottle. The price is 30/- per dozen bottles for cash.' The two sole agents appointed were Alec's brother, Alfred Hood, and his old friend, Derek Keppel, and a sharp little postscript in the prospectus reminded its readers that: 'this wine is not to be confounded with another Sicilian wine bearing a somewhat similar name.'

To celebrate its launch, Hood gave a large lunch-party at 'The Ship and Turtle' in Leadenhall Street, which was widely reported in the press. *The Morning Advertiser* effused: 'it can scarcely fail of achieving a prominent place in the wine-markets of the world. A remarkably fine specimen was served at the table yesterday . . . a pale tinted wine of good body and pure flavour . . . and the low price at which it is offered ought to recommend it.'

Nevertheless, despite this promising start, the experiment proved a failure. It was expensive to export, advertise and distribute, while the costs of making the wine (for it was never bottled under seven years' maturity), plus those of distilling the spirit to maintain it, made the whole venture impractical. Eventually, the wine was once more sold at six months old, following local custom. The vineyards produced abundant harvests until the dreaded phylloxera disease appeared in Sicily around 1900, eventually destroying three quarters of the Duchy vines.

In terms of the broader political picture the government in Rome had concluded that crime and political corruption were indivisible in the island; when in 1876 the Prime Minister, Marco Minghetti, attempted to introduce legislation to break the power of the Mafia, left- and right-wing Sicilian deputies combined to bring down his administration. Indeed, overall very little had changed for the better since the Risorgimento.

It was at least in the Duchy's favour that it lay in the east of the island, where society was more open, Mafia-style boss rule less widespread, and enterprise and investment somewhat greater. There people were described as 'rarely going armed', whereas in the western areas it was 'universal'. Moreover Messina and Catania with their flourishing foreign communities were setting the tone for the rest of Sicily in commercial and intellectual attainments. Against this background can be set Alec's achievement in putting the estate on a more viable economis basis and making of Maniace in Consul Stigand's words: 'with the palace of the Prince Baucina at Montemaggiore the only veritable country house in the island'. As the century drew to an end, Hood was to find other distractions both in his social life and in a job at Court in London. For now he felt he had consolidated the Duchy. In Stigand's description: 'it is indeed gratifying to find such evidence of what English energy, intelligently directed, can do in a district which was formerly one of the wildest and most deserted in Sicily.'

Sir Alec Nelson Hood

CHAPTER XVI

'A little bandbox duke'

'Quite a pet like a little bandbox duke on the stage', was how the Irish authoress, Edith Somerville described Alec in a letter to her sister, after visiting Maniace in February 1920. It seems doubtful that he would have particularly appreciated the description; for he did not have much of a sense of humour about himself. But by then Alec had become quite a literary and social figure, one of the most senior and respected members of the British community in Sicily, who could also look back on almost thirty years of service at Court in London.

By the 1890s Hood was seeking wider horizons than those provided by running the Duchy. He had always spent three or four months in England every summer, initially content to stay within the bosom of his large family. In summer 1882, however, some friends of his had founded the Royal Italian Opera Company, and knowing that Alec was fluent in Italian had invited him to join it on a part-time basis. He welcomed the opportunity, for it gave him some occupation and income during his summer visit. He proved himself so competent an administrator that in 1883 he was asked to stay on and manage the Company throughout the winter, while the two principal directors were in America. This he agreed to do – apart from a brief trip to Sicily – and his knowledge of and involvement in the world of opera grew fast. Music was one of the chief loves of Hood's life, as his collection of autographs, including those of Verdi, Gounod and Meyerbeer and many famous singers show. But despite his efforts the company folded in 1884, while he lost his own investment of £2,000.

He had no desire to enter politics as his eldest brother had done, but in view of the family's connection with the Court, a job there was the obvious solution. Alec had already helped his father with arrangements for the Queen's Jubilee celebrations in 1887, and was fascinated by the mystique of royalty. At a Fourth of June party at Eton in 1890 he met Princess May of Teck, and they got on so well that he was invited to her home, White Lodge in Richmond Park, and in August to join her party to see the Passion Play at Oberammergau. Alec's suitability as a courtier was noted, and in 1892, Princess May's mother, the Duchess of Teck, appointed him her Equerry and Comptroller. Princess Mary Adelaide, descended from George III's seventh son, Adolphus, she was the sister of the eccentric Duke of Cambridge, for so long Commander-in-Chief of the British Army. Reputed to weigh seventeen stone, she was in every sense larger than life. Ebullient, impulsive, extravagant and warm-hearted, she was adored by the public. In the words of her daughter's biographer: 'She had a gift for inspiring a wild affectionate enthusiasm amongst the London crowds, which relished 'Fat Mary's' stout benevolent appearance and her jovial yet imperious manner. It was this gift which had never been entirely welcome to her first cousin, the retiring widowed Queen.'

Princess May's engagement to Prince George, heir-presumptive to the throne after the death of his older brother, the Duke of Clarence, meant that the family's prospects were transformed. The Duchess of Teck was now the mother of the future Queen of England. As such she needed a discreet and reliable adviser and Victoria was probably involved in the appointment of the son of one of her favourite courtiers. Alec's new job was certainly to prove no sinecure. There was much to be done before the wedding and Hood proved an admirable Comptroller. After the splendid service in the Chapel Royal, one newspaper noted: 'now the wedding is over a word may be spared for a man who played a considerable part in it, although the greater portion of his work lay below the surface . . . Mr. Hood is about forty years of age, and is so quiet and unostentatious that his record has brought him little or no fame.' But his royal patrons were aware of his merits for the Queen had appointed him an Extra Gentleman Usher in 1892 to ensure a continuing connection with the Court.

Although he still spent six months a year in Sicily, Alec became indispensable to the Tecks' household and devoted to the Duchess. He quickly learned to couch his suggestions for economies in suitably diplomatic terms and managed to effect some improvement in the family's finances. He often travelled with them – to St Moritz, to Bad Nauheim for the cure and to visit the Queen's eldest daughter, the Empress of Germany, at Friedrichshof. But the Duchess's health was failing and she died of heart failure on October 27th 1897. Hood was recalled from Maniace by a telegram from Princess May, now the

Duchess of York, returning only to find that his employer had not left a will. He quickly set to work to try and sort out her affairs, successfully settling her many debts and resisting politely any interference from the Queen.

It was not only the Teck family's affairs that worried Alec. His father remained as great a favourite of the Queen's as ever, who confided to her Journal: 'good old Lord Bridport yesterday completed his fiftieth year in my service. He is the only one amongst all my numerous gentlemen who has served me so long and so continuously. I wrote to announce to him that I would give him my picture.' But because the demands of life at Court absorbed so much of Bridport's attention, his estate at Cricket St Thomas suffered in consequence.

Problems had reached such a pitch by 1895, that when Bridport's youngest daughter, Rosa, married the much older owner of a neighbouring estate, Herbert Evans of Forde Abbey, her father conceived the idea of moving in with them and letting the Cricket estate. However, no suitable tenant was found and that autumn the decision was taken to sell the entire property. The house itself was bought by a Mr. Fry from Bristol. In Alec's view: 'the great grief of my father's life was the sale of his family home with many of the pictures, Nelson relics and plate and some of the furniture, a sale enforced by the rascality of the family lawyer (Wynne) who embezzled trusts of which my father was a trustee'. Indeed Bridport even had to auction the presentation plate, enamelled gold boxes and sword hilts formerly belonging to Nelson and inherited through his mother, of which the Treasury purchased eleven items for display at Greenwich.

According to Hood, he had personally saved Maniace for the family, since Wynne, after running through the trust funds, thought of the Duchy which he had once visited, and suggested to Bridport that the estate should be developed by means of a company with outside investors, over which he, Wynne, would exercise effective control. When no precise information as to how the family would benefit was forthcoming, Alec intervened. Wynne then disappeared after a fraudulent bankruptcy owing some £250,000 and ruining many people. All of which went to demonstrate that Bridport was certainly no businessman.

Within two years, Rosa's marriage to 'that curious and unsatisfactory man', in Hood's words, was on the rocks, and both she and her father needed a new home. At this point the Queen intervened, offering Royal Lodge in Windsor Great Park for the remainder of Bridport's life. It was next to his old home at Cumberland Lodge, and here he lived until his death in 1904, occasionally visited by Victoria and friends from Court.

Life at Court and family affairs were not Hood's only pre-occupations. Now that the Duchy was running fairly smoothly, much of the day to day management could be left in the hands of the reliable Charles Beek, who had been engaged as Agent General in 1891. Until then Alec had been very much in charge by himself, for Monsieur Fabre was solely director of the wine-making operations, while William Grisley faithful old Samuel's son, had come to a sorry end. A handsome, elegant man, married to Cecilia Spedalieri, a girl from a good Brontese family, he was also a confirmed gambler. Being averse to hard work as well, he had left the Duchy's employment around 1880, and had proceeded to lose all his own and much of his father-in-law's money. When the latter declined to pay, Grisley committed suicide at a hotel in Catania in 1887.

Hood's new job inevitably distanced him further from Duchy affairs, so when he was in Sicily for his winter visits, with the house modernised and the garden expanded and beautified, his main occupation was entertaining a stream of guests at Maniace. Many were his family's friends, but others reflected his own literary, musical and artistic interests. The novelist F. Marion Crawford and his wife, long-time American residents in Italy with a house at Sorrento, came to stay, enjoying themselves so much that his novel, *Corleone*, describing an attack by brigands on a country house, was largely set, suitably enough, in the neighbourhood. Mr and Mrs William Sharp, 'he so good-looking and attractive', also became frequent visitors. Under the pseudonym Fiona MacLeod, Sharp wrote many Gaelic poems, and prose as well. Sharp became a close friend of Alec, and his articles on the Duchy were printed in the *Pall Mall Magazine* and *Atlantic Monthly*. That indifferent Poet Laureate, Alfred Austin, was a guest in 1898, his effusions in verse being nicknamed by the press: 'Alfredocles on Etna'.

Several single female visitors stayed, like Miss Maude Valérie White, the composer of such quintessential Victorian songs as *Home Thoughts from Abroad*, *Ye Cupids*, and the unfortunately named *Soft Lesbian Airs*. During one stay she dedicated a new composition, *Buon Riposo*, to Hood, with words by William Sharp describing the native evening salutation. Some guests were less welcome; as Hood recalled: 'In 1892 a tiresome English woman, married to an Italian "patriot", and she herself a socialist, by name Jessie White Mario invited herself. A bit of a firebrand, I had to correct her sharply when she began to criticise adversely Queen Victoria (of whom she knew nothing).'

As he approached middle age, Alec, a 'confirmed bachelor', also sought the company of some racier members of society. Hamilton Aïdé, reputedly the son of a Greek diplomat (or of Lord Melbourne according to some accounts), a novelist, playwright and artist, fascinated him. So did Robert Hichens, ten years Hood's junior, a good-looking and prolific author, who was an odd mixture of melancholia and humour. He was the son of a Kent clergyman, who had originally wanted to become a musician, but whose parallel talent for writing prevailed. Trained as a journalist, he had scored a definite success with *The Green Carnation*, published in 1894, a satire on Oscar Wilde and his circle.

In an article entitled 'Telling my Fortune', Hichens recounted how a clairvoyant had predicted that he would shortly go and stay in an ancient castle, far away and set in mountainous country. He had scoffed, but soon afterwards had met Alec at a lunch-party in London, and had been invited out to Maniace that autumn. Thus began a long-lasting and intimate friendship, which was to survive for over forty years. Evidently Hichens possessed much charm: Maude Valérie White was infatuated with him – a vain quest of course, as his proclivities lay in other directions. Tina Whitaker's diary noted in November 1906: 'She is pining to get away to her Robert in Taormina – he of course is with his Alec Hood at Maniace'.

Alec still fulfilled his local duties at Maniace, as President of the Bronte Working Men's Club, and attended their functions regularly. He was also President of the Collegio Capizzi in Bronte. This institute had been founded in 1778 to commemorate Ignazio Capizzi, an 18th century priest and painter who had fostered an artistic tradition in Bronte, producing several competent local artists, such as Nicolo Spedalieri, a fellow member with Wincklemann, Mengs and Canova of the neo-classical Arcadia Academy in Rome. It was very much the prestigious seat of learning in a small hill town, and Hood was proud to be elected its President, frequently visiting the college and giving speeches *'con accento inglese, ma in bella forma italiana'*. The completion of the Circumetnea Railway had been first projected in the 1880s to link Catania and Taormina round the landward side of the volcano. Alec wrote to the Catania press, emphasising how much this would relieve poverty and unemployment in the island but he had to wait until September 1895 for the inauguration of a route, which also enormously improved Maniace's communications with the coast.

In January 1901, Queen Victoria died, and her grand-daughter-in-law therefore became Princess of Wales. Now in need of a Private

Secretary, she wrote to Hood, requesting him to accept the post. He agreed, delighted to be back actively employed at Court, although on the same basis as before – that he should spend the winters in Sicily. This arrangement worked well, and Alec kept the job until George V's accession in 1910. As the demands of being Private Secretary to the Queen were far greater, 'and knowing that I could not fulfil the duties of that post under the altered circumstances, consistently with my six months' absences in Sicily, I begged leave to retire'. Queen Mary did not want to lose his services altogether, so he agreed to stay on as her Treasurer. Following the example of his father, who in over sixty years at Court left behind no notes or memoranda, Hood was a model of discretion, and no records of those years, in which as a privileged spectator he observed the conduct of affairs of state, survive.

The turn of the century also saw Hood's years of commitment to Maniace rewarded. On June 4th 1904 Lord Bridport died in his ninetieth year at Royal Lodge, poisoned by the smell of new paint, for workmen were then redecorating the house. 'He was the beau idéal of an English gentleman and greatly beloved,' wrote his adoring son. Alec had become the favourite child, 'my father was always indulgent and affectionate towards me', and by the terms of the will, which he disclaimed any part in drafting, he inherited everything. To quote from the wording: 'It is right you should have the Duchy, for you have worked so hard there'. Thus in mid-1904 did the fifth Duke of Bronte succeed to his title and estate, reiterating the terms of the original grant that the holder might leave both to whomsoever he chose.

Of all his family Alec was anyway the one best fitted to inherit. In his 'Recollections', he described his brothers and sisters: 'About Arthur, the eldest, who was one of the handsomest men of his day, there is not much to relate.' Interested neither by soldiering nor by his twelve years in the Commons, 'he was witty by nature and might have risen to a position in the state had he wished to do so'. Still he had a son, Maurice Henry Hood, born in 1881, who would eventually inherit the Bridport title. 'The next brother, Horatio, died early in life (aged 29 in fact), from smallpox contracted on a shooting excursion in China, when in command of HMS *Pegasus*'; while William and Alfred were constantly in financial difficulties, the former, involved in the tea trade, after leaving the East; 'only succeeded in losing his younger son's portion and the amount of a legacy left him by a godmother'.

Indeed only the youngest, Victor, named after the Queen, his god-mother, had shown any promise. In his twenties he had emigrated to the United States and found employment as Manager of the Texas

Guano Company. In 1887 he was mentioned in the press there for organising a Jubilee Festival in Victoria's honour, which was held in the Bat Cave in Nueces Canyon, presumably the source of much of his Company's raw product. By 1890 he had moved to Mexico, where the government granted him a concession to build a railway in the northern state of Coahuila; 'this crescent-shaped road will traverse one of the most productive regions on earth'. His *hacienda*, San Ysidro above the Sabinas river also attracted attention, for its 2,000 acres were entirely fenced, while it comprised magnificent woods, orchards and even a pack of foxhounds. Its practical purpose was as a specialist hog-breeding and slaughtering enterprise, shipping 50 to 100 animals a week, and curing or smoking them as well. By 1894 however, his spirit of adventure still unsatisfied, he had sold up and moved on to Australia, where he soon abandoned commercial enterprise and gained respect and popularity as Private Secretary to successive Governors.

Alec Hood had a much higher regard for his sisters, writing of the eldest, Nina, 'perhaps the most reserved of the four', that: 'she and Rosa were the best-looking, and uncommonly good-looking too.' Nina married a Scottish landowner, George Ferguson of Pitfour, and became one of the Queen's Women of the Bedchamber. The next down, Mary, married Hugh, Lord Hertford; 'She worked indefatigably for others and was always busy.' Sadly she died quite young, aboard ship en route home from Egypt. Adelaide married an ex-Naval officer, Herbert Gye, who became Consul at Brest; thereafter the couple lived at Paris, then Folkestone. The baby of the family, Rosa, had nursed her father until his death; 'Now her devotion is transferred to me, bless her', and she spent much of her time with her beloved brother in Sicily.

His own master at last, Hood was able to buy a permanent base in London, so he bought a house in Chelsea, at No 13, Pelham Crescent. The remaining family pictures, papers and memorabilia were taken there from Royal Lodge or shipped out to Sicily. Furthermore a new idea began to form in his mind. Alec had always worshipped the sun, and the Duchy, at an average altitude of 2,000 feet plus on the slopes of Etna was often cold in winter. Surely the solution was to find a property down by the sea; the obvious place was Taormina, then growing in popularity as a fashionable resort.

Taormina's rise to fame had started some forty years before, when a young Prussian artist, Otto Géleng, had arrived there to convalesce. He found the town's setting enchanting and began to sketch the Greek

Theatre and the other sights. From his lodgings in the house of Giuseppe La Floresta, just off the main street, the Corso, Géleng discovered many charming memorials of earlier civilisations. After some months' stay having fallen in love with a Taorminese girl, Filomena Zuccaro, he returned to Germany. Encouraged by friends, he arranged an exhibition of his works in Paris, where the beauty of the subject matter and the splendour of the colours aroused both interest and incredulity, for it seemed remarkable that the trees should be in full flower while Etna was covered with snow. Géleng, realising he must confound his critics, cleverly invited three of the bitterest to come to Taormina and see for themselves, offering to pay their expenses if they were disappointed. As the town then only boasted one extremely modest inn, the Bellevue, he persuaded the La Florestas to put up his guests, painting a sign 'Hotel Timeo' (after the legendary founder of the city), which was placed above the door, even though his landlady tried to obliterate it with her mop.

The three French journalists arrived and were quickly captivated by the charms of Taormina, on which they reported rapturously. The news soon spread, and French and German tourists began to arrive, initially much to the annoyance of the natives. But cupidity triumphed over their habitual xenophobia, and several houses were converted into hotels or pensions, the Timeo foremost among them.

There were undeniable drawbacks; the roads were dirt, the drainage primitive and the lighting non-existent. Yet Géleng, who had made his home in Taormina, taken Italian nationality and married Filomena Zuccaro, was tireless in organising improvements and agitating for more. Finally in 1872, a delegation of the leading townspeople suggested he should become *prosindaco*, or first citizen, without any election, as he best understood the problems involved. For the ensuing two decades, Géleng worked hard to publicise Taormina, inviting celebrities from all over Europe to visit it, and undertaking promotional trips himself.

These efforts paid handsome dividends. By the 1890s Taormina was established as a winter resort, where sunshine could nearly be guaranteed. Not all the people it attracted were entirely respectable. Wilhelm von Glöden, another German, had originally been persuaded to come for health reasons, but decided to stay to indulge tastes which were definitely frowned upon in his native country. He bought a house at the southern end of the town, near the San Domenico convent, where he entertained lavishly and kept exotic pets, reputedly including a talking crow and a tame bumble bee. When scandal overtook his family, and his stepfather, Baron Von Hammerstein, was ruined and imprisoned for libelling the Kaiser, Glöden needed to earn some money. Thus he began to use his photographic talents to produce postcards of Taormina, soon graduating to portrait studies of local boys.

His own protégé and assistant, Pancrazio Bucini, found the models and arranged their poses. In fairness most of them were taken with their clothes on, often in classical dress, although the boys were occasionally in female attire, and all had to use a lotion of fresh milk and other unguents to make them appear even more youthful. Girls posed for him too, the niece of the priest from Castelmola pretending to be Eleonora Duse, who because of her age had refused to be photographed. The great actress was actually visiting the town at the moment, so Glöden presented her with the picture and an inscription which read: *'Ecco, Divina, l'immagine della vostra adolescenza!'* Not surprisingly with such skilful sales techniques, his photographs became well-known in much of Europe. Reflecting the spirit of the age, they helped to draw a further stream of travellers to Sicily.

The winter season lasted roughly from November until Easter, after which the tourist season ended. But some foreign visitors began to buy houses in Taormina, and a few of them lived there on a more permanent basis. Among the first British arrivals were Sir Edward and Lady Hill, who purchased a fine property called Santa Caterina in 1898. Their maiden daughter, Miss Mabel Hill, was an early bene-factress of the youth of the town. Seeing that so few means of employment existed, she founded a school of needlework and embroidery for poor local girls at her own expense, starting what is now an established industry. She continually badgered the Salesian fathers to open a home for indigent boys, even gaining an audience with the Pope on the subject; and the home eventually opened in 1911. Her sister married Inigo Triggs, an architect who designed several villas for foreign clients.

Another early resident was Miss Florence Trevelyan, who according to gossip had been asked to leave England because of a scandal involving the King. On arrival at Taormina she went straight to the Timeo, where the La Florestas objected to her entourage of five large dogs. After protracted haggling a deal was struck, whereby she agreed to extend the hotel at her own expense provided she could keep her pets. When one of them fell ill, as there was no vet in the town, she asked a local surgeon, Professor Salvatore Cacciola, for help. He cured the dog, fell in love with its owner and married her. Now that she was settled permanently in Taormina, she became a lady of good works, paying for dowries for needy girls and medical treatment for the poor.

Florence bought several properties, including a farm on Monte Venere, and the enchanting islet of Isola Bella in Mazzarò Bay, often travelling between them in quasi feudal state preceded by bagpipes and dispensing alms. Unfortunately she collapsed and died in 1907 while taking a bath too soon after a large dinner; the funeral procession to her grave on the mountain was followed by a crowd of Sicilians throwing flowers on her coffin. Her chief memorial is the splendid public garden she created in the town.

It was not only the growing foreign community which attracted Hood to Taormina. With his romanticised vision of old Sicily, he found much to appeal to him there. Many of the people were still unspoilt, living in primitive dwellings, while on the slopes towards Etna the peasants still cultivated their land, mostly for fruit, in traditional fashion. At least they wore shoes, whereas the fishermen at Mazzarò wore none, and continued to use the old style nets, the *shabicca* which took twenty men to operate. The little town with its one main street, the Corso Umberto, was gradually spreading along the hillside as villas and hotels were constructed. But there were still many open spaces with glorious views over the sea, its three little bays indenting the coastline, and the straggling houses of Giardini stretching down towards the promontory of Naxos and away to the south – while on a clear day, the snow-capped cone of the volcano framed the horizon.

In about 1903 Alec found the perfect site for his dream villa, just below the main road winding from Taormina down to the sea and roughly half-way down the hill facing towards Etna. He bought a large plot of land and drew up designs for the house himself. Experience of altering the buildings of Maniace had given him an adequate knowledge of architecture, so he needed little help with the plans. Soon afterwards work began, and Hood was often at Taormina, staying at the Timeo, and erecting a tiny shed for shelter from the rain or burning sun so that he could monitor progress. Since he was simultaneously making the garden, putting in three wells to catch the water running down the hillside and numerous trees, while operations were virtually suspended during his summer absences in England, progress was inevitably slow. As he later proudly recollected: 'the planning and designing of the house, inside and out, and writing the contracts, was all done exclusively by me.'

In 1912 he began to move in and engage staff, although the villa was not completely finished until 1913, and with the advent of old age he spent ever more time there. Every week a cartload of provisions was brought down, and the house was immaculately kept with five indoor servants and three gardeners. Indeed 'La Falconara' as he had christened it, increasingly replaced Maniace as Hood's home in Sicily. During the years before the First World War, Taormina's reputation as a winter resort was at its height, often being visited by royalty. In 1905 the Kaiser returned for the third time and even the King of Siam stayed there briefly. In 1906, Edward VII visited the resort with a large entourage. In spring 1909 the royal yacht was once more in Sicilian waters with the King, Queen Alexandra, Princess Victoria and his sister-in-law, the Dowager Tsarina, Marie Feodorovna aboard. Hood remembered: 'His Majesty had telegraphed ahead to me from Malta to meet him and I dined on board, being received with much kindness.' Determined to be their guide round Taormina, he had also tentatively arranged lunch at Maniace, which the Queen and her sister-in-law wished to see. Unfortunately the Italian Ambassador to London, Marchese di San Giuliano, had already organised the schedule, 'a long railway journey of about six hours round Etna with no stopping followed by tea at his home near Catania; and the plans could not apparently be changed'. Alec noted maliciously: 'I afterwards heard that the royal party were bored to death, cooped up in that red plush Circumetnea saloon with a hot May sun beating fiercely down on the roof and I do not wonder.'

Certainly there was no lack of society in Taormina ranging from the royal to the downright disreputable. The Americans had also discovered Taormina and two of them were to become Alec's friends. Charles Wood, nicknamed 'King Carlo', was a painter and a veteran Italophile who had bicycled through most of the country, and decided to settle there. His first modest house on the Corso served as a convenient shop window for his art, but soon he began building a magnificent villa and studio at Madonna della Rocca, where every Sunday he put on concerts, which were free to all the townspeople. A successful painter, albeit 'of the almost blossom type' in Tina Whitaker's words, he only returned to the USA to organise his exhibitions, rushing back to Sicily as quickly as possible. In his memoirs, *Yesterday*, Hichens recalled that: 'Wood's profession was the reproduction of Etna on canvas. He invited everybody he met to lunch or tea in his rooms, and each one before leaving had to buy one of his pictures as a memento'. Wood's compatriot, Harry Bowdoin, had been on his way to Malta, but on impulse had decided to settle in Taormina instead. Son of the first American ambassador to a United Italy in 1870,

Bowdoin was a man of endless good works, who endeared himself to the natives by working tirelessly for the victims of the Messina earthquake.

This appalling natural disaster destroyed the even tempo of life in pre-war Sicily. The earthquake of December 28th 1908, killed at least 80,000 people, civil order collapsed and near-anarchy followed. As Hood wrote to the Princess of Wales: 'I pen these few lines (for they say it is useless to think of telegraphing as the wires are broken throughout), to tell Your Royal Highness that I am in the land of the living, although that alas cannot be said of many poor people in the neighbourhood.' After saying that no damage had been done at Taormina or Bronte, he went on: 'at 5.15am this morning all here were awakened by the earth shaking violently and the hotel heaving. That went on certainly for half a minute . . . and the shocks continued, I counted six in one hour'. A double shock had occurred, the two foci under the sea bed being less than eight miles apart. Cracks opened in the earth, up to five feet wide in some places; along the Corso Garibaldi 98 per cent of the houses collapsed immediately; vast clouds of dust arose, which were turned to mud by the steadily falling rain. The sea retreated, and two giant tidal waves formed to the south of the straits, which were over thirty feet high by the time they passed Giardini. They flooded Messina to a depth of 500 yards, completing the devastation. Of the city's fifty churches, including the 11th century Cathedral, all but one were destroyed. All communications to the mainland and the interior were severed; twenty-four hours later fires were raging despite the continuous rain.

Efforts to reach the stricken city were in vain, as Alec discovered, for all the roads were blocked with debris. 'I shall never forget the scene I saw to my dying day. The panic was almost sadder than the havoc. People were camping out in shelters formed of empty wine casks with sheets for a roof, in boats drawn up on the main streets with a sail for covering, in and under carts, anywhere in fact except inside the remaining houses . . . one old man was sitting on a heap of ruins which had been his home, speaking of the three children he had lost, crying: "if the sea has not got them, they are lying here beneath me".' In practical vein, Alec realised what needed doing: 'I have ventured to telegraph to the Lord Mayor in the hope that he will be induced to start a public fund, should he not already have done so . . . and I have volunteered to act in the distribution of the money sent to avoid its disappearance into the pockets of the distributors as happened two years ago with the earthquake in Calabria'.

Two days later when the King and Queen arrived to inspect the damage, their journey was compared to Dante's through the Inferno. Cold seismic rain was still falling, dead bodies floated in the harbour, while the magnificent façade of the Palazzata was standing, an empty shell. Organised gangs had formed, after the surviving convicts had escaped from the wrecked gaol, and were looting shops and wealthier houses. Murder was rife and although martial law had been imposed, only gradually did the international fleet lying in the harbour manage to restore order and feed the population.

Thanks to Alec's intervention, the Lord Mayor's Fund raised £160,000, which was properly distributed. Thanks again largely to its foreign residents, Taormina offered shelter and relief to many of the homeless. Emergency operations were performed there and the patients sent on south; while collection centres were set up for the free milk and bread which poured in from all over the island. It had been a traumatic experience. Hood wrote in mid-January 1909: 'the last fortnight has been an evil, hideous nightmare, in which I believe the very depths of misery have been reached. The pen of a Euripides would fail to give a true notion of it. All the horrors of the universe: fire and water, with the upheaval of the earth in all its fury, and every affliction humanity can suffer: loss of family, friends, clothes, possessions came upon the poor inhabitants who the day before were merry making at the time of peace and goodwill towards men'.

Alec was grateful to have escaped so lightly, reporting from Maniace: 'practically no damage here. There are cracks in the hall ceiling and the corridor, some plaster came down in one of the arches below, also in four bedrooms, but nothing beyond that'. Consciousness of this seemed to make him redouble his labours for the victims of the earthquake, and Hood richly deserved the decoration 'Grand Official of the Crown of Italy' which was bestowed upon him.

Apart from the catastrophe which befell Messina, these were uneventful years on the scale of the island's turbulent history. Life at Maniace was uneventful and even the Brontesi were relatively quiescent. After twenty years of hard work to get the Duchy running smoothly, Hood made few changes there in the next twenty, following his posts at Court and Beek's arrival as agent. The vineyards produced abundantly until the advent of phylloxera, and after the abandonment of attempts to market it in England, the wine found a ready market in Sicily. Indeed even after phylloxera had struck, wine from the estate was being sold to supplement depleted production at Marsala. But reliable as Beek was, he did not try to farm any of the land in hand or alter the system of letting through the few large *'gabellotti'*, so the agriculture remained static.

Alec went on adding to the contents of the house, especially after his father's death, bringing many family items over from England, and beautifying the garden. In 1905 he erected an obelisk in Bridport's memory, standing forty feet high at Serraspina, the highest point on Duchy property, 5,000 feet above sea level, and bearing the inscription: *filius amore impulses hoc signum posuit*. That same year the little cemetery among the almond trees on the slope above the Saraceno and facing the castle was inaugurated, first receiving the body of Bridport's old valet. Almost immediately afterwards William Sharp, who had died after a few days' illness while staying at Maniace, was buried there too at the age of only fifty. Two quotations from his writings were carved on his tombstone: 'Farewell then, to the known and exhausted. Welcome to the unknown and unfathomed', followed by: 'Love is more great than we can conceive, and death is the keeper of unknown redemptions'.

Sharp had been responsible for persuading Hood to write his first book. Entitled *Adria*, it was a historical novel, 'aimed at describing the beauty of Venice, that incomparable city, typified by a young girl whose love for liberty and her country made her a heroine against the domination of Austria in the days of the patriot Manin'. It took Alec seven years to complete, after regular autumn visits to Venice for inspiration. Published in 1904, and kindly received by the critics, 'the net result of sales after deductions for copies supplied to me was the sum of £3.1.8!' *Tales of Old Sicily* published by John Murray in 1906 fared somewhat better, netting its author some £30, which from a sale price of 6 shillings per copy was not too bad in his opinion. It contained four stories, entitled: The Great Mother, Venus of Eryx, The Divine Philosopher and Cyane, all of which illustrated Alec's fondness for and knowledge of the island and its past.

Nine years later Hood published his most ambitious work *Sicilian Studies* through George Allen & Unwin which he dedicated to Robert Hichens. This comprised fifteen stories and essays in all, mainly factual and based on his own views and experiences. One piece was entitled The Spirit of the Mafia. Here, as well as analysing the state of mind which gave birth to it, Alec included a glossary of Mafioso terms with their veiled meanings – *serenata* (an evening's entertainment) meant a drawing of knives; *cantare* (to sing) meant to betray; *ballare* (to dance) meant to fight. The phraseology was picturesque, 'keep the knife sheathed' was to discuss matters calmly; 'he blew out the candle' (he murdered someone); 'the priest is among the guests' (blood will be spilled).

The most instructive essay described the customs and superstitions of the island. Hood produced a glossary of the various Sicilian greetings in use, *Biniricitu* (Benedicite) from the younger to the elder person being answered by *Santu* (Salute). A peasant might say *Gesu e Maria* to a stranger; the reply was *San Giuseppe v'accompagni*. On parting *Cirurnativi* (take care of yourself) elicited *Raccumandatami u Signuri* (commend me to the Lord), while knocking at a door *Ddorazia* (Deo Gratias) should have *Trasiti cui siti* (whoever you are, enter) as its response. The *Mal Occhio* or 'Evil Eye' was still considered important, as were dreams, especially if occurring on a Monday or Tuesday. White grapes signified tears, black grapes fecundity; similarly white figs equalled misfortune and black figs prayers for the souls in limbo. A black dog brought good luck, a white one loss or theft, a reversal of modern beliefs. Pears presaged punishment, wheat torment, raw meat approaching death, and chickens a treasure trove. In this essay, Alec showed how intently he had observed Sicilian life and ways over many years.

By the time this third and last book was published in 1915, the world had changed dramatically. Most of Europe was embroiled in war. Taormina was bereft of its tourists; most of the foreign residents had left, barring a few like Bowdoin who had joined the Red Cross; those from Germany like von Glöden preferring voluntary exile to internment. Maniace, too, was closed to guests, although on several occasions between 1914 and 1918 Hood managed to get out to Sicily from England and back again safely. Many of the young men on the Duchy had been conscripted although there remained enough to keep the estate running under Beek's supervision. And when the dust finally settled and the carnage ceased, nothing in Sicily, as in the rest of the world, would ever be quite the same again.

CHAPTER XVII

An uncertain succession

On the 1st August 1929 Alec wrote a memorandum for his heirs: 'I think it well to write this letter to be read by you after my death, for you will readily admit that after more than half a century of experience in Sicily and management of the Duchy of Bronte, the welfare of the latter and its future are of great moment to me . . . I feel anxious that its future should be in good and capable hands, so that it may, DV, be kept intact and treasured by those who come after me.' By now Hood was over seventy-five, and his constant preoccupation was that Maniace and the estate should remain the Bridport family property after his death.

Among the havoc wreaked by the First World War, the loss of heirs to great names and titles was a commonplace. Maurice Henry Nelson Hood, the only surviving son of Alec's eldest brother, had married Miss Eileen Kendall, or Eileen Orme to use her stage name for she was an actress, in 1908. The young couple emigrated to Canada and had a son and a daughter. At the outbreak of war Maurice had returned to England to join up, and had been posted to the Hood Battalion which formed part of the Second Brigade of the Naval Division. Early in 1915 they were sent out to join the allied forces engaged in the Dardanelles Campaign. During May Maurice had been in action, as his letters home show. On June 3rd he wrote: 'I got several letters yesterday in the trenches. We were up there for four days, and came down at 2 am this morning. It was awfully hot and very cramped. Our brigade has been chosen, as reliable, to do an advance and take a Turko trench, which has been annoying us lately'.

To quote from General Sir Ian Hamilton's despatches: 'At 8 am on June 4th an artillery bombardment began, and the infantry advanced at noon. The Second Brigade of the Royal Naval Division rushed forward with great dash; the Anson battalion captured the southern face of a Turkish redoubt, which formed a salient in the enemy's line; the Howe and Hood Battalions captured the trenches fronting them. By 12.15pm the whole Turkish front line was in our hands'. From this assault Maurice did not return, and it was not until October that it was finally confirmed that he had been killed in action. The Divisional Chaplain wrote to Lady Bridport: '. . . The last that was seen of your son was when he was leading his men right into the Redoubt which was captured. Then unfortunately we were forced to retire, leaving many dead on the field'. It appeared that Maurice had been shot in the jaw and collapsed into a trench. Thus died the heir to the Bridport title and probably in due course to the Duchy of Bronte.

This was but one of the losses Alec suffered during the four years of war which destroyed the Victorian and Edwardian world he had loved so dearly. As he wrote in his 'Recollections': 'During the Great War the Queen desired to retain my services, and as I was over age for the Army, I dedicated myself to her works of Mercy.' In Sicily, he offered to continue his good works, but was frustrated by mismanagement and incompetence.

One journey he made to Sicily from England, on September 26th 1918 took him via Le Havre, and then Paris. 'The excellent news from the battlefields is reflected generally in the bearing of the people.' After a brief stop, he continued his journey, arriving at Taormina on October 5th. Back at La Falconara his reflections were bitterly anti-German: 'it should be remembered that the Huns are devoted to pig meat and the flesh of geese; from the one they have probably developed their crass pigheadedness, from the other their extreme folly'. He mused: 'it will be interesting psychologically to see how the Huns will take their beating'; but when up at Maniace he heard of the Armistice being signed, he rejoiced: 'There is a little "Te Deum" chanting in one's breast which is none the less grateful for being sung solo rather than in chorus'.

That autumn Alec spent six weeks up at Maniace. He was in low spirits, being anxious about the running of the Duchy: the faithful Charles Beek had died in May 1917, and been buried in the Abbey Church, while his replacement, Edwin Hughes, son of a schoolteacher in Rome, was new to the job, having arrived only a few months earlier. But Hughes' health was a worry: 'a weak heart and now a clot of blood in the groin where an operation is impossible it is said', did not, as his employer observed, augur well, and no good substitute agent was available. The solution was obvious; the proprietor must spend more time in Sicily than in the past twenty-five years, otherwise the well-being of his estate would suffer. Hood wrote to the Queen offering to resign from his post as Treasurer, and with the New Year came a reply: 'need I assure you how reluctantly I part with such an old friend of my family, nor how grateful I am to you for many years' faithful service as well as the kind interest you have taken in my affairs'.

One result of his increased free time was Hood's five volumes of 'Recollections' that he compiled over the next eighteen years. Part memoir, part diary, part commentary on current events, they were never intended for publication. In the words of the Introduction to Volume I: 'This is a private record and not for perusal by the crowd'. There are plenty of comments and aphorisms which reveal much about their author's character and prejudices. 'What a delightful place the world would be if there were no cranks or fanatics; but it would not be so amusing', or: 'I can understand a nobody wishing to be a somebody. But that a somebody should desire to be always climbing passes my comprehension'. A propos snobs: 'Thank God for them. The world would not be nearly so amusing without them. And how many there are in all grades of society! Some of the greatest snobs I have known are those at the top of the tree. I wonder why?' Occasionally his comments were downright crotchety. Female fashions and short skirts were decried for 'revealing spindle shanks and big feet unashamed to the public gaze'; while 'low-cut bodices unduly expose throat and chest to the benefit of the doctors'. With many women in Hood's opinion: 'the more bizarre the costume, the better they are pleased. That used to be confined to courtesans – but tempora mutantur!'

Better news from Bronte cheered Alec early in 1919; 'I am less anxious as to the management of affairs for Hughes seems better in health, although I fear rather a shaky reed to rely on'. Moreover young George Bulloch, who had worked under Beek and 'knows the ways of the place' had returned after serving in the Army. Thus heartened, Hood left for London in May. After a busy summer, he made a quick tour of the West Country, mainly to see the churchyard at Cricket where his parents were buried. 'It pained me to see the neglected state of the Park. Where once all was trimness and tidiness, now nettles and thistles have exuberant growth'.

On his return to Sicily in October, with his sister Rosa, Alec found his peace of mind about the Duchy had been ill-founded. He learned that Bulloch had developed fits, and was uttering threats of vengeance for imaginary ills, so his father had to be telegraphed to remove him.

Hughes' health still did not permit him 'to get about', and the accounts were seriously in arrears. On November 30th Alec returned to Taormina after five weeks of hard work at Maniace: 'to Rosa the rest and quiet were not only pleasant but beneficial, whereas I had little of either'. Realising that he was too old himself to take on the entire management of the estate, he wired to his brother Victor in Australia, suggesting that he should come and live at Maniace.

Victor arrived that spring 'to help in managing affairs; he seems to take an interest in what is going on', and Alec again spent a pleasant summer in England. But during his absence news reached him that a horde of landless peasants were occupying Duchy land. The situation was less serious than it sounded, however, and Victor had behaved with great tact in a difficult situation. In due course the furore died down: most of the peasants decamped peacefully, but it was an indication of how unsettled the world had become.

The First World War had done much damage to the Sicilian economy by cutting off most of its export markets, while few war industries had flourished there. With the need for cheap food, official wheat production had declined and prices soared on the black market, while high inflation had diverted investment from agriculture to commerce. Change was, however, in the air, and in mid-1922 the Rome Parliament passed the Micheli Law, permitting the state to expropriate uncultivated parts of large estates, where improvements were deemed possible. This helps to explain the appeal of Fascism as a counter-revolutionary force both to businessmen and landowners, as well as to those intellectuals who pointed out how little sixty years of unification and Parliamentary rule had done for Sicily, and for some years, many people like Alec looked on Fascism with a benevolent eye.

In a world beset with so many troubles, one place at least had regained its pre-war charm and escapist gaiety. Soon after the return of peace, Taormina was re-established as a fashionable resort. The exiles returned, their appetite for pleasure sharpened in many cases. The Transatlantic residents were back too, a new one being Robert Percival Campbell, a rich Canadian who evinced his desire to blend into the surroundings by learning the dialect and frequenting the town's bars.

Needless to say Hood held himself largely aloof from such raffish society. His closest friends in Taormina were Americans: King Carlo Wood, with whom he regularly visited Syracuse to see performances of classical Greek drama in the theatre there; Leader and Lilyan Williams who had an antique shop; Bowdoin; and M M Oppenheim.

He was also on quite friendly terms with some newer residents: Charles Williams, Bobby Pratt-Barlow (even though the latter's habits were closely akin to the German 'baroni') and Robert Kitson, a talented water-colourist whose work had originally been admired by Géleng. One couple he saw frequently had recently moved from Catania; Percy Trewhella and his wife Gertrude who had lost their infant son in the 1908 earthquake. They bought the site of Sant'Andrea down on the bay at Mazzarò where they built a large villa for themselves and their two small daughters.

Sadly for Alec, the closest of all his friends, Robert Hichens, had ceased coming to Sicily after the War. He had met a Swiss couple and they had set up what amounted to a ménage à trois, firstly in England and Switzerland, deciding in the early Twenties to move to Egypt for eight months a year. Alec regarded the relationship with some cynicism tinged with bitterness: 'of friend Hichens I hear little these days. He is always with his fidus Achates (let us hope he is fidus)'.

In 1920 Maude Valérie White brought a new acquaintance to meet him, Dame Ethel Smyth, the composer 'whose cleverness and versatility are beyond dispute'. The latter came to stay at Maniace, accompanied by Edith Somerville, joint authoress of *The Irish RM*; 'kind, thoughtful, unselfish, with a fund of Irish humour and very intelligent – also be it said a master of hounds', in Hood's description. A very different sort of guest was Prince Felix Youssoupov, one of Rasputin's assassins, who came to lunch, predicting the imminent collapse of the Bolshevik regime in Russia, so reinforcing some of his host's sillier views.

Needless to say the most celebrated resident of Taormina at this period failed to get on with Alec and vice versa. Early in 1920 D H Lawrence and his wife Frieda rented a villa just outside the town; 'I have found such a charming house here in a big garden . . . Fontana Vecchia means old fountain – the name of the property'. Soon afterwards that March he wrote: 'I must say I like this place. There are a good many English people but fewer than Capri and not so all-overish – and one needn't know them'. In July: 'We are still here; I live in pyjamas, barefoot all day . . . we do our own work, I prefer it and can't stand people about . . . behold me in puris naturalibus performing the menial labours of the day.'

Although by that autumn he was complaining: 'Everywhere seems very far off . . . Sicily at the moment feels like a land inside an aquarium – inside all water – and people like crabs and black-grey shrimps creeping on the bottom', on the whole Lawrence loved the climate and the scenery: 'Etna herself, Etna of the snows and secret changing winds, she is beyond a crystal wall. When I look at her, low, white, witch-like under heaven, slowly rolling her orange smoke and giving sometimes a breath of rose-red flame, then I must look away from earth, into the ether, into the low empyrean . . . Pedestal of Heaven'. He was, however, less enthusiastic about Messina: 'Oh horrible Messina, earthquake-shattered and renewing your youth like a vast mining-settlement, with rows and streets and miles of concrete shanties, squalor and a big street with shops and gaps and broken houses still'. His opinion of the Sicilian peasants, whom he found full of hatred and malice, was equally low: 'These maddening, exasperating, impossible Sicilians, who never knew what truth was and have long lost all notion of what a human being is – a sort of sulphurous demon'; and again: 'They never leave off being amorously friendly with almost everybody, emitting a relentless physical familiarity that is quite bewildering to one not brought up near a volcano'.

Lawrence soon met Alec, and was invited to Maniace, as he reported in a letter to Cynthia Asquith in May 1920: 'Did you ever hear of a Duca di Bronte – Mr Nelson-Hood descendant of Lord Nelson (Horatio), whom the Neapolitans made Duca di Bronte because he hanged a few of them? Well Bronte is just under Etna, and this Mr Nelson-Hood has a place there – his ducal estate. We went to see him – rather wonderful place, mais Mon Dieu, M le Duc – Mr Hood I should say. But perhaps you know him?

> Tell me where do Dukedoms lie,
> Or in the head or in the eye?

That's wrong

> Tell me where are Dukedoms bred
> Or in the eye or in the head?

If I was Duca di Bronte, I'd be tyrant of Sicily. High time there was another Hiero, but of course money maketh a man; even if he was a monkey to start with.'

Lawrence's biographer, H T Moore, gives an even less polite if more fanciful account of the visit: 'As the Lawrences and their friends approached the Castle, all of them riding mules, six or seven lackeys of the Duke tottered out to meet them, ageing shepherds whom Hood had arrayed in costumes like those of the Pope's Swiss Guard. One of these collapsing retainers who knew English doffed his cap, bowed and presented greetings from his master. The party entered the castle whose authentic Norman façade clashed with the furnishings of the interior, although these were appropriate to the appearance of Hood's sister, who affected the style of Queen Alexandra. The Duke himself went around staring at his guests through a monocle fastened like a pince-nez to the bridge of his nose. Lawrence in his exasperation roughed out the scenario of a skit on the place, but before long his humour gave out altogether and he had to escape.'

As the decade progressed, Hood's thoughts increasingly turned towards the spiritual, in part, no doubt, due to the personal losses he was suffering. In 1921 on his way back from his summer sojourn in London, he heard of his brother William's death from dropsy. That winter, cold and wet, saw his sister Rosa taken ill. Her condition worsened, and she died on March 17th 1922, being buried at La Falconara in the newly completed double tomb. 'My loss, Oh God, is very great,' lamented Alec: 'I loved her more than anyone on earth. And if I have not recognised it more fully until now, may God forgive me'. She was followed by her eldest sister, Nina Ferguson, in summer 1923 and by Arthur Bridport at his home in Guernsey on March 29th 1924. Neither Alec nor Victor went to the funeral; fraternal relations had anyway been strained. The 13-year old Peter, son of Maurice Hood, who had died in action at Gallipoli, thus succeeded both to the title and as head of the family.

In December 1922, Edwin Hughes 'finally succumbed to a variety of diseases' at Maniace. His employer rushed up from Taormina in an open lorry through a raging blizzard: 'arriving with my cap and fur coat collar frozen stiff with snow and quite numbed'. At the age of sixty, Victor was too old to run the Duchy single-handed, so a new deputy, Major Richard Forsyth Gray, ex-Royal Army Service Corps, was engaged. This succession of shocks, and Rosa's death in particular aged Hood considerably and left him withdrawn and depressed, reflecting: 'At best death is peace, rest and a blessed change, at its worst a not-to-be'.

One pleasure that Alec still enjoyed was his writing. He confided his earliest memories to his 'Recollections', from soon after his birth on June 28th 1854, including the landmarks of his infancy: hearing the minute guns firing for the Prince Consort's funeral; watching the arrival of Princess Alexandra for her wedding from a stand on Castle Hill; and later the fire at Cumberland Lodge in November 1868. Queen Victoria drove over in the afternoon to inspect the blaze, which had begun in the housekeeper's room, and was accidentally drenched by a hose, at which she merely remarked: 'I think we had better move away'. Seen through his own eyes: 'I was a shy boy in my early days, diffident, affectionate by nature, somewhat pensive, anxious to make friends, sympathetic . . . I did not learn much at schools and gradually acquired a love of reading and for Art, especially for Sculpture. Later he added: 'solitude has little terror for me, which is fortunate, because from the age of 19 onwards for nearly twenty years, I lived very much alone for eight months of every year at Maniace . . . I feel inwardly as youthful as fifty years ago, and that has been assisted by the good health that Divine Providence has given me'.

In May 1924 Hood produced his pamphlet on the Duchy, which he had privately printed. It began with a potted history of Maniace up to Alec's first visit there in 1868, continuing with a detailed description of the house and its contents as arranged by him, then with the changes and improvements he had made to the estate. To this pamphlet Alec appended chunks of two articles William Sharp had written on the Duchy twenty years earlier. Similarly when composing an article, 'Nelson's Duchy of Bronte', which appeared in *Country Life* in August 1929, he quoted extensively from Sharp, and put in disappointingly little about the buildings' architectural evolution. The article concluded with a paean of praise for the Fascist regime: 'The country has now been rescued from lawlessness by the firm rule of Prefect Mori of Palermo, directed and supported by the iron will and clear-sighted statesmanship of Signor Mussolini, who . . . has taken the place of those effete and self-seeking politicians whose so-called democratic government had nearly brought the nation to communistic dissolution. Italy has had a second Renaissance'.

Interestingly Hood's approval of Mussolini was sincere and long-lasting. He was full of praise for Fascism in 1922: 'It is evidence of sound moral intention and clear-sightedness and if wisely guided will be of untold benefit'; being in Rome at the moment of Mussolini's march: 'One felt that right (politically) had at last come into its own in this outburst of patriotism both moving and restrained. In 1927 Hood chaired a conference in Taormina discussing Fascist policies in English for the benefit of foreign visitors. His speech ended: 'I think you need have no fear because when a lofty patriotism, springing from the hearts of men goes hand in hand with integrity, there can be no fear for the future. That is why I revere the name of Benito Mussolini and the work of Fascismo of which he is the Creator'. This attitude would remain unchanged until well into the 1930s.

Perhaps the single event in all these years which gave Alec the greatest pleasure was the visit King George V and Queen Mary paid to Sicily in spring 1925. The trip followed the King's collapse from influenza and bronchitis, so was supposed to be both convalescent and private. On April 1st a telegram summoned Hood to Messina just as the royal yacht, *Victoria and Albert* steamed into harbour. On board were the King and Queen, his sister, Princess Victoria, and their younger son, Prince George, later Duke of Kent. Alec stayed on board that night, and the next day a walk was taken round the old port of Messina. On the 4th a special train took the entire royal party to Taormina, where they were driven up to La Falconara to inspect the house and garden. 'I could entertain but ten in all . . . the rest of the Household and officers lunched at Mrs Dashwood's or in the town.'

Following a Sunday spent at Messina visiting the British cemetery, the yacht with Hood still aboard left for Syracuse on the Monday, and after a two day stay there steamed through the Straits to Palermo in 12½ hours. The Easter weekend was spent in and around the city, while Alec ignored all his other commitments and stayed on until the following Saturday. In his farewell message, the King mentioned: 'the utmost pleasure derived from our stay in an island which will always be connected with the life of Britain's greatest naval hero'.

The royal visit confirmed Alec's status as the senior British resident in eastern Sicily, a position he took seriously. Lilyan Leader Williams, wife of the antique shop owner and vice-chairman of the Church Committee, wrote him a touching tribute: 'I wonder if you ever think how much we all appreciate having you for the head of our little colony here. Your thoughtfulness and real kindness to us all is something that I am quite sure we should not find in anyone else'.

Life at Maniace continued through the 1920s at a fairly even tempo. Victor was an efficient and popular Agent. But his brother remained worried about the succession to the estate. Should it be left outright to his great-nephew, Peter Bridport? In 1925 Alec noted with satisfaction: 'Peter, who is now head of the family, has passed for the Navy, a relief to all concerned . . . May it be a good training school for the boy'. That August, during his visit to London, Hood recorded: 'Peter Bridport came to stay with me for two nights. I found him intelligent, gentle with good manners and healthy ideas, fond of his profession and tall for his age (14); in fact promising as far as I could perceive in the short time he was with me'. He had told the boy that: 'if he behaved properly he might eventually and under certain contingencies succeed to the Duchy of Bronte, but that would depend on him and how he shaped'.

219

In 1928 he was further gratified when visiting the *Victory* at Portsmouth and subsequently being given lunch in the mess of HMS *Nelson*, to learn that his great-nephew was to join the ship direct from Dartmouth. A letter soon arrived from Peter to say that: 'he slung his hammock over the case of Nelson relics, and one night narrowly missed putting his foot through the glass'. By 1929 a young naval officer, based on Malta, got three days' leave which he spent at La Falconara with a shipmate friend, 'too short a visit from that nice boy', who returned for another visit in 1930 during the Carnival. Time was to sour this favourable opinion.

Even if Hood regarded young Bridport as his ultimate heir, he was still contemplating leaving the Duchy to his brother, Victor, in the meantime. In February 1928 the latter suddenly announced his engagement to Mrs Violet McBean, a widow from New South Wales then living in London. Alec commented: 'this should not make any difference in looking after the estate. It is an affair of long devotion, and I am glad he will have someone to care for him when I pass on'. The wedding took place in July at St Martins-in-the-Fields, but the honeymoon was cut short by the news from Maniace that Major Forsyth Gray had died, meaning that Victor had to hurry back to supervise affairs. When his elder brother returned in October, he found 'Shrimp', whose childhood nickname was still frequently used, had been up at Otaiti for the preceding two months, and had hired a new assistant, George Dubois Woods, who had worked at Marsala as an apprentice for Woodhouse from 1922 to 1926. This was just as well as Victor's own health was failing. It was a wet cold winter, ushered in by a major eruption of Etna: subsequently, the Saraceno river in full flood swamped the bridge at Maniace and completely destroyed it.

Throughout the winter months Victor was ailing and depressed that his wife had refused to join him at Maniace. In early April 1929, Alec with Dr Sinclair collected him in a closed car, 'we found him with both lungs congested and took him back to Taormina as good care and nursing were essential'. Although his lungs improved, Victor's mental state did not. 'I knew from conversation with him how grievously disappointed he was that married life had not proved the happy companionship which he had looked forward to . . . indeed he felt this so keenly that he was considering an annulment on grounds of non-consummation'. He remained bedridden at La Falconara for a month and died on May 1st. Hood lamented: 'I have lost one who was a good and dear brother to me; he was my right hand at Maniace. I committed all my affairs to him, and he gave unlimited devotion. He was deeply attached to the Duchy to which he would have been my successor'.

Now there was no alternative to appointing Peter Bridport his direct heir, and that summer Alec made a new will. In an accompanying memorandum addressed to 'Peter and my future heirs whoever they may be', he recommended them to supervise its management in person, always to employ a British agent (at that moment Woods seemed 'very active and reliable') and sub-agent as well. The Duchy was unencumbered by debts save for three mortgages. He wished all family relics and pictures in his three homes 'to be saved from the desecration of the sale room if possible', while his parents' and the other graves should be maintained. Lastly he wanted a stone obelisk to his and Victor's memory erected on the apex of the hill known as the 'Fondaco Mandorleto', at the end of an avenue of trees facing the house.

Death was very much in Alec's mind in these years, but his enjoyment of life had not vanished. Having resented Robert Hichens' desertion, Alec had found a new and fairly constant companion, Gilbert Barker, 'whose charm of an unusual personality, sympathy combined with a rare intelligence, unusual and unselfish affection, a keen appreciation of the beauties of this land with a love of books endeared him to me greatly'. Another of his guests was 'Beverly Nichols, fresh from his triumphs as a Cochrane Review writer both of words and music – a mental tour de force. He was with me several days, proving himself a delightful companion and a fair pianist'. They had already met once at a party in London, about which Alec recorded an entertaining story: 'Nichols told me that he had loved Sicily especially Taormina. "Dear old Alec Hood, the Duke of Bronte you know was awfully nice to me. I almost lived at his villa". When we were parting, he said: "By the way, do tell me your name. I should so much like to meet you again". "I am dear old Alec Hood, the Duke of Bronte you know," I replied'. There also came to Maniace: 'Noel Coward, that singularly lucky young man, playwright, author, actor and musician, who it is said is making £1,000 a week from his work. A pleasant and amusing person'.

Entertaining a stream of guests kept the ageing Hood active, as did his self-appointed role as guardian of the family's heritage and Nelson's good name. In 1925 he was enraged by the publication of Norman Douglas' new book of essays, which resurrected the controversy over Caracciolo's execution. Alec ferociously defended his ancestor: 'To Nelson loyalty to constituted authority and duty were paramount. It was not for him to extend clemency to a rebel whose conduct he abhorred'. He found Mrs Barrington's biography, *Divine*

Lady, equally infuriating: 'All my family have decried the notion that Horatia was the Hero's daughter, and perhaps not even of Lady Hamilton'. As late as 1936 he was writing a rejoinder in trenchant terms to Compton Mackenzie's article in the *Daily Mail*, which referred to the events of 1799 at Naples as 'that ghastly business when the Victor of the Nile murdered Francesco Caracciolo', and to 'the deplorable behaviour of Lady Hamilton and her blithering old husband'. 'Permit me to protest strongly that a pen like yours, deservedly popular, should parrot-like perpetuate scandal-mongering gossip and lying assertions'.

Not only did he do his utmost to defend the family name, but he also promoted a rapprochement with members of the Nelson family, healing the long coldness after the lawsuit in the 1840s. 'I have stayed at Trafalgar with Horatio, 3rd Earl, who being a minor at the time could hardly be held responsible for the litigation. He was a man of kindly disposition and a High Churchman. His son, Merton, now the 4th Earl, is very friendly; and I entertained him with his nephew at Maniace and Taormina some three years ago. He reverted to Rome and was at one time a priest, I believe'.

Towards the end of his life, the regime in Italy was beginning to alienate Hood. His enthusiasm for Fascism had been long-lasting; indeed he had even enrolled in the Liverpool branch of the British Fascist Movement. But he had gradually come to realise that Sicily was no better governed than before. Departing for England in 1933, he felt: 'not sorry to leave behind the increasing difficulties of a landowner in Sicily, where government aggression in the shape of taxation and silly socialistic meddling makes life in that island increasingly irksome'.

During his last years, Alec's affection for Taormina remained undimmed. He still adored the climate, as well as the countryside, driving up the newly completed road on Etna to a height of 4,500 feet, but by this time, his health was failing and during the spring of 1932 he was laid low with pneumonia.

Notwithstanding his illness, Alec paid his normal summer visit to England in 1932, lunched with the Queen and saw numerous plays. The next three winters, Alec went on cruises to warmer climates. The first took him to Ceylon; the second, to Ceylon and Burma, this time escorted by Peter Bridport. His great-nephew had just resigned from the Navy as a lieutenant, and Hood was hoping to persuade him to come and live at Maniace, to learn about running the Duchy. Their journey together was not a success. On the way out, Alec complained: 'I saw little of Peter throughout the fortnight's voyage. He devoted himself assiduously to a girl friend on board and her party (evidently sickening for the love disease which attacked him later). The young man is obviously self-centred or in other words egoistic'. In early March they parted in Kandy, and Peter en route home sent a letter to Hood; 'I posted a long reply to London, where as he announces he intends to go and not take up work at Maniace, alleging he is unable to make a sacrifice of social engagements. Although he denies female involvement, he is evidently on a string ... such foolishness and selfishness of youth blind to future interest is a disappointment to me for I had though better of him'. Despite these fulminations, Alec did nothing to alter his will, and was delighted when Bridport got engaged to Pamela Baker, sister of his brother-in-law, later that year.

Alec's third and last cruise took him to Egypt, where he saw Robert Hichens. But the trip was a failure, for he hated the boat, and ill for a month with bronchitis he saw little. Sadness at Princess Victoria's death that December was engulfed by news of the King's death on January 20th 1936. Hood composed an emotional farewell: 'Fond Memory brings the light of other days around me ... vivat Rex et Ave!' He added 'I recall the fact that I was the first "commoner" (excepting doctors and nurses) to see the little Prince, now King Edward whom God direct and preserve'.

Edward VIII's abdication horrified him. 'As an astounding bolt from the blue comes the scandal of the King and the American woman. It has stirred the Empire to its foundations'. Nonetheless, Alec wished the new King and Queen long life, happiness and prosperity, although: 'I as an old courtier cannot but regard with some disfavour that a commoner, good as she may be as all say, should occupy the exalted seats of Queen Victoria, Queen Alexandra and Queen Mary ... But times have changed, and we must hope for the best. At least a welcome domesticity has returned to the throne'.

Alec's 'Recollections' closed in February 1937, with a table concerning the lineages of the Hood and Nelson families which he had just sent to his friend, the Duca di Carcaci in Catania, who was preparing a book on the noble families of Sicily. For several months Hood had virtually been confined to the house. On March 29th Woods rushed down from Maniace in response to a telegram to be informed that his employer's days were numbered. Peter Bridport hurried out from England, arriving in Taormina five days later, and staying nearly a fortnight. But the old man lingered on until June 1st. His funeral took place at La Falconara on the 3rd, in accordance with the will, and was attended by the Mayors of Bronte and Taormina, the British Consuls at

Messina and Catania, a bevy of lawyers, agents, nearly every Duchy employee and large numbers of local people. Alec was buried in the garden in the same tomb as his sister Rosa. As Woods wrote to Peter Bridport: 'I would like to say how much the Duca's passing has been felt, for his loss is not only one to his family, but to the Duchy, Taormina and Sicily'.

CHAPTER XVIII

Life in the Duchy between the Wars

'The revenue of the Duchy has been steadily rising since the property was committed to my charge, and though taxation has become very grievous and difficult to meet, there should be hopes of prosperous times ahead'. So Hood wrote of the estate in his memorandum of 1924. It is interesting to take a closer look at life in the Duchy in the inter-war years, before the coming of War followed by radical reforms transformed it forever. Little had changed at Maniace since around the turn of the century; indeed the notes prepared by George Woods for the new apprentice, Anthony Heath, show that the estate was run following a set pattern. Woods divided the activities into four categories: fruit growing, agriculture, forestry and vines.

The first, fruit growing, was the most profitable. After abandoning the attempt to manage the orange gardens directly owing to the high costs of cultivation and the difficulties of preventing pilfering, they were let out in 1924 *a mezzadria* – i.e. on a sharecropping basis to men who tended the trees, saw to the manuring and usually kept a third of the produce. This worked well; gross revenue from the sale of the fruit varied from about 300,000 to 750,000 lire, and there seemed little incentive to alter the system. Woods did however feel that a carriage road between the two properties with their 30,000 trees was desirable, and that the other landholdings at Marotta, comprising almond, olive and pistachio trees, might be cultivated directly by the estate in due course, a presage of things to come.

As for agriculture: 'the Duchy does little or no direct farming of the land on its own account and must avoid doing so as it does not pay'. Thus the settled policy originally laid down by Alec was faithfully adhered to, except for a small amount of land kept in hand to provide pasture and fodder for the estate animals. The number of farms let had risen from thirteen to thirty-four by subdividing the old fiefs into more practicable units, and all tenants had to guarantee two years' rent in land and property or cash. Nevertheless for the customary six-year leases for the period 1926–32, twenty farms were let to eleven farmers. As Woods later wrote: 'The disadvantages to the Duchy under the old system were as follows: in the first place the farmers who rented more than one farm naturally had the best ones, and were able, being rich and powerful, to keep away any new tenant who might like to make an offer for a farm. In the second place, with the fewer people making offers, they were able to control in great measure the rents, keeping them always at a low figure, not to say a very low figure.'

Changes here could be made only gradually. In negotiating the 1932–38 leases, Woods was able to let twenty-five farms each to a single tenant, with five farmers controlling the remaining nine, while in the new leases for 1938–44 he completely abolished the multiple letting of farms, in some cases further dividing them for letting directly to the smallholders. But in a time of worldwide depression the rents, averaged out over the first two six-year periods, only rose from an annual 525,000 lire to around 600,000 lire, while the proportion paid in wheat and kind rather than cash rose sharply. Only from 1938 did Woods reckon that rental income should rise enormously to an estimated annual figure of over 1,100,000 lire.

The other two categories presented a less encouraging picture. Despite the planting undertaken by Hood thirty or forty years before, the forests had not been maintained due to labour shortages caused by the First World War, nor had many decaying or over-mature oaks and beeches been felled. A contract had been signed with a timber merchant whereby replanting would be undertaken in return for his taking all the wood he cut. Therefore, although the forestry was now on a sounder basis, it was making no contribution to estate income. It was a similar tale of woe with the vines. Phylloxera had in the end destroyed three-quarters of them, while the remaining stocks of Duchy wine had been sold cheaply during the War. In the 1920s as the only alternative to a massive replanting programme, all the vineyards had been let on a twenty-eight year lease at a modest rent of 40,000 lire per annum provided the vines were replaced and a fixed amount of wine was guaranteed to the estate.

The traditional quit rents still remained on the books, but in practice the Duchy had virtually given up all attempts to collect those that were not paid. There was also some property in Bronte: the Palazzo Ducale itself, the Carabinieri barracks and eleven other houses or warehouses on which rents were paid. Yet the costs of repair had become so prohibitive that during the 1930s most were sold outright. This anyway provided a welcome source of ready cash in an era of heavy taxation, when the estate had to maximise its assets to stay profitable. The Fascist regime's inheritance laws, which imposed a 50 per cent duty on the value of the entire Duchy, were equally fierce, and were only evaded by Hood formally adopting his great-nephew, Peter, as his heir after 1930.

Alec's desire to reduce costs was not helped by his brother, Victor, who although a competent administrator, wished to run things along old-fashioned lines. In 1928, the Duchy employed forty-five staff, about some of whom Victor (in his introductory notes for Woods' information) was less than complimentary. Babbo Carastro the Yard odd job man, whose sole duties were to blow bellows in the forge and clean the courtyards and stables, was described as 'half-witted'. 'Attina, a rather useless person, does odd jobs anywhere. Was a rough carpenter and possibly cooper'. Lawrence Hughes, son of the late Agent, 'speaks better Sicilian than English . . . has no head for figures, is casual and apt to give ill-considered replies to questions so that his statements have to be checked and verified'. There were five full-time household servants, although they were scarcely needed for most of the year. But no reductions in staff were proposed, even if Victor recognised the true character of some of them. It is a tribute to Woods' quiet efficiency that within eight years he managed to reduce the number of Duchy employees to twenty-six, with almost half of the departures being through voluntary retirement.

The year at Maniace, like the week, was divided up in time-honoured fashion. After the completion of La Falconara, Alec normally visited England from June to September and came to Maniace twice a year in spring and autumn for stays of several weeks. When his car was spotted entering the driveway, the Duchy flag was raised, the *campieri* paraded by the main gate, while the other staff stood under the arches of the entrance. The administrator was the first to greet his employer, followed by all others present, in due order of precedence, with most Sicilians kissing Hood's hand. Apart from these visits in April/May and October/November, Alec would sometimes drive up from Taormina for the day with guests. Otherwise few people were entertained at the Castello.

Every summer, during July, August and early September, the Duchy's administration retired up to the healthier air of Otaiti, as the environs of Maniace were still considered malarial, while other employees were sent to Bronte. As Victor's memorandum complained: 'It is not necessary for all *impiegati* (office staff), to go up every night. Some must sleep down here for one or two nights in succession – as others already do. They must take turn about, with the rooms being allocated accordingly – though the trouble is their bedding!' Endless hours must have been spent on the treks up and down to Otaiti. Yet a scheme to refurbish a small house down in the orange groves, so that workers could stay there during the fruit-picking season and save the long journeys to and from Maniace, was delayed for years on grounds of expense.

The week's routine was equally invariable. On a Monday morning carts arrived from Bronte with any estate employees who did not live nearby. An eight-hour day was worked, the bell to begin being rung at 7.30am. At midday an interval of one hour was allowed for luncheon, and work recommenced until 4.30pm. In summer the lunch hour was doubled to allow for a siesta, so the day ended at 5.30pm. Every evening the clerks had to present the list of the day's work and issues of food, olive oil, wine or fuel to the administrator and sub-agent. On Saturdays the weekly pay sheets were checked and initialled, those staff returning to Bronte were transported back there in the evening, while a 'garrison strength' cadre was left at Maniace over the weekend.

Life's even tenor was seldom disturbed by dramas, such as the 19th century bandit scares. The floodwaters which washed away the bridge over the Saraceno were an exceptional event. Equally so was the fire at the Castello on January 21st 1933. Woods was awakened by farm tenants hammering at the main gate, shouting that the roof of the straw store was ablaze. Dividing his force of twenty-one into two parties, to prevent the fire spreading to the granary or the residential wing, and with only buckets of water available once the chemical extinguishers had been used, he managed to bring it under control within six hours, although the roof's blazing timbers collapsed and the horses were extricated from the adjacent stables with difficulty. 'Luckily there was no wind to fan the flames . . . we were fortunate, and our fire fighting equipment must be much improved. Being miles from the nearest village or town, and having no electricity or telephone, we must "be prepared"!'

More dramatic was the attempt to murder Lawrence Hughes. On July 8th 1937, Woods noted in his diary that he was just getting up at Otaiti, when Hughes arrived at the door covered in blood. He had been riding down from the forests, when somebody had fired at him from the undergrowth, hitting him in the elbow, which fortunately, as his arm was holding the reins, was at an angle covering his heart. The assailant had quickly vanished. The initial suspect, a recently dismissed forest guard, had a foolproof alibi, as he was found in bed at his house in Bronte. The *Carabinieri* immediately began investigations, establishing that the shots came from specially prepared rifle bullets. The other obvious suspects were the family of a Duchy employee, with whose wife Hughes had had a liaison of some years' standing, but they were all on such obviously friendly terms that this theory seemed implausible.

Suspicion eventually fell on another forest guard, Portaro, who had not come down to Maniace when summoned, and whose accounts of his movements that day were confused and contradictory. Also implicated were the Lupicas, the tenants of Gatto farm, whose lease was not being renewed the next year. They were not deemed to be of good character, and as Woods observed; 'one must remember that some of the biggest troubles here arise over the question of land'. Moreover there had been several other incidents in the preceding months – the Forest Guards' barracks at Petrosino had been broken into and set alight; hay and straw ricks had been burned on several farms; and the sub-tenant at Otaiti had been discovered drowned in the small fountain in front of the house. Since it was no bigger than a good-sized bath, and he had already been beaten up, as a bruise on his temple indicated, murder was suspected. On July 14th the *Carabinieri* reported that the youngest of the four brothers, Vito Lupica, had confessed to all these crimes, save the Otaiti death. He had further-more implicated Portaro, and the tenant of the Boschetto farm, who apparently 'knew all about it'. The Duchy moved swiftly to have the Lupica family's goods sequestrated and there the matter rested, for the trial was forever postponed on various pretexts.

After so long a period of tranquillity, this incident also highlighted the anti-British feelings prevalent in Italy by the mid 1930s, a portent of change to come. The Fascist authorities were scrupulously correct in their dealings with the Duchy, but life inexorably became more difficult. Wheat and other produce now had to be sold through co-operative societies, who took their commission on all business trans-acted. During the Abyssinian crisis it was impossible to change lire into sterling by legal means; Woods was grumbling justifiably that his salary was paid in lire at fluctuating rates of exchange, whereas his contract was in sterling. Indeed the rates of exchange, fairly constant while Britain was still on the Gold Standard at around 92 lire to £1, had dipped to 60 to 70 lire, then risen to over 100.

After Heath's precipitate departure in 1935, it was thought inadvisable to appoint another English sub-agent. The resentment at the reforms introduced by Woods into the negotiations of new farm leases was very evident. Several of the *gabellotti* made anonymous denunciations of the Duchy to the authorities; although numerous smallholders visited Hughes when he was recovering in hospital, only one of the larger tenants followed suit. This combination of factors presaged an uncertain future at the moment of Peter Bridport's succession.

The estate was admittedly still operating at a profit. Yet the balance held at a variety of banks only just covered total expenditure, which ran at an annual rate of between 435,000 and 675,000 lire during the five years to 1937. Economies in scale, such as the reduction in the number of employees, were counterbalanced by rising wages and state insurance contributions. By Woods' reckoning there were four mortgages on the property, not the three Hood had claimed, and he estimated the interest payments at nearly 100,000 lire per annum rather than the 50,000 mentioned by his employer.

Over this same period in the 1930s bank overdrafts varied between 65,000 and 228,000 lire. Only on the January 1938 figures did revenue exceed expenditure by the handsome sum of over 550,000 lire, while the overdrafts had been discharged. In such circumstances whoever owned the property could not afford to take large sums out for their personal expenses, nor in fairness had Alec ever done so. In the ten years up to his death, the Ducal Drawing Account, which financed the upkeep of La Falconara and his own lifestyle, never amounted to more than 210,000 lire per annum, and once sank as low as 90,000. Usually no moneys were remitted to England, indeed his estate there was assessed at a modest £2,300.

Peter Bridport had been assured by his great-uncle that possession of the Duchy was not a sure passport to great riches, an assertion borne out by the facts. Nevertheless thanks to good management the estate seemed by 1938 in a fairly healthy condition. And the charms of Maniace, by all appearances virtually unchanged since the 19th century, remained undiminished.

In talks he gave in Canada during the Second World War, Woods vividly described the Castello's Victorian interiors: the drawing-room with 'the walls covered with wine tinted damask and hung with pictures in heavy gilt frames ... and numerous autographed photographs of Queen Victoria, British and European royalties including the last Czar and Czarina of Russia'; the dining-room 'whose walls are panelled in dark wood, the design being based on the frieze of old Spanish leather altar frontals, six of which are hung on the walls above'; with the gardens 'a riot of colour in the early Sicilian spring'. What was needed was the devotion and commitment of a new generation to guide the Duchy successfully into the mid 20th century.

The Modern Era

CHAPTER XIX

War and expropriation

'In a suitable place near the Castello the rural village Francesco Caracciolo will be built – the centre of civic life, with its post and telegraph office, school, medical dispensary, health office, Fascist branch and institute for after-hours recreation ... thus the Fascist regime, despite Nelson, replies by raising the shining light of the patriot Caracciolo, and by achieving social justice through the revolutionary means of a far-reaching land reform'. (Doctor Francesco Pollastri of the *Ente di Colonizzazione del latifondo Siciliano*, in the magazine *L'Universo*, Spring 1943.) This purple prose described their plans for the Duchy, recently expropriated by the Italian government. History certainly appeared to have been turned on its head.

The situation at Maniace had become increasingly tricky in the two years or so between Hood's death and the outbreak of the Second World War. George Woods felt distinctly uncomfortable in the prevailing anti-British atmosphere, and handed in his resignation to Bridport during the latter's visit to Maniace in October 1937. It took some time to find a replacement, but eventually George Niblett, a land-agent with no previous experience of Sicily, was engaged, and arrived in early February 1938. Six weeks later Woods accompanied by his wife Margaret took ship from Naples for his native Canada. His employer paid him a fitting tribute on departure: 'I find that it is impossible for me to find words to express my gratitude to you for all that you have done for the Duchy during your time in Sicily'.

It was unfortunately a most unpropitious moment for Bridport to get to know the island, its language, people and customs, which he obviously had to do in order to understand the Duchy. In fact he and his wife, Pamela, only paid four brief visits there altogether before the outbreak of war. Matters were further complicated by the birth of their first child, Peter Peregrine Nelson Hood in May 1938, who sadly died at a few hours old. Moreover Bridport had been appointed a Lord-in-Waiting by Baldwin's government, and although he had left the Navy in 1933, he was still on the Emergency List and likely to be recalled to active service if hostilities commenced.

Ironically on August 5th 1939, the *Evening Standard* reported on: 'Lord Bridport, who is to spend the Parliamentary recess on the Sicilian estates which he inherited together with the Dukedom of Bronte ... they are the only British-owned estates in Sicily, and are remarkable for the fact that they are the first in the island to put Mussolini's new peasant-farming policy into active operation. Soon after he inherited it, Lord Bridport began to split up his land into peasant farms. He now only awaits the promised financial assistance from the Italian authorities to pursue this policy further ... He also owns a beautiful villa in Sicily, which he is at present trying to sell'. Efforts to sell La Falconara had so far proved unavailing. The trip was actually called off at the last minute, as the international situation darkened ever further, and later that month Bridport was recalled to the Navy and posted to HMS *Newcastle*.

On September 3rd 1939, Great Britain declared war on Germany. Although officially neutral, no one doubted where the Italian government's sympathies lay, and in Sicily anti-British propaganda rose to a shrill crescendo. Poor Niblett, who had never had a chance to find his feet, beat a hasty retreat to England, leaving Lawrence Hughes, now promoted to Sub-Agent, in charge of the estate. On June 10th 1940, with the fall of France imminent, Mussolini entered the war, hoping to divide the spoils with his Axis ally. The Fascist regime wasted little time. Within a month Ciampani, the Prefect of Catania, had declared the Duchy sequestrated as belonging to an enemy alien, although the news did not reach the London press until mid-July, when the *Daily Mail* carried a large headline – 'Duce Seizes Peer's Land – His Anti-Nelson Touch'. It is doubtful that Mussolini himself was responsible for this, although his son-in-law Ciano, the Foreign Minister, was certainly interested in the property, for he subsequently tried to buy it for a sixth of its real market value. Hughes, the sole Englishman on the spot, was packed off to an internment camp near Parma, where he was to remain for the next three-and-a-half years.

In Taormina too the Anglo-American colony had dispersed. Almost all its denizens had managed to reach home in time, save for 'King' Carlo Wood, who stayed behind, loudly denouncing his compatriots for bombing Italian towns. Thanks to his many influential friends he escaped internment as an enemy alien, and died in his own bed, in April 1942, lamenting the fate of his adopted country. Perhaps the most adventurous journey of all was that undertaken by the Trewhellas, who had only left Sicily in early 1940, after repeated admonitions from their children, had been delayed in Lausanne and arrived in Paris to witness the fall of France. That December with other British subjects they were sent to an internment camp at Besançon, where conditions were primitive but not cruel. Eventually Mrs Trewhella, and then her husband, were released and permitted to return to Paris. There they spent the remainder of the war, only returning to England after the Liberation.

Most Taorminesi however remained as staunchly Anglophile as they had been in the late 1930s, when at the wedding of the Trewhellas' daughter, Gwennie, the townspeople had lined the streets and pelted the happy couple with flowers. The stern humourless attitudes of the Fascists had found little reflection here. Almost everyone was outraged when Bucini, the protégé and heir of von Glöden, who had died in 1931, was prosecuted for keeping 'pornographic' photographs, i.e. those taken by his master, although his defence that they were works of art had secured his acquittal. Now they were saddened to see the expatriates' houses, including La Falconara, seized and administered by the Banco di Sicilia as enemy property.

It had originally been intended that the Bank of Sicily would be given the Duchy as well. Indeed its officials were so eager to take it over that they offered four million lire outright for the property, which was handed over to them on August 6th, only to be taken back again four months later. The Fascist authorities had changed their minds, and it was presented to the ECLS, the office for the colonisation of the Sicilian *latifondi*.

Mussolini on his visit to Sicily in 1937 had promised sweeping reforms and the abolition of the *latifondi*. In fact very little had been done, as many of his supporters considered such measures socialistic. But a confiscated estate owned by an enemy alien seemed the perfect place to put such rhetoric into action. A group of Fascist functionaries descended on Maniace to divide up the estate into smallholdings. The protests of Duchy employees that this had been the policy for some time, even producing the plans to prove it, were ignored. There was some debate whether the Castello should be turned into flats, and what kind of new houses should be built for the peasants. Then the functionaries departed, taking with them the granite cross from the courtyard which Hood had had erected to Nelson's memory.

Soon afterwards a swarm of engineers, masons, plumbers and carpenters descended on Maniace, and the construction of the Borgo Francesco Caracciolo, virtually under the walls of the Castello, was begun. This eyesore, which marred the beauty of the landscape, was unquestionably undertaken from propaganda rather than practical motives. *Il Tempo* published grandiloquent phrases, such as: 'The new landed property which will be created at Maniace, far from having a philanthropic or demagogic character, will have a strong feeling of conquest about it'. In its article, entitled 'From slum dwellers to Landowners', it was claimed that: 'we are not just creating land-holdings but men as well', while: 'it is obvious that words alone do not suffice to transform seven thousand hectares of land'.

The unpalatable truth was that this dogmatic policy had already failed. Elsewhere in the island eight villages lacking any proper infrastructure had been hurriedly constructed, to which no Sicilian was prepared to move. Nevertheless the building of the Borgo Caracciolo continued; new houses, a Fascist office, a school, a hospital, hotel and cinema were all planned, plus a post office, despite the existence of one next door in the Castello since 1914. But the work had not progressed very far, at the most halfway, before the collapse of the regime which had promoted it.

In fairness some of the ECLS' ideas for agrarian reform were not without merit. Practical measures to improve the land were under-taken; near Maletto for example some ingenious earthworks were designed to prevent the annual flooding of the fertile fields round Lake Gurrida by the River Flascio. Twenty-nine peasant houses were built on the Duchy; each was supposed to hold two families, with out-buildings to shelter crops and livestock (six cows per family). Actually these houses could barely each fit in six people, while they were never plastered externally. It was rightly felt that the planting of trees in irrigated areas would prevent erosion, yet the peasants' protests that it would hinder their cultivation were allowed to prevail, although some olive and almond trees were eventually planted and flourished.

The trouble was that the whole programme was put into effect far too quickly to let it work properly. Regarding both the *gabellotti* and the sharecroppers as parasites, the Fascists wished to encourage a mass of smallholders to cultivate the land on their own account. This was, however, fundamentally impractical. To provide adequate amounts of land a large proportion of the population settled on the Duchy would have had to be turned out. Since this was impossible, the smaller parcels of land allotted to each family necessitated intense cultivation, the raising of livestock or the creation of small-scale cottage industries. As it was, the parcels of land were not big enough anyway – four hectares of arable and under an acre of vineyard was insufficient to raise the living standards of any family.

Fascist bombast continued undeterred. Pollastri's article, published in April 1943, boasted of what had already been achieved. It was full of historical inaccuracies: Normans, not Norwegians under Harold Hardrada, had helped Maniakes defeat the Saracens; King William the Bad could not have accompanied his wife, Queen Margaret, to Troina in 1173, for he had died seven years earlier. An imaginary Abbey of Bronte was claimed by Pollastri to have been united with Maniace in 1418, while he wrote that Nelson had also been invested with the lands belonging to the Monastery of San Filippo di Fragala. He waxed unduly lyrical about the countryside, to say that: 'The earth here has brought out all its gifts in such profusion, to which the hand of man has added a miracle', was really stretching the imagination.

Some of his statements were pure lies, for instance that none of the English owners had ever bothered about their estate, or that the farmhouses were unfit for human habitation, although he did have a point when he said that much of the abandoned pasture or even lava land could be reclaimed for cultivation. There is a distinctly empty assurance at the end that under Fascism, everything would soon be different; 'for there is no better technical Institute than ours created by the good nature of the Duce'. Doubly empty indeed, because at last the tide of war had begun to turn.

On January 31st 1943, Robert Kitson, then living near Leeds, had replied to a letter from George Woods in Canada. He had recently tried again to write to a friend in Taormina, and had just received an answer to say that his home was in good condition. Apparently the Fascists had given Woods a splendid funeral; 'of course he was thoroughly pro-Fascist, practically the only one in Taormina.' Otherwise he had heard little news, and he was missing Sicily and its climate dreadfully. 'After forty winters abroad I have found it rather awful to have to be here, at the moment in a cold gale, so that one's hands can hardly write, but I have survived and am now looking forward with hope to the time we can get back again'. His wish was to be granted within a few months.

The Allies invaded Sicily on July 10th 1943 and by July 23rd had bisected the island and mopped up all resistance in the west at trifling cost. Mussolini's fall from office took place on July 25th, when the Badoglio ministry seized power. This news convinced the Germans that their ally could no longer be relied on; Field Marshal Albrecht

Kesselring, as overall commander in Italy, was ordered to send no more German troops to Sicily and arrange for the evacuation of the 70,000 already there. On July 30th General Hans Hube assumed command of all Axis forces on the island. The outlook was not encouraging. After intensive aerial bombardment over 1,100 Axis aeroplanes had been damaged or destroyed, and he had only 25 German aircraft left at his disposal. Similarly four out of five train ferries across the Straits of Messina had been sunk.

In Eastern Sicily, however, the British were having a much less easy time, for the Germans had effectively taken over the fighting from their demoralised Italian allies. German paratroops held up the British advance on to the plain of Catania for over a fortnight from July 15th. But the whole of Sicily had fallen to the invaders by the end of the month, save for the long isosceles triangle in the north east corner. Centuripe had been captured by a brilliant north-westward thrust by the British 78th Division, while Patton's troops were advancing along the north coast and inland towards Etna, thus forcing Montgomery to shelve his plan to advance along both sides of the mountain. Kesselring decided to abandon his *Hauptkampflinie*, and the British finally captured Catania on August 5th, with its streets blocked with debris but its harbour intact. Meanwhile the Germans regrouped along a new line, christened the Hube, stretching through Cesaro and Randazzo down to the sea at Riposto. The area round Etna was to see the hardest fighting of the whole campaign.

Operation Hardgate as the Allied thrust to split the enemy's defence lines and capture the land mass of Etna was called, was already under-way. On August 4th Montgomery ordered 30th Corps to advance northwards through Aderno and Bronte to Randazzo, while 13th Corps was to advance in parallel formation, avoiding heavy losses if possible. It took three days' sharp fighting however, and incessant air attacks on enemy lines of communication, before the Allies entered Aderno unopposed early on August 7th; 450 sorties had been flown against the town to prevent Panzer formations from moving up in daylight. Troina and then Cesaro were captured by the Americans. Meanwhile the British had cleared Bronte, meeting light resistance. However Maletto itself only fell after an assault had been mounted in brigade strength, and on August 13th Allied troops entered Randazzo. The fine old mediaeval town lay in ruins; 85 per cent of its houses and many of its historic landmarks had been destroyed, for it had been the target of 1,200 sorties by Allied aircraft.

As the battles raged around Maniace, the British press suddenly remembered the Nelson connection. *The Times* commented: 'what a coincidence it would be if the present Viscount Bridport were now serving in the naval forces operating off the Sicilian coast'. The *Daily Telegraph* correspondent's inaccurate reporting moved George Niblett to put pen to paper from Earley, Berkshire: 'The seat of the Duchy is not the town of Bronte but the Castello di Maniace . . . The Duchy is a vast estate situated some miles away from the town of Bronte, and it has no property or other interests in the town. That Bronte is about the only clean and well-kept small town in Sicily is news to me . . . there is not the slightest difference as to cleanliness between Bronte and the many other Sicilian towns of similar size I know'. AP reported more accurately: 'On the western slopes of Mount Etna, squarely in the path of the British and Canadian advance, there is the town of Bronte. And just outside of Bronte there is a large estate that still legally belongs to the heirs of Lord Nelson, renowned British admiral'.

The Duchy had in fact escaped remarkably lightly. As the fighting grew closer, the Castello had been taken over by the Germans as a divisional headquarters from which the fallback to the Hube Line had been partially directed, and which Kesselring had visited on a flying visit to Sicily. Once Bronte had fallen to the Allies, a rapid evacuation was necessary, although they retired in good order, taking only two small pictures and ruining the scanty contents of the estate's armoury. The first Allied soldiers actually arrived at the castle as the Germans were still in sight retiring up the hills towards Randazzo. The first Englishman inside the house was, amazingly enough, one with Sicilian connections – Ivor Manley, who had married Gwennie Trewhella, and who had been attached to the American Seventh Army for the campaign. Knowing Maniace from visits in the 1930s, he had determined to be the first to get there, and formally retook possession of the estate as British property. After an ecstatic welcome from the Duchy employees, he, plus an accompanying American officer with their corporal driver, dined and slept at the Castello. Reputedly Ivor Manley proposed a toast to Nelson, to which his colleague responded with one to Abraham Lincoln.

Taormina was abandoned by the Germans on August 13th, and the next day was recaptured by the Allies in singular fashion. Major Geoffrey Keating, chief of Montgomery's photographers, had outdistanced the advance guard, and, driving towards Taormina, found Italian soldiers manning machine-gun posts, which blocked the narrow mountain road up to the town. 'I told them to hand over their revolvers and guns, but they were reluctantly disagreeable at first', he was quoted as saying. 'They apparently thought I was a German. Then one of them said: "Oh, you are English", and they all dumped their guns in front of me.' Keating summoned the Colonel commanding, and ordered him to send the garrison, totalling 400 altogether, to the prisoners' cages, assuring him the Allies had already surrounded the town. This was done immediately, and British troops found Keating firmly in possession of the San Domenico, the former convent and grand hotel, which had served as the Wehrmacht's headquarters.

Soon afterwards Manley got to Taormina, and going down to his parents-in-law's villa, affixed a notice to the gates of the Sant'Andrea, which had been used as the Luftwaffe headquarters, proclaiming it to be British property. The townspeople greeted their liberators effusively, as a cutting from the *Montreal Daily Star*, which was sent to Lady Bridport in London, showed. In their war correspondent's words: 'We walked into the town up a steep hill, through the hanging gardens of villas, whose inhabitants welcomed us with broad smiles and salutes. Earlier, as we drove through the outskirts, people came out to clap and cheer, and a priest raised his hand in benediction. In the town I was approached by a local man speaking English, who had been for years in the employ of Viscount Bridport, heir to the Duke of Bronte . . . the Sicilian's first question was as to the whereabouts of his old master. He hoped his employer soon would be back in Taormina. Then he asked if the British would bring food. He said the towns-people had only been given the equivalent of two slices of bread per day for several days.'

That man was Girolamo Quattrocchi, the butler at La Falconara ever since it had been built. Until the German occupation the villa had been left undisturbed, while the Banco di Sicilia had paid the staff regularly. Thereafter officers had been billeted at the house, which they did not use as a mess since they ate in the Timeo. Apart from silver photograph frames, very little had been taken; fortunately much of the furniture had already been sent up to Maniace for storage.

The Sicilian campaign had almost ended. On the night of August 16th, American troops were the first to enter Messina, for the British were delayed by mines and demolitions along the coastal road. The Germans had organised their evacuation to the mainland with meticulous efficiency, ferrying across most of their equipment and an estimated 60,000 German and 75,000 Italian soldiers, an operation which the Allies despite overwhelming air superiority had failed to prevent. General Hube crossed the Straits on the last ferry to leave the island. Within thirty-eight days of their first landings the Allies had reconquered Sicily, although the enemy, recovering from the initial surprise, had fought stubbornly. Especially in the north-eastern corner the damage done had been enormous, some villages had been nearly obliterated, while much of Palermo and Messina had been destroyed by bombing, and Taormina had suffered over a hundred deaths in air raids.

The Duchy had escaped extremely lightly, although it must be admitted that English and Canadian troops, billeted in the Castello, did more damage than the Germans had ever done, even using the portraits of several of the family's naval ancestors for bayonet practice. In Taormina they behaved better. There were few recorded instances of looting, and the main memorials to the military occupation are to be found on the walls of the English church, one dedicated to: 'The Officers and Men of 30th Corps, who gave their lives in the cause of freedom. Their name liveth for evermore'. Another tablet to the 50th (Northumberland) Division's dead: 'has been placed in this church by their comrades, many of whom worshipped here.'

Italy officially ceased to be a belligerent, when the Armistice was broadcast by both Badoglio and Eisenhower on September 8th. The next day the Allied Armies landed at Salerno; the War had moved on, and for Sicily peace had returned. But the island remained under the jurisdiction of the Allied Military Government (AMGOT), while life slowly returned to normal. As Woods commented in his correspondence from Canada: 'I see from the papers that London policemen have been sent to Sicily with A.M.G.O.T.! I am afraid that they will have a hard time of it after the first flush of the Sicilians' pleasure at our arrival dies down'. After many years' experience, his scepticism about the islanders' fondness for any kind of foreign authority was well justified.

The Duchy had been placed under AMGOT's control as early as August 18th, although with so many other matters to distract their attention, the official decree of confiscation, dated September 1941, was not formally revoked until February 25th 1944. Luckily several of the estate's senior employees, Mario Carastro, who understood every facet of its administration, Dottore Alfio Nicolosi, who had managed the orange gardens since the 1920s, and Giuseppe Ciraldo, in charge of selling much of the produce, had remained at Bronte or Maniace throughout the War. When the Castello had been occupied by troops, they had contrived to conceal many of its treasures and archives, even though various files, books and documents, particularly from Alec Hood's time, did disappear. Now that the ECLS's control had been

243

removed, they quietly resumed their management of the Duchy, supervised by British officials from Catania.

At the end of 1944 they were rejoined by Hughes, who after escaping from his internment camp had spent nine months behind enemy lines before successfully getting back to Maniace.

In 1945, following the end of hostilities in Europe, AMGOT officially handed back the Duchy to several of its employees, who had been nominated as Peter Bridport's representatives. The owner himself had still not returned to Sicily, although he had sent everyone on the Duchy a long telegram on April 27th 1945, to inform them that as soon as he was released from the Navy he would return to make his home at Maniace for most of the year. The telegram concluded: 'I am ever mindful of the memory of my illustrious ancestor, Admiral Viscount Nelson, the first Duke of Bronte . . . inspired by his example of honesty and fair dealing, I intend in the years to come, to work to my utmost endeavour to bring a greater security and prosperity than has ever been known before to all those who live and work on the fair lands of the Duchy of Bronte'. Bridport had spent four years in the cruiser *Newcastle*, mostly in the Indian Ocean and Pacific, where he had seen action on a number of occasions and had been promoted Lieutenant Commander. After the *Newcastle* had been torpedoed, he had been posted back to London, working in the Press Division of the Admiralty until he was demobilised at the beginning of 1946.

By this time his marriage had broken down, Pamela Bridport had remarried Major Alexander Scratchley in December 1945, while Peter himself wed Sheila van Meurs, the widow of Wing Commander J D Little, in January 1946. Later that year, accompanied by his new wife, Bridport sailed in SS *Empress of Australia* from Liverpool. The story that on driving up the approach to the Castello the couple was greeted by a triumphal arch in which the inscription 'Viva il Duce' had been clumsily altered to 'Viva il Duca' is doubtless apocryphal, but there was no mistaking the warmth of the greeting. Nevertheless after the traumas of the preceding years, the happy, secure world of the 1930s could never be recreated.

CHAPTER XX

Land reform and modernisation

'Modern Italy's land reform programme may cost a great grandson of Lord Nelson the vast estate which grateful Sicily once granted to the famous Admiral and his heirs "forever" . . . Two actions are coming to a climax this month to determine whether he may lose all his Sicilian lands, two thirds of them – or none at all.' (Associated Press, Palermo, March 1956). Although over-simplified and inaccurate, this reporting highlights the difficult course the Duchy had to steer between the Scylla of land reform and the Charybdis of too hasty a modernisation in the post-war years.

Peter Bridport had returned to Maniace in 1946, aged only thirty-five, determined to pursue the reformist policy which had been initiated in the 1930s. At the time of the confiscation of the Duchy, twenty-three new houses were being built for the peasants; gradually, more were constructed after 1946. The unfinished eyesore of the Borgo Caracciolo was abandoned, but the estate put up a variety of buildings for its dependants. In 1946 a small surgery was opened with a resident doctor and midwife, and a tiny hospital was set up the following year. A priest came to live permanently among the community of Fondaco, the hamlet across the Saraceno barely a mile from the Castello, and conducted services in the Abbey church in place of the visiting clergy from Bronte. A club and non-profit making shop were opened in 1948, while thanks to the Duchy's generosity a new school was completed in 1949. A village post office replaced the single room at the Castello, and the modern flour mill at Fondaco, finished in 1950, was used by the neighbouring small farmers as well as by the estate. The bridge across the Saraceno was rebuilt no fewer than three times at this period after violent floods and storms, without any help from the state.

Outside commentators remarked on these improvements. The *Daily Telegraph* published an article from its special correspondent, Martin Moore, in November 1948, entitled: 'Marshall Plan will transform backward Sicily'. In it the *latifondi* were fiercely condemned under such heading as 'The Wasted Interior' – 'vast estates' – 'village slums' and 'vicious exploitation'. The Duchy was, however, singled out for special praise. Moore wrote: 'Bronte sets no example of mechanised modernity. A donkey and an ox yoked together were ploughing a stony field as I drew up at the manor house. It has no electricity, no telephone and a telegram might take two days to come from Catania. The methods of agriculture are as old as the brown hills, it is the attitude of man to man and man to land that differs here. Instead of slum villages among unpeopled acres, the country is dotted with individual house built by the Duchy for its tenants. The estates supports 10,000 people (a decided exaggeration) in decency and comfort'.

A still more laudatory report appeared in the periodical *L'Italia Industriale – Commerciale – Agricola* in 1949, which describes Bridport as 'a pioneer of the island's agricultural renewal'. It stated that 2,278 hectares were leased to some 700 families of smallholders, a further 551 hectares were let out among 132 families of sharecroppers, while 400 hectares of pastureland had also been broken up into small units. The total population supported by the estate was estimated at 5,000 (a more realistic figure, if still on the high side), each family living in its own house rent-free. Even if the writer admired the Duchy too uncritically, it showed how far the reforms started by Woods had already been taken.

Of course much remained to be done. The Castello itself was decidedly primitive, with no modern services and only one bathroom. From 1947 it was slowly modernised and redecorated; three bedrooms were converted into bathrooms, while the upper floor of the north wing, above the offices of the administration, was turned into nurseries. For the first time in its history, Maniace had an infant in residence. On March 17th 1948, Sheila Bridport had produced a son and heir, Alexander Nelson Hood. In November the baby arrived in Sicily for the first time accompanied by his nanny. But some of the improvements had to wait a while longer. The Castello had no telephone until 1955, while only in 1962 was it wired for electricity and a generator installed.

One important success in sorting out his affairs was achieved by Bridport in 1948, when he sold La Falconara to the northern industrialist, Count Marzotto. In consequence that April the remains of Alec Hood and his sister, Rosa, were brought up to Maniace and reburied in the private cemetery there. Others of the same ilk followed suit; Count Giorgio Cini, for instance, bought the large villa which had once belonged to the Hills. The character of Taormina was changing, as those expatriates, like Kitson and Pratt-Barlow, who returned after the war, discovered. Foreign tourists continued to flock there, indeed more so than ever as the number of hotels grew; and the Trewhellas, finding the need to make their property pay, turned the Villa Sant' Andrea into a hotel in 1951. Meanwhile a new summer season for visitors was supplementing and by degrees eclipsing its traditional reputation as a winter resort.

The expatriate community had sadly dwindled; Kitson died in 1947, von Stempel, the last of the *baroni*, aged 90 in 1951. Percival Campbell, originator of so many amateur theatricals at Casa Campobello, died in 1963, although Miles Wood lived on until 1972, after which their house with its heterogeneous collections from all over the world was inherited by their manservant. At Pratt-Barlow's death in 1959, his obituary eulogised: 'one of the rare band of Englishmen abroad who have been in the best sense – dilettanti'. That same year the Trewhellas were killed by a car on the road outside the Sant'Andrea;' in the words of their epitaph: 'They died united as they had lived'. A few new foreign residents, mostly American, did settle after the war, such as Eugene Bonner, a longtime visitor who was to publish *Sicilian Roundabout* about the island, and Culver Sherrill from California, who was the first to install a swimming pool in his garden at Villa San Vincenzo. But they did not affect the changes mostly alas for the worse, which had already overtaken the town.

Taormina was not the only place in the dreary post-war world where links with the past were being severed. In England the state pension of £5,000 per annum, which the government had paid every year to the Nelson family since 1805, was abolished by the Socialists. In November 1945, in response to a private member's question, the Chancellor of the Exchequer had stated that to date the family had received some £700,000. The member, Wilson Harris, then wrote to *The Times* pointing out that 'the descendants of the Revd. William Nelson DD' had received this sum plus the £90,000 voted for purchase of an estate. He went on: 'May I say that in raising this matter again, I do not suggest for a moment that the payment to the present earl, who will be 88 next month, should cease. I should hope they could also continue during the lifetime of his brother and heir who is 85. But thereafter the nation may well feel that its debt to the victor of Trafalgar has been adequately discharged – particularly since Lord Nelson's own conception of the expression of his country's gratitude by no means contemplated the ennoblement or endowment of his elder brother. It pointed in quite another direction.'

He was promptly answered by Carola Oman, authoress of a superb biography of the Admiral. She reminded *The Times'* readers that the First Earl had left no male issue; therefore the family since his death had in fact descended from Horatio's eldest sister, Susannah Bolton. She concluded: 'It is true that with his dying breath Lord Nelson commended Lady Hamilton and his daughter Horatia to the generosity of his country, but he also, when articulation was becoming difficult, repeatedly reminded his chaplain-secretary of a message to the Rt. Hon. George Rose regarding an appointment for the husband of his sister, Susannah. The last sentence of his last codicil, written a few hours earlier, runs: 'My relations it is needless to mention – they will of course be amply provided for.'

Nevertheless the damage was done. In 1947 the Labour government terminated the pension without compensation after the lifetime of the Fifth Earl, who had succeeded his brother that year. Combined with the incidence of death duties, this had disastrous consequences. The Nelsons decided the only solution was to sell Trafalgar and its surrounding estate of some 3,400 acres by public auction. 'Were we a rich family,' the Earl's heir was quoted as saying, 'we should welcome the opportunity of making a gift to the nation of the house and property, but this is far from the case'. After some deliberation, the government had refused to purchase Trafalgar as a naval establish- ment, although the National Maritime Museum did agree to buy 140 Nelson relics for the nation. The auction took place in June 1948; Trafalgar itself was bought by Associated Electrical Industries as a residence for its chairman, and the family's connection with it ceased entirely. Since then attempts to reinstate the pension have proved unavailing, while there have been five holders of the Nelson title in almost sixty years, whose connection with the Admiral has become ever more tenuous.

Understandably enough Peter Bridport might thus consider himself the sole remaining guardian of what remained of the family heritage. It was his misfortune to play this role in an environment that was both alien and often hostile to him. For Sicily was not an easy place for anyone trying to manage a large landed estate in the 1940s, although the Anglophobia inspired by Fascism had vanished. At the end of the

Second World War the island was economically prostrate, its export markets closed, with widespread food shortages and a rationing system that had completely collapsed. The black market flourished hand in hand with crime which had largely grown thanks to those rehabilitated *Mafiosi*, who had returned on the back of the victorious American army, and now with their confrères occupied positions of power throughout Sicily. Indeed on some properties, although not at Maniace, landowners had called in Mafia assistance to evict hordes of landless peasants who had remained as squatters.

By the 1948 elections the Christian Democrats had become the majority party for good. The political situation was now stable, but the problems were not necessarily solved. And with the poorest peasant entitled to a vote, the pressure for agrarian reform remounted inexorably. At the end of the war 1 per cent of the population in Sicily still owned 50 per cent of the land, while laws from Rome which provided that the peasants could utilise uncultivated land on the 'latifondi' had been ignored. It was now enacted that estates over 500 acres, which refused to carry out improvements, could be expropriated. But this was not enough; for the importance of agricultural issues on an island containing 10 per cent of Italy's population and a mere 1.3 per cent of its industry in 1949 could scarcely be overrated. To maintain electoral popularity, to justify the existence of a cumbersome and expensive bureaucracy in Palermo, massively subsidised from Rome, to satisfy expectations which had already been raised and could never be fulfilled; for all these reasons land reform had perforce to be extended universally, even to those estates which were endeavouring to improve things on their own.

Bridport's task of reconstruction in the 1940s had been further complicated by the condition in which he had found the Duchy. Before the War a simple biennial crop rotation had been practised, with beans or vetch as the staple alternative to wheat, barley, oats or rye. During the Fascist occupation, with a scarcity of grain, the land had been cultivated for an annual crop, and the arable area extended by 1,000 hectares, often on to poor soil. Furthermore much of the woods had been cut down, exacerbating the eternal problem of erosion, and making some good land infertile. At this period the Duchy was still exactly the same size as after the 1861 Transaction, and the 6,594 hectares were divided up as follows:

1,886 Ha of forest
  260 Ha cultivated in hand
  553 Ha cultivated by sharecropping
      (with 50% of the produce given as rent)
2,886 Ha Arable ⎱ all tenanted, two-thirds
1,009 Ha Pasture ⎰ of it to smallholders.

─────

6,594 Ha

In 1948 the 1,886 hectares of forest were leased to the Italian Forestry Commission, a decision made imperative as they became less of a source of income and required more capital expenditure. Moreover much of the area registered as woodland had lost its trees entirely, due to over-felling and natural wastage, so a major replanting programme under expert management was needed. This was a sound move and had it been matched by equally decisive action on the land under cultivation, many subsequent problems might have been averted. Unfortunately Hughes, who had been appointed Agent in 1945, despite long familiarity with the country, was neither imaginative nor dynamic enough to recommend a radical solution while there was still time, and what was done was too little too late.

Shortly before the Agrarian Reform Law was due to come into effect in 1950, the Duchy offered to sell or lease some 1,700 hectares to the smallholders, who were then occupying the land. Knowing that the law provided for the owner to keep an equivalent amount to that offered for sale plus a further 200 hectares, it was calculated that this was sufficient to satisfy its requirements, since much of the lava land used for pasture, as well as the vineyards and orange groves were anyway exempted. This was less of a device to evade the law than an honest attempt to ensure that the land became the property of those who had lived on it for decades, many from the villages of Tortorici and Maletto, rather than of the native Brontesi, to whom the state would probably have assigned it. As evidence of good faith, the price asked was around a third of the current market value. Facilities were offered to purchasers to pay over five years, without interest charges being incurred, while annual instalments could partly be paid in kind. The terms offered to potential tenants were yet more advantageous; a twenty-year lease would only cost a sum equivalent to two-and-a-half years' rent at market prices, and again payment could be made in kind.

This scheme was approved by the province's Smallholders' Association and the Prefect of Catania. But the Ente di Riforma Agraria

Siciliana contested it saying that they only recognised as valid transactions completed before December 27th 1950 – the qualifying date under the new law. This involved a mere 283 hectares out of a total of 1,691 originally offered. Both sides filed suit, and the litigation began, leaving all the transactions under the scheme in suspension. Furthermore, another suit was filed contesting the family's very ownership of the estate. In few places outside Sicily could such a situation arise; that the authorities were simultaneously suing the same person for the expropriation of some and the confiscation of all of the same property.

Peter Bridport wrote: 'During the whole 150 years that the property has been British, the owners have never had any preferential treatment on account of their nationality. The British Embassy has not and indeed should not ever use influence or pressure to obtain special treatment for the owners'. Nevertheless, in confronting this Hydra of damaging litigation, he felt he must have recourse to his compatriots, and the British Embassy in Rome willingly co-operated. Five years of negotiations were finally resolved in 1956. The Italian government agreed to recognise the validity of what they described as the 'ad hoc' administrative provisions under which the Duchy had been returned in its entirety in 1945. In return, Bridport abandoned his counter-claims for war damages and for income lost in the years of the Fascist occupation; and, while his ownership of the Borgo Caracciolo was accepted, he had to undertake to use it for the benefit of the local population. Both parties would pay their own costs and expert witnesses' expenses. The Borgo Caracciolo was quietly demolished as unsafe in 1964, the material being used for building roads and houses. Peter Bridport's right to the estate was at last established, yet – somewhat unfairly – he had aroused resentment by invoking the aid of the British authorities.

The lawsuits over the application of the Land Reform proved even more intractable and as litigation dragged on, the Duchy was accused of obstructing progress. One of its most bitter critics was the author Carlo Levi in *Words are Stones* (1955). He described Bronte as 'a large village without any beauty of architecture, but with good houses along its main streets . . . for lack of drainage streams of foul water flow along the ground, through the alleys and the sloping courtyards, and the smell catches you in the throat'. For this at least he did not blame the Duchy, although his emotive account condemned it on every count: 'the land has changed masters, but its peasants have continued to live in the same straw shacks unchangingly for a thousand years'. He

251

derided the estate's offer to sell to the peasants, 'for they had to pay the expenses on the deed of acquisition, whereas Horatio Nelson when he received Bronte as a gift, was exempted by the generous Bourbon from paying the sum due for the title of investiture'. Meanwhile the regional government moved to expropriate 1,189 hectares of the woodland leased to the Forestry Commission. This left islands of forest, still belonging to the estate, which were quite uneconomic to manage; therefore the remaining 697 hectares were sold in 1962.

Hughes retired in 1960 and was succeeded as Agent by Frank King. The latter had come to Maniace in 1951 as Sub-Agent, and had soon acquired a thorough understanding of the Sicilian mentality. It was thanks to his energetic approach that a settlement was reached in 1962. He advocated the sale of any Duchy land which was not in his opinion an economic asset, to release funds to improve the rest. So in 1962, 52 hectares of pistachio trees were sold, as well as a further 206 hectares to smallholders who had occupied it for years. The estate, now reduced by 5,384 hectares altogether, either from voluntary or forced sales, amounted in the mid-60s to some 1,208 hectares of which 929 was let and the remaining 279 in hand.

The land reform programme had nearly finished its work on the Duchy. One hidden blessing in the drastic cut in size of the estate was that it focused attention on improving what was left. Widespread replanting of the vines had started in the 1950s. New trees were planted in the orange gardens from 1960 to replace ageing stock, and irrigation pipes were installed, while under King's enthusiastic supervision a new experiment was begun at Maniace. The Duchy had grown citrus fruits for years, as well as grapes, olives and a variety of nuts, but, apart from a brief experiment of cultivating strawberries in the 1890s, had never tried to grow other fruit in commercial quantities. Admittedly the altitude presented a problem, for the Castello stood some 2,000 feet above sea level, but with proper protective measures this seemed a risk worth running. Thus peach trees were planted for the first time in 1960, and the first of 23,000 pear trees in the following year.

Eventually apples, apricots and cherries were grown too, while a sophisticated irrigation system by drip and microjet was installed. Over the next two decades the estate would become a model fruit farm.

Modernisation continued apace, and the Castello acquired the trappings of a comfortable English country house. A tennis court was built in 1961, and a splendid swimming pool three years later. The gardens and grounds were extended and beautified, while the landscape benefited from the demolition of the ugly Borgo Caracciolo. In 1961 renovation and repainting of the Castello commenced, and the building was brought up to scratch; shortly afterwards it was connected to mains electricity. Nearby communications were improved by the authorities: the main road from Randazzo to Cesarò and Bronte, which passed within a mile of the Castello, was tarred and widened; a bus service from Tortorici and Randazzo to Bronte, which stopped at Maniace to pick up passengers from the hamlets along the Saraceno valley, had existed since the 1950s.

The Duchy also continued its public works. In 1954 nine new houses were put up, despite the fact that they might be liable for expropriation with their surrounding smallholdings in the future. When in 1955 the wooden bridge over the Saraceno was washed away yet again, it was replaced by the estate since no money was on offer from local government. It was not until 1968 that the state resurfaced the road and built a concrete bridge. That same year a church was built adjoining the school at Fondaco. In 1964, the Commune of Bronte took over responsibility for the dirt roads down the valley and the river bridges. The Fondaco flour mill was bought from the estate and the village school was presented to the Commune.

Most important of all perhaps was the restoration of the Abbey church in the 1960s. When the Fascists had confiscated the Duchy in 1940, they had expressed their intention of restoring the church, the fabric of which was by then in need of repair. A sum of money was set aside for the purpose, and the Superintendent of Ancient Monuments had undertaken a study of the problem, also recommending that all items of interest in the Castello should be transferred to a Museum of the Risorgimento. Nothing was done, however, and twenty years later the work had become urgently necessary. As the church had always been recognised as the Duchy's private property, provided it was kept open for public services, the Duchy alone had to undertake it.

Extensive works began in 1966, walls were strengthened, many of the ceiling beams were replaced and some of the pillars supporting the nave were reconstructed. Windows in the church, which had earlier been blocked in, were opened up, and the magnificent carvings on the pillar capitals and around the main doorway were now seen to best advantage. The large Palladian plaster arch behind the main altar was removed, revealing part of the earlier stone masonry and foundations for pillars extending into the barn behind. Although the three naves were not lengthened further, the priest was now able to say Mass from behind the main altar facing the congregation, while the casket containing the remains of the mysterious *Beato Guglielmo* was moved and placed behind a glass panel under the South Altar in plain view of the worshippers. Technically the permission of the Archbishop of Catania should have been sought first, but he made no comment when he finally rededicated the church on July 12th 1967.

This major achievement perhaps marked the apogee of Peter Bridport's stewardship of the Duchy. Throughout these often difficult years he had spent more than nine months of every year in residence at Maniace, taking a close interest in all the developments on the estate. Apart from his annual summer trip to England, he went away less than he had in the 1950s, when he frequently travelled with his wife and young son. But as his marriage drifted on to the rocks, and with Alexander away at boarding school in England, he was often alone at Maniace. It was his misfortune that no part of his upbringing had ever been in Sicily, the fault also of his great-uncle, Alec, for not having nominated him sooner as the heir to the Duchy. For despite Bridport's deep love for his home, his knowledge of the Italian language and of the island in general was always limited, while his natural shyness prevented him from feeling at ease in local society (in the way the Trewhellas' daughters, for example, instinctively did). By the 1960s his main relaxation was in escaping for weekend visits to Anglo-American expatriates in Taormina.

He remained however a tenacious guardian of the family's heritage, deciding to give a number of Nelson relics in the Castello, including the Admiral's will, correspondence and signed receipts from Lady Hamilton, and the book on naval signalling by Captain Bligh of *Mutiny on the Bounty* fame which had been presented to Nelson, on permanent loan to the National Maritime Museum at Greenwich. But the cut-glass decanter and two wine glasses from the day cabin on HMS *Victory* stayed at Maniace, as did the wonderful collection of naval pictures and portraits relating to the Hoods as well as to Nelson. A quite unfounded rumour persisted, and was relayed into print by a French journalist, that the Castello also housed the infamous rope with which Caracciolo had been hanged. Whenever material concerning any of them appeared in the press or magazines, he was an indefatigable correspondent, taking endless pains to defend the good name of his ancestors.

When Finley and Mack Smith's monumental three volume history of Sicily was published in 1968, Bridport felt impelled to take up his pen once more in this cause. In a spirited exchange of letters in the columns of *The Times*, he objected to the references made to the Duchy, in one of which Lord Bridport was referred to as its owner in 1820 rather than his father-in-law, while the assertion that the estate doubled rather than halved in size during the 19th century was entirely incorrect. Neither was it fair to accuse his ancestors of illegally enclosing land at this period, nor to label them as absentee landlords after 1873.

He concluded: 'I find Mr Dennis Mack Smith's two volumes of absorbing interest, and in my view they will in all likelihood become the standard works in the English language . . . I sincerely hope that the author will see fit in the interests of posterity and historical accuracy to make corrections along the lines I have indicated.'

His impassioned attempt to vindicate his family was sadly to be one of Peter Bridport's last acts. In failing health the Sixth Duke of Bronte died on July 25th 1969, at the young age of fifty-eight. He was buried in the private cemetery at Maniace, while a plaque 'In Loving Memory' was erected in the English church at Taormina where he had regularly worshipped. Alexander, who had recently come of age and had begun a career in merchant banking in London, succeeded to the estate. With no near Hood cousins, the future appeared somewhat endangered, but in January 1972 he married Linda Paravicini, and they had a son, Peregrine, two years later. The Duchy would not fade into history for lack of an heir.

By the early 1970s the general outlook for the estate was by no means gloomy. The economic situation was improving in Sicily, especially in the east of the island, although Palermo as the centre of the bureaucracy which administered the state contracts showed signs of growing Mafia influence, with crime, drug-smuggling and political assassination all commonplace occurrences. The mass emigration of up to ten per cent of the population in the 1950s and 60s to seek jobs elsewhere was slowing down, and had already led to higher wages for those left behind, and a reduced pressure on the land, some of which did beneficially revert to pasture.

Any efforts at land reform were widely considered to have failed, as the size of the holdings distributed to the peasants – three hectares on average – was too small to provide even a modest living. When added to the sheer discomfort of rural life, the often excessive distance from the villages, and the lack of any help from the authorities in improving the land or increasing its yield, it was scarcely surprising many fields were deserted and houses abandoned. This had happened less on former Duchy land, owing to the tenacious character of the Tortorici settlers, who were fiercely attached to it, and were especially resourceful in raising livestock and finding employment as day labourers. The last demands by the Demanio Forestale of the Regional Government on the estate were in 1975, when 884 hectares of poor lava land were expropriated to form part of the National Park of Etna.

King carried on as Agent with his task of modernising the Duchy. The quality of the wine had been improved, and in 1973 six cement tanks were built in the store at Boschetto which, along with additional barrels brought the total storage capacity to 325,000 litres. Sheds were constructed to house equipment, and in which fruit could be sorted. The vintage was now pressed entirely by machine, while the renewal of some of the vines continued. Huge stainless steel containers were bought to store olive oil, and new tractors to plough between the fruit trees. Experiments which proved unprofitable, such as rearing 5,000 turkeys, were dropped.

On the farm communications were maintained by means of short-wave radios; and mechanisation also came to the Castello, where, on the retirement of the doorkeeper and last former Duchy guard in 1977, electric gates were installed. The sale of 45 hectares of pasture in 1979 was a further step towards rationalisation, marking the demise of the last tenants of the estate. A less happy event was the sale in 1975 of the 70 hectares of orange gardens on the other side of Bronte, to settle family inheritance problems following Peter Bridport's early death. But even this brought some benefit for the sheer distance at which the groves were situated from the rest of the farm had made their cultivation inconvenient and expensive.

Nor in this era of change had Maniace lost its old-fashioned charm. The Castello was still run along the lines of a comfortable country house, now equipped with all the necessary amenities of the late 20th century. The gardens were re-landscaped and much new planting was done. And the customs and ceremonies of former times persisted, such as placing a wreath on the cross in the courtyard every year on October 21st, Trafalgar Day.

Every year the third Sunday of May saw the Feast of Saint Sebastian, patron saint of Tortorici, a tradition which had begun in the 1930s. The band always arrived early by bus from Tortorici and started to play outside the castle. The crowd grew until at 11am the parish priest arrived, and wine was dispensed. Half-an-hour later a procession left the church, formed by the women carrying large candles, to which were stuck banknotes, and a swarm of children. They marched down as far as the bridge and back, chanting as they walked. At midday Mass was celebrated, after which the vividly coloured statue of Saint

Sebastian, numerous arrows adhering to him, was ceremonially borne in its casket out of the church on the shoulders of an enthusiastic crowd. Within about an hour the horde of onlookers, many of whom had milled about outside patronising the many stalls set up for the occasion, had dispersed. But at about 7 o'clock in the evening more fireworks heralded the noise of an approaching band escorting the Saint's statue back to the church, where it would remain for another twelve months.

The underlying problems had not, of course, vanished. The profitability of the Duchy was a perpetual worry. In 1971 a hard winter had meant a bad financial year for the estate, and now that it was primarily dependent on fruit-growing, it was correspondingly the more vulnerable. In 1974 a heavy frost in mid-April destroyed 95 per cent of the total production. Capital to finance the improvements had to be raised by borrowing from the banks, while the money owed by ERAS for the expropriation of so much land trickled in interminably slowly. The first amount, £52,000, was in fairness paid quite promptly in 1964, but thereafter repeated requests had to be made to the government to squeeze out further payments. Although nothing dramatic had happened, the political climate appeared threatening; at the least the uncertainty it engendered discouraged further investment. On the 209 hectares, which was all that remained of the Duchy in 1979, almost everything possible had been done to turn it into a viable economic unit. But the future could not be guaranteed; it would need both faith and luck as well as human endeavour.

CHAPTER XXI

The sale of the Duchy and afterwards

'The deal with Nelson's heirs is already confirmed – Catanesi will acquire the Admiral's Duchy.' (Headline from a local Sicilian newspaper, *Diario di Catania*, 18th July 1980 – and somewhat premature, as it turned out.)

Alexander Bridport had decided to cut his losses. He was no longer prepared to risk any further investment in the property, particularly in the uncertain economic and political climate that prevailed in Italy in the late 1970s. Interestingly, Peter Bridport had considered selling up back in 1966, but having been advised that the price fetched would be a fraction of the Duchy's market value, had changed his mind.

When Alexander Bridport put the property on the market, he could not find a suitable buyer for the whole estate. Despite an early flurry of international interest, there did not seem to be any potential non-Italian buyers. A prominent local businessman with important underworld connections had expressed interest in buying the castle, but when his overtures were rejected, he had resorted to such Mafia signs of displeasure as a bloody severed sheep's head being tossed into the courtyard. Under the circumstances, few other local buyers were prepared to risk expressing an interest themselves.

Alexander was eventually obliged to split up the property, selling the land separately to local farmers. The high standards established in recent years by the Duchy administration were, sadly, not maintained. Furthermore, much local building then took place, most of it *abusivo* (in other words, without permission), especially across the Saraceno and along the valley leading to the private cemetery, still owned by the Hood family today. The village of Maniace, tiny in the 1970s, grew to a massive extent, destroying the area's previously rural atmosphere.

Understandably, when the property was sold, Alexander Bridport wanted to take the contents of the Castello with him – perhaps to furnish and decorate a future home. He assumed that what was essentially an English naval family's series of pictures and memorabilia, albeit combined with some good Sicilian furniture, would be of scant interest to the Italian authorities. However, the ineptitude of the then Christies' representative in Rome so irritated the Italian heritage lobby that the government slapped a *vinculo*, or chain, on the entire transaction, thus prohibiting the collection, as a part of Italy's national heritage, from leaving the country. This inappropriate response to what was merely a houseful of contents with no relevance to Sicily's history proved irreversible, and only a tiny proportion of the collection was able to be salvaged by the family. It also meant that the only likely buyer of the property was the state – and pressure for the state to buy was mounting in Sicily, with Maniace being described as 'an asset of inestimable artistic and historical worth'.

So it was that the castle of Maniace, most of its contents and 15 hectares of land surrounding it were bought by the Regional Government of Sicily (for less than £600,000). This body then decided that the municipality of Bronte was the most fitting new owner for the Castello, its contents and grounds, and therefore, in September 1981, Bronte was presented with the property. A closer study of the Duchy's history, and of the long-standing hostility between the town and the neighbouring estate – far predating the Nelsons' and Hoods' ownership and indeed, going right back before the days of the *Grande Ospedale* – might well have led outside observers to question whether Bronte was in fact the most suitable recipient of this gift.

A museum was opened in the house in spring 1982, though it consisted merely of some of the rooms exactly as they were left by Alexander Bridport. But its inaccessibility, on the landward side of Etna and still over an hour's drive from either Catania or Taormina, ensured that once people's curiosity had been assuaged, visitor numbers would decrease.

In April 1983, I paid my first visit to Maniace since the sale. While staying with friends in Taormina, we had driven up for the day to see how the place looked under new ownership. At Boschetto, our first port of call, neither wine press was operational. The former Duchy storekeeper, who had bought two hectares of vineyard himself, lamented that all the other six larger proprietors took their grapes away to make the wine. Almost all the old casks had been removed, apart from several he had managed to save, and the big shed, now used as a storehouse by the Municipality of Bronte, was locked.

We took our picnic up to Otaiti, and ate it in the walled garden. The wind was as strong as Mrs Elliott had noted over a century before, but this scarcely detracted from the beauty of the view. Sunshine illuminated the whole valley spread out beneath us with the Castello as its focal point, and the slopes of Etna behind it still covered in snow. From such a lofty vantage point little had changed. Yet on the drive back down the hillside we realised how much building was in progress in the villages, most of it only half-finished, but evidence of the steady growth in population. One particularly ugly house was rising right on the west bank of the Saraceno directly opposite the Castello.

The ex-Duchy bookkeeper, now employed by the Municipality of Bronte as head caretaker at the Castello, met us at the front gate. Fervently denying the accuracy of the reports in *La Sicilia*, he showed us into the church. It was certainly not in ruins, but chinks of light were visible through the roof, and there were several pools of water on the floor. In the adjacent corn magazine the damage was far worse, as part of the roof had come down altogether. Fortunately the restoration completed by the Duchy in the 1960s was intact, and his assurance that repairs would be undertaken proved for once not to be just empty rhetoric.

The main block of the house seemed in reasonable repair. It did, however, lack any sense of being lived in, although at least one of the three caretakers always slept in what had been the Agent's old rooms. The pictures and furniture were all in their original positions, while other items such as packs of cards, a hairbrush, even a half-full tin of talcum powder, gave the impression that the former occupants could still return at any moment. But the atmosphere was fusty, the dust lay thickly and everything bore labels as in a saleroom. There were apparently plans to open all the reception rooms and several bed-rooms too with a rope across the doors, perhaps also to convert the kitchen into a library and use the outbuildings for conferences. We were assured that since opening the previous May, between six and seven thousand visitors had been to Maniace, and that if properly publicised over ten thousand should come in a year, for the Castello was open all the twelve months, on every day except Mondays, and tickets cost a mere 1,000 lire (about 50 pence). To point out how relatively inaccessible it was, and how far from the main tourist routes, seemed unkind.

The garden was quite well kept, although no new planting had been done, and the swimming-pool was out of bounds, except to the town dignitaries of Bronte. It was good to see the cemetery, the sole piece of land remaining in the Bridport family's possession, looking so tidy; the gravestones were clean, and the grass had recently been cut, even if a cynical observer might have remembered that we had given a week's notice of our visit. But the fruit trees, once the pride of the Duchy, had not been cared for and the irrigation system was obviously not working. With this reminder that things in Sicily could revert all too quickly to their primitive state, we took our leave.

Little was done during the 1980s to maintain the interior of the Castello, although repairs had been undertaken to the roof and outbuildings. In fact over £200,000 was voted for these purposes up until 1989, when a further £350,000 was allocated. A further £1,000,000 had been spent from 1988 in consolidating the foundations of the Castello along the Saraceno river, while the cultural *soprintendenza* of the Province of Catania had spent some £165,000 on restoring the Abbey church in the 1980s. But to a casual visitor like the author in the early 1990s, it was far from obvious where all this public money had gone. True, the outbuildings with new cedar doors and windows looked very smart, but the house seemed as sad as it had some ten years earlier.

At last, in the mid-1990s, things began to improve. A further sum of well over £500,000 was voted for restoration purposes and a start was made on restoring both the house and garden to their former state. By the millennium, much progress at Maniace was apparent, and a further public contribution of £2,000,000 was set aside to complete external and internal restoration work. A fascinating museum of volcanic stone was founded along the colonnade underneath the *piano nobile* rooms of the Castello, while the vast Duchy archive was put into digital form.

A visit to Maniace in Spring 2005 confirmed this good news, though much still remains to be done to bring the property up to the standard of historic houses on view elsewhere in Western Europe. There is a guidebook, but it lacks proper descriptions of the past owners and of the contents, while there is a lack of descriptive labels in any language. The Abbey church with its precious icon remains in fine shape, while the garden, though perhaps lacking inspiration in layout and planting, is not as neglected as before.

Rechristened 'Castello Nelson' by the Sicilian authorities, the intention is that Maniace should become a major site of tourist interest, an integral part of the Nebrodi park and a major conference centre as well. There are now comprehensive facilities for large delegations, and a good shop in the courtyard selling local specialities such as pistachio nuts and their various derivatives, along with Sicilian wines, oils and cheese.

Of course, to a visitor remembering the old days of private ownership, things can never be quite the same again. A symbolic end to the old order came with the death of Frank King, the erstwhile dedicated Duchy administrator, in Catania in September 2003. Yet there is now a local sense of optimism that the whole place can make an impact both culturally and economically, while becoming one of the focal attractions of the Province of Catania. From the Bridport days, two former members of staff still work in the castle administration, while another runs a delightful restaurant nearby.

The story of Maniace through the centuries has been a chequered one, when spells of hopeful development have alternated with periods of gloomy stagnation – but there are grounds for believing that it is far from over yet. The best hope for the future is that now the foreign connection – the source of so much xenophobic controversy – has ceased, Maniace may come to be appreciated by a sufficient number of Sicilians who care about a unique and priceless survival from their past. Then indeed the dreams of Queen Margaret, who founded a great monastery in a wilderness; of Nelson, who wanted to retire to the estate he had so justly earned; and of Alec Hood and Peter Bridport, who saw it as their family's precious heritage, may not have been in vain.

In 1983, on our way back to Taormina, I remember the lava's track down Etna in the direction of Randazzo was clearly visible. An extraordinary effect had been created where it had stopped, partly surrounding a house and encroaching unevenly on some vineyards. A pathetic attempt had been made to grow prickly pears on the lava; otherwise it lay in black heaps, offering no hope of reclaiming the land underneath. Another reminder, if needed, of how often the malign fates in Sicily, natural as well as human, have been too powerful for anyone to combat with lasting success.

I can only hope and pray Maniace will never present a scene of such desolation. Otherwise I would echo the words of the poet:

Better by far you should forget and smile
Than that you should remember and be sad.

Bibliography

Myth & Classical Times

Diodorus Siculus	*Universal History*	
Thucydides, Polybius & Livy, in various translations		
Cicero	*Verrine Orations*	
Plutarch	*Lives*	
A H M Jones	*The Later Roman Empire*	1964
M I Finley	*Sicily to the Arab Conquest*	1968

The Dark & Middle Ages

M Amari	*Storia dei Mussulmani di Sicilia* (3 vols)	1854–72
G Buckler	*Anna Comnena*	1929
J B Bury	*A History of the Eastern Roman Empire*	1912
Vincent Cronin	*The Golden Honeycomb*	1954
J J Norwich	*The Normans in the South*	1967
J J Norwich	*The Kingdom in the Sun*	1970
Michael Psellus	*Chronographia*	Tr. 1953
E Gibbon	*Decline & Fall of the Roman Empire*	Ed. J B Bury 1896
E Curtis	*Roger of Sicily*	1912
S Runciman	*History of the Crusades* (3 vols)	1954
S Runciman	*The Eastern Schism*	1959
G Ostrogorsky	*History of the Byzantine State*	Tr. 1956

The Monastic Era

There is a mass of papers in the Collegio Capizzi at Bronte, partially collected together into two volumes (Bronte 1906–36). These proved an invaluable help in deducing relationships between the Brontesi, the Grande Ospedale di Palermo and the Monastery of Maniace itself.

C Waern	*Mediaeval Sicily*	1912
L J White	*Latin Monasticism in the Middle Ages*	1938
L Genuadi	*Il Comune del Medioevo in Sicilia*	1821
S Runciman	*The Sicilian Vespers*	1958
F Scaduto	*Storia e Chiesa nelle Due Sicilie dai Normanni ai Giorni Nostri*	1887
H Koenigsberger	*The Government of Sicily under Philip II of Spain*	1951
D Mack Smith	*Mediaeval Sicily [800–1713]*	1968
P Brydone	*A Tour through Sicily & Malta in a Series of Letters to W. Beckford*	1773

Nelson

Among primary sources I have consulted the Bridport papers in the British Museum, the Hamilton and Nelson papers (privately printed, A Morrison, 1893–4), and N H Nicholas's *Despatches of Lord Viscount Nelson*.

Otherwise:

A Bryant	*The Years of Endurance*	1942
T Coleman	*Nelson: The Man*	2001
J S Corbett	*The Campaign of Trafalgar*	1910
J Ehrman	*The Younger Pitt*	1983
A Foreman	*Georgiana, Duchess of Devonshire*	1987
B Fothergill	*Sir William Hamilton*	1969
F Fraser	*Beloved Emma*	1986
J Galt	*Voyages in Sicily*	1809–11
E M Keate	*Nelson's Wife*	1939
E C Knight	*Autobiography* (2 vols)	1861
B Lavery	*Nelson & The Nile*	1998
Hallam Moorhouse	*Nelson in England: A Domestic Chronicle*	1915
C Nelson	*The Nelson Encyclopaedia*	1999
C Oman	*Nelson*	1947
T Pocock	*Horatio Nelson*	1987

T Pocock	*Nelson's Women*	1999
Victoria, Duchess of Sermoneta	*The Locks of Norbury*	1940
C White	*Nelson's Last Walk*	1996

The Duchy & the 19th century

The two volume *Memorie Storiche di Bronte* has been of great help in tracing the history of the Duchy of Bronte and its relationship with the townspeople. The Duchy records, for accounts, buildings, crop experiments and many other matters are essential to consult for the 19th and 20th centuries.

Winifred Guerin	*Horatia*	1970
M Eyre Matcham	*The Nelsons of Burnham Thorpe*	1911
Harold Acton	*The Bourbons of Naples*	1956
Harold Acton	*The Last Bourbons of Naples*	1961
Lady Blessington	*The Idler in Italy*	1839
F Brancaccio di Carpino	*The Fight for Freedom in Palermo*	1860
Norman Douglas	*Old Calabria*	1915
Dennis George	*A Handbook for Travellers in Sicily*	1864
Mrs Minto Elliot		
Rear-Admiral H	*The Diary of an Idle Woman in Sicily*	1881
Winnington Ingram	*Hearts of Oak*	1879
G M Trevelyan	*Garibaldi & The Thousand*	1909
Augustus Hare	*Cities of Southern Italy & Sicily*	1883
Christopher Hibbert	*Garibaldi & His Enemies*	1965
Giuseppe Tomasi di Lampedusa	*The Leopard*	1960
Giuseppe Tomasi di Lampedusa	*Two Stories & A Memory*	1962
Edward Lear	*Landscape Journeys in Southern Italy*	1852
D Mack Smith	*Garibaldi*	1982
George Martin	*The Red Shirt & The Cross of Savoy*	1970
Marquis of Ormonde	*An Autumn in Sicily*	1858
Walburga, Lady Paget	*Embassies of Other Days*	1923
Walburga, Lady Paget	*In My Tower*	1929
Leonardo Sciascia	*Nino Bixio of Bronte*	1963
Christopher Seton Watson	*Italy from Liberalism to Fascism (1870–1925)*	1967
Sidney Sonnino	*I Contadini in Sicilia*	1877
R Trevelyan	*Princes Under the Volcano*	1972

World War & Modern Times

Luigi Barzini	*The Italians*	1964
Danilo Dolci	*To Feed the Hungry*	1969
Edith Clay	*Ramage in South Italy*	1965
Raffaele da Cesaro	*La Fine di un Regno*	1918
Lord Ronald Gower	*Old Diaries*	1902
Christopher Hibbert	*Benito Mussolini*	1962
Robert Hichens	*Yesterday*	1947
Sir A N Hood	*A History of the Duchy of Bronte*	1924*
Carlo Levi	*Words Are Stones*	1959
Norman Lewis	*The Honoured Society*	1964
D Mack Smith	*Mussolini*	1954
D Mack Smith	*Modern Sicily after 1713*	1956
Gavin Maxwell	*The Ten Pains of Death*	1959
Gavin Maxwell	*God Protect Me from My Friends*	1956
Pietro Nicolosi	*I Baroni di Taormina*	1973
Manfred Pedicini Whitaker	*A Record of English Families in Sicily*	1970*

* Privately printed

Index

Abbey Church of Maniace, *see* Santa Maria di Maniace
Abd' Allah, Emir, 4, 5
Aboukir Bay, 63, 64
Abu Hafa, 3
Acland-Hood, Charles, 155
A'Court, Colonel, 119
A'Court, William, 115
Acton, Sir John, 59, 62, 68, 74
Acuto, Commander di, 112
Adelaide, Princess Mary, *see* Teck, Duchess of
Aderno, xxii
Agamemnon, HMS, 56, 60
Aidala, Rosario, 168, 170, 171
Aidé, Hamilton, 199
Al Akhal, Emir, 3
Alexander II, Pope, 11
Alexander VI, Pope (Roderigo Borgia), 33, 34
Alfonso V, King of Aragon and Sicily, 29, 33
Allied Military Government (AMGOT), 243, 244
Anagani, Givanni da, Abbot, 27
Anthony, Abbot, 22
Arabs, xxvi–xxvii, 3, 4, 6
Arduin, 4

Arnaldo, Archbishop of Monreale, 22, 23
Attina, Arcangelo, 168, 170
Austen, Jane, 104
Austrian empire, 46, 61

Baker, Pamela, *see* Hood, Pamela
Banks, Sir Joseph, 79
Barker, Gilbert, 221
Barlow, Catherine, 57
Barrett, Bryan, 119–21
Barrett, Martha, 121–2, 123–4, 127, 128–30
Basilian order, 10, 17, 37, 78
Beek, Charles, 198, 212
Belmonte, Prince Antonio Francesco, 114
Benedict XIII (Antipope), 29
Benedictine order, 10, 17
Bentinck, Lord William, 113–14, 115, 116
Biosa, Don Gregorio, 116–17, 120
Bixio, General Nino, 171, 172, 173
Bola, xxiv
Boleyn, Anne, 48
Bolton, Frances, 103
Bolton, Susannah, 98, 99, 101, 157–8

Bolton, Thomas, 98, 99, 101, 102, 157–8

Bolton, Tom (later 2nd Earl Nelson), 102, 103, 105, 158

Bonamico, Abbot, 27

Bonamico da Randazzo, 21

Bonaparte, Joseph, 111

Boniface VIII, Pope, 22

Bonner, Eugene, 247

Borgia, Roderigo, *see* Alexander VI, Pope

Borgo Caracciolo, 235, 238, 245, 251

Bowdoin, Harry, 205–6, 214

Bridport, Alexander, 1st Viscount, *see* Hood, Alexander (1726–1814)

Bridport, Alexander, 1st Viscount, *see* Hood, General Alexander (1814–1904)

Bridport, Alexander, 4th Viscount, *see* Hood Alexander Nelson (1948–)

Bridport, Arthur, 2nd Viscount, *see* Hood, Colonel Arthur (1839–1924)

Bridport of Cricket St Thomas, Peter (Rowland Arthur Herbert Nelson) 3rd Viscount, *see* Hood, Peter (1911–69)

Bridport, Samuel, 2nd Baron, *see* Hood, Samuel (1788–1868)

Bridport, Sheila, Viscountess, *see* van Meurs, Sheila

Bronte, xxiii, 12–13
  under the Romans, xxiv–xxv
  in the 13th century, 19–20
  in the 14th century, 25, 28, 29
  conflict of Easter 1502, 35

and closure of the Abbey Church, 37–8

rivalry with Randazzo in 16th century, 39–43

and eruptions of Etna (1500–1800), 43–4

relations with the Hospital, 44, 45, 46–7

in the 18th century, 49–50

as Horatio Nelson's Duchy, 75–9, 82–4, 86, 87–9, 91–2, 96

under William Nelson, 104–6, 109–13, 115–25, 127–37, 139–45

in the 1820 uprising, 131–2, 133

and forestry dispute (1825), 140–1, 145

under Charlotte Bridport, 158–9, 175, 178

in Revolution of 1848, 161

in Revolution of 1860, 163, 167–73

Transaction of 1861, 173–4, 176

under Alexander Bridport, 176,181, 190, 197, 198

under Sir Alexander (Alec) Hood, 200, 213, 225–31

under Peter Bridport, 235–6, 241, 244, 245–6, 248, 249–57

in the Second World War, 237–44

under Alexander Bridport, 255–7, 259–60

under the Regional Government of Sicily, 260–3

Brydone, Patrick, 48

Bucini, Pancrazio, 202

Buonaparte, Napoleon, 60, 62, 111

Bulloch, George, 213

Byzantium, xxvi, 3, 4, 5

Cacciola, Salvatore, 203
Cairone, Don Antonio, 46–7
Calabria, Duke of, 130
Calafato, Giovanni, (12th century) 7
Calafato, Giovanni (13th century) 18
Campbell, Robert Percival, 214, 247
Campo Formio, Treaty of (1797), 61
Cannata, Antonio, 169
Cannata, Ignazio, 169
Cape St Vincent (battle 1797), 61
Capizzi, Ignazio, 50, 199
Caracciolo, Marchese Domenico, 47, 48, 50, 59, 69
Caracciolo, Commodore Francesco, 61, 64, 66, 70, 221–2, 235, 254
  trial and hanging of, 72–4
Caramanico, Prince of, 48
Caraprino, Don Ignazio, 49
Carastro, Mario, 243
Caserta, 79
Castelcicala, Prince, 115
Catania (Katane), xxiii, xxiv, xxv, xxvii, 12, 190
  uprising of 1837, 159
  Revolution of 1848, 161
  Revolution of 1860, 163, 167
Causton, Colette, 142
Causton, John, 134, 142, 143
Cesare, Nunzio, 167
Championnet, General Jean Étienne, 66, 67, 70
Charles I, King of Sicily (Charles of Anjou), 19
Charles II, King of Spain, 46
Charles III, King of Spain (Charles VII, King of Naples andSicily), 50
Charles V, Emperor, 39
Cimbali, Antonio, 161, 169–70, 172
Cini, Giorgio, 247
Ciocchis, Gianangelo de, 37
Circumetnea Railway, 199, 205
Ciraldo, Giuseppe, 243
Clary, General, Tomaso, 163
Clement V, Pope, 23
Collera da Naso, Antonio, 36
Colonna, Cardinal Pietro, 23
Collegio, Capizzi, 199
Constitution of 1812, 114, 115, 130
Copenhagen, Battle of (1801) 85
Coward, Noel, 221
Crawford, F. Marion, 198
Cucco, Vincenzo, 132
Cyclops, the, xv, xxii

della Catena, Brigadier Prince, 131–2
di Martino, Joseph, 121, 124, 127, 132–3
di Martino, Rosario, 121, 124, 129, 130, 134
Diodorus Siculus, xxi
Dorians, xxiii
Duse, Eleonora, 203

Edward VII, 205
Egypt, 62–3
Elgin, Lady, 80
Elizabeth I, Queen of England, 55
Elliot, Frances, 185–7
Elliot, Sir Gilbert, 61, 85
Ely, Lady, 187
Empedocles, xxiii
Etna, Mount, xv, xxi, 12

in Greek legend, xxii–xxiii

eruptions, xxv, 12, 16, 43–4, 47–8

in Christian superstition, 14–15

and Anne Boleyn, 48

and Elizabeth I, 55

as seen by D. H. Lawrence, 216

Evans, Herbert, 197

Fabre, Louis, 179, 186, 189, 198

Fazzello, Tomasso, 36

Featherstonhaugh, Sir Harry, 84

Ferdinand I, King of Sicily and Aragon, 29

Ferdinand I, King of Two Sicilies, (formerly Ferdinand IV, King Naples and Ferdinand III, King of Sicily), 50, 58, 75, 81, 87, 88, 103

character of, 59, 60

capture of Rome (1798), 65–6

evacuation to Sicily (1798), 66–7

rule in Sicily, 69, 70

return to Naples,(1799) 72, 74

and British occupation of Sicily, 111, 113, 115

abolition of 1812 constitution, 130

death of, 145

Ferdinand II, King of the Two Sicilies, 145–6, 159, 161, 162

Filangieri, General Carlo (Duke of Taormina), 161–2

Finley, M. I., 254

First World War, 209, 211–12

Forcella, Cavaliere Antonio, 87, 89, 91, 109, 110, 112, 116, 117, 118, 120, 141

Foote, Captain Edward, 71, 72

Fox, Charles James, 74

Francavilla (battle 1719), 46

Francesco, Abbot, 22

Francis I, King of the Two Sicilies, 114, 145

Francis II, King of the Two Sicilies, 162, 173

Frederick II, Western Emperor (Frederick Hohenstauffen), 17–19

Frederick III, King of Sicily, 25

Frederick IV, King of Sicily, 27

Frederick, Marquis of Randazzo, 26

Gallo, Marquis de, 62, 67

Garcia, Abbot, 27

Garcia IV (Ramirez), King of Navarre, 9

Garibaldi, General, Giuseppe, 163, 167, 171, 173, 177

Géleng, Otto, 201–2

George V, King, 219

Giacomo, Abbot, 19, 20

Gibbon, Edward, 3

Gibbs, Abraham, 87–8, 89, 90, 91, 92, 109, 110, 112–13, 116–18, 119, 120

Gibbs, Mary, 90, 98, 119

Goethe, Wolfgang, 35, 49

Gorgone, Francesco, 168

Graeffer, John, 79, 82–4, 86, 87, 88, 89

Graeffer, Mrs, 79, 88, 90, 101, 109,110–11, 112, 120

petition against, 116–17

Gravina, Admiral Don Carlos, 92

Gray, Major Richard Forsyth, 217

Greeks, xxiii

Greville, Charles, 57, 65, 67, 86

Grisley, Samuel, 177, 178–9, 198
Grisley, William, 178, 198
Guisxard, Robert 7

Hamilton, Lady Catherine, 57, 58
Hamilton, Emma, Lady
    (formerly Amy Lyon), 57,
    65, 75, 76, 79, 80, 86, 92
  relationship with Maria
    Carolina, 58, 60–1, 80, 81, 87
  relationship with Nelson, 62,
    64, 68–9, 71, 81, 82, 84, 85, 91
  and Nelson's will, 92–3,
    99–100, 104–5, 110
  relationship with Nelson's
    family, 96–7, 98
  decline and death, 100–2
Hamilton, Sir William, 57, 58, 60,
    61, 62, 65, 70, 71, 75, 76, 80,
    84
  evacuation to Sicily, 67–8
  and Nelson's relationship with
    Emma, 68–9, 81, 82, 85–6
  withdrawn from Sicily, 81
  death of, 86–7
Hardy, Admiral Sir Thomas, 62,
    92
Harris, Wilson, 247
Hart, Emma, 57
  see also Hamilton, Emma, Lady
Haslewood, William, 84, 85, 99,
    104, 106, 109, 110, 119
Hauteville, Robert de, 6, 7
Hauteville, Roger de (Roger I), 6,
    7, 12
Hauteville, Roger de (Roger II), 8
Hauteville, William de, 4
Heath, Anthony, 225, 230
Hichens, Robert, 199, 205, 215,
    221
Hiero I, xxiv

Hiero II, xxiv
Hill, Sir Edward, 203, 247
Hill, Mabel, 203, 247
Hill, Lady Mary, see Hood, Lady
    Mary
Hohenstauffen, Henry, (Henry
    VI, Western Emperor), 13,
    14, 17
Honorius IV, Pope, 21, 22
Hood, Adelaide, 201
Hood, Alec see Hood, Sir
    Alexander Nelson
Hood, Alexander (1726–1814),
    1st Viscount Bridport, 149,
    150, 151, 152–4
Hood, Alexander (1758–1798),
    151, 154
Hood, General Alexander
    (1814–1904), 1st Viscount
    Bridport (cr.1868)
  and Bronte, 175, 178–80, 183
  as a courtier, 175–6, 183–5,
    196–7
  death of, 200
  memorial to, 208
Hood, Sir Alexander Nelson
    (Alec) (1854–1937), 189–90,
    198–9
  and Maniace, 175, 177–83, 185,
    186–7, 188, 199, 207–9, 212,
    214, 227
  and Duchy of Bronte, 176, 181,
    189–90, 197, 198, 200, 213,
    219–21, 227
  as a courtier, 195–7
  inherits Duchy, 200
  at Taormina, 201, 204–6
  and Messina eartquake, 206–7
  as an author, 208–9, 217,
  sympathy with fascism, 218,
    222

death and will of, 223–4, 247, 254

Hood, Alexander Nelson (1948–), 4th Viscount Bridport xvi, 246, 254, 255, 259–60

Hood, Alfred (1858–1918), 183, 190, 200

Hood, Arthur (1824–1901), (Lord Hood of Avalon), 155

Hood, Colonel Arthur (1839–1924), 2nd Viscount Bridport 175, 200, 217

Hood, Horace, 156

Hood, Horatio (1843–81), 200

Hood, John, 149

Hood, Lady Mary (nee Hill), 175, 183

Hood, Mary (later Lady Hertford), 200

Hood, Maurice Henry Nelson (1881–1915), 156, 200, 211–12

Hood, Nina (later Ferguson), 201, 217

Hood, Pamela (later Lady Bridport), 223, 235, 242, 244

Hood, Peregrine, 255

Hood, Peter (1911–69), 3rd Viscount Bridport, 217, 219–20, 221, 222, 223, 224, 227, 230, 236, 241, 244, 245–6, 248–9, 251, 254–5, 256, 262

Hood, Peter Peregrine Nelson, 236

Hood, Rosa, 183, 185, 197, 201, 213, 214, 217, 247

Hood, Samuel (1724–1816), 1st Viscount Hood, 56–7, 60, 150, 151–2

Hood, Sir Samuel (1762–1814), 151, 154–5

Hood, Captain Samuel, 63

Hood, Reverend Samuel (1689) 149

Hood, Samuel (1788–1868), 2nd Baron Bridport, 103, 136, and the Bronte estate, 143–4, 145, 149, 154, 155, 157, 174, 175

Hood, Tremor, 149

Hood, Victor (1862–1929), 183, 200–1, 214, 217, 219, 220–1, 227, 228

Hood, William (1848–1921), 175, 200, 217

Hospital, see Ospedale Grande e Nuovo di Palermo

Hotham, Admiral Sir William, 61, 95

Hughes, Edwin, 212, 213, 217

Hughes, Lawrence, 227, 228–9, 230, 236, 244, 250, 252

Hutchinson, Julius, 119, 122, 123, 124, 127, 137, 139, 140, 141, 142, 145

Innocent VIII, Pope, 34

Jeans, John, 171

Jervis, Admiral Sir John, 61, 62, 65

John, Marquis of Randazzo, 25, 26

Katane see Catania

Keating, Major Geoffrey, 241, 242

Keith, Admiral, Lord, 81

Keppel, Derek 190

King, Frank, 252, 256, 261

Kitson, Robert, 215, 239, 247

Knight, Miss, 67, 70, 81

Knight, George, 104

La Floresta, Giuseppe, 202, 203
Lanza, General, Ferdinando, 163
Lauria, Roger di, 20
Lawrence, D. H., 215–17
Leanza, Antonino, 167
Leghorn expedition (1798), 65–6
Leghorn expedition (1814), 115
Lentini (Leontinoi), xxiii, xxiv
Lentini, Simon of, 29
Leotta, Rosario, 170
Levi, Carlo, 251–2
Linton, Lynn, 187–8
Little, Wing Commander J. D., 244
Liuzzo, Giuseppe, 167
Lock, Cecilia, 69, 74
Lock, Charles, 68–9, 74–5, 80–1
Loffredo da Baucco, 22
Lombardo, Giuseppe, 117–18
Lombardo, Nicolo, 167, 168, 169, 170, 171, 172
Lombardo, Placido, 167, 173
Luca, Gesualdo de, 78
Luca, Sebastiano de, 172
Lupica, Vito, 229
Luzzi, Prince di, 69, 77
Lyon, Amy, see Hamilton, Emma, Lady

McBean, Violet, 220
MacDonald, General Jaques Etienne, 70, 71
Mack, General Karl, 65, 69
Mack Smith, Dennis, 38, 254, 255
Maddelena, Nicolo di, 28
Mafia, 190, 208–9, 249, 255, 259
Maida (battle 1806), 111
Maio of Bari, 9
Malta, 62, 65, 80
Manfred of Hohenstaufen, King of Sicily, 19

Maniace, xv, xvi, xxi, xxvi, 8, 12, 13, 14, 15, 48, 136, 143
  in the 13th century, 19, 20
  in the 14th century, 25
  disappearance in the 15th century, 28–9
  and eruptions of Etna (1500–1800), 43
  Abbey church, see Santa Maria di Maniace
  under Graeffer's stewardship, 79, 88, 109
  under Mrs Barrett's stewardship, 122
  under Thovez's stewardship, 141
  in the 1820 uprising, 133
  Charlotte Bridport's visit, 157
  and the Revolution of 1848, 160
  and the Revolution of 1860, 170
  under Alec Hood's stewardship, 175, 177–8, 183, 185, 186–7, 188, 199, 207–9, 212, 218, 219, 225
  Castello at, 177, 179–81, 188, 227, 228, 230–1, 237, 241, 243, 245, 246, 252–3, 256, 260
  vineyards at, 133–4, 142, 179, 181–2, 187–8, 189–90, 207, 226, 256
  in the Second World War, 235, 237, 238–9
  under Peter Bridport's stewardship, 252–3, 254, 259
  under the Regional Government of Sicily, 260–3
Maniace castle (Syracuse), 18
Maniakes, George xv, 3, 4–7
Maniscalo, Salvatore, 162, 163

Manley, Ivor, 241, 242
Margaret of Navarre, Queen, xv, 9–10, 11, 12, 13
Maria Carolina, Queen of Naples and Sicily, 75, 76, 79
 relationship with Emma Hamilton, 58, 60–1, 80, 81, 87, 101
 and Nelson, 64
 evacuation to Sicily, 66–7, 69
 return to Naples, 72
 visit to Vienna 81–2
 and British occupation of Sicily 111–12
 exiled to Vienna (1813), 114–15
 death of, 115
Mario, Jessie White, 198
Marmossolio (monastery), 22
Martin I, King of Sicily (Martin of Aragon), 28, 29
Martorana (church), 10
Martorana (painter) 50
Mary, Queen (formerly Princess May of Teck), 196, 199–200, 213, 219
Marzotto, Count, 247
Matcham, George (Nelson's brother-in-law), 98, 99, 101, 102, 105
Matcham, George (Nelson's nephew), 103
Matcham, Harriet, 103
Matcham, Katherine, 98, 99, 101
Mazzarrò, 204, 215
Medici, Luigi de, 140
Meli, Bernardo, 167, 168, 173, 189
Messina, 4, 12, 41, 47, 70, 190, 243
 revolt of 1232, 18
 earthquake of 1783, 49
 Revolution of 1820, 130

 Revolution of 1860, 163
 earthquake of 1908, 206–7
 as seen by D. H. Lawrence, 216
Michael the Paphlagonian, Emperor, 3, 5
Milazzo (battle 1860), 163
Minessale, Don Gennaro, 79
Minghetti, Marco, 190
Minissalle, Carmelo, 160, 172, 173, 174
Minissale, Silvestro, 160, 172, 173, 174
Misilmeri (battle 1068), 6
Monreale, 11, 12
 cathedral, 10, 13, 22
 archbishopric of, 27
Montferrat, Boniface, Marquis of, 14
Moore, Martin, 246
Morrison, Alfred, 106
Murat, Marshal Joachim (King of Naples), 113, 115
Mussolini, Benito, 218, 237, 239

Naples, 57, 59, 60, 62, 88, 162
 capture by Ruffo (1799), 71–2
 capture by the French (1806), 111
 revolution of 1820, 130
Naxos, xxiii, xxiv, xxv
Nelson, Charlotte (later Lady Bridport), 95, 96, 97–8, 100, 103, 104, 105, 115, 149
 and the Duchy, 157, 175, 178
Nelson, Edmund, 56, 85, 96, 99
Nelson, Frances, Lady, 56, 60, 64, 68, 84, 85, 86, 96, 97, 98, 99, 100, 149
Nelson, Hilaire, Countess, 104
Nelson, Horatia, 84, 91, 92, 93, 98, 99, 100, 101–2, 105–6

Nelson, Admiral Horatio,
    Viscount Nelson of the Nile,
    xv–xvi, 60, 74–5, 90, 151
  and slipper legend, 55–6
  victory at Cape St Vincent, 61
  relationship with Emma
    Hamilton, 62, 64, 68–9, 71,
    81, 82, 84
  pursuit of French to Egypt
    (1798) 62–4
  Leghorn expedition, 65–6
  recapture of Naples, 70–2
  treatment of Caracciolo, 72–4,
    221–2
  and Duchy of Bronte, 75–9,
    82–4, 86, 87–9, 91–2, 96
  death and will of, 92–3, 99–100,
    109, 115–16, 247–8
  relationship with William
    Nelson, 97, 98, 99
Nelson, Horatio (nephew, later
    Viscount Trafalgar), 91, 95,
    99, 100, 102, 105
Nelson, Horatio (later 3rd Earl
    Nelson), 104, 222
Nelson, Maurice, 99
Nelson, Sarah (later Countess
    Nelson), 95, 98, 102, 103, 104
Nelson, Tom (2nd Earl Nelson)
    see Bolton, Tom
Nelson, William (later 1st Earl
    Nelson)
  early life, 95–6
  and the Bronte estate, 96,
    104–5, 109–13, 115–25,
    127–37, 139–45
  relaitionship with his brother,
    97, 98, 99
  and Horatio's will, 99–101
  inherits Earldom, 102–4
  death of, 157–8

Niblett, George, 235, 236, 240
Nicholas, Archbishop of
    Messina, 11, 12
Nicholas, Sir Harris, 106
Nichols, Beverley, 221
Nicolo di Cipro, 29
Nicolosi, Doctor Alfio, 243
Nile, Battle of the (1798), 63–4
Nisbet, Fanny see Nelson, Fanny,
    Lady
Nisbet, Josiah, 60, 65
Normans, 4, 6, 7

Oman, Carola, 248
Oppenheim, M. M., 214
Orde, Sir John, 90
Ospedale Grande e Nuovo di
    Palermo, 33–4, 35, 36, 38
  relations with Bronte, 40, 44–5,
    46–7, 141
  creation of Nelson's Duchy, 77
Otaiti, 227, 228, 229

Pace, Matteo, 41, 42
Paget, Sir Arthur, 81
Palermo, 41, 47, 243
  and 'Sicilian Vespers', 20
  rising of 1647, 45
  arrival of Neapolitan court
    (1798), 67
  riot of 1800, 80
  riot of 1812, 114
  uprising of 1820, 130–1
  revolution of 1848, 160, 161
Pallio, Edigio, 66, 71
Palmieri, Colonel, 131
Pancrazio, Abbot, 10
Paravicini, Linda, Viscountess
    Bridport, 255
Pepe, General Florestano, 130–1,
    132

Peter I, King of Sicily (Pedro III, King of Aragon), 20
Peter of Blois, 11
Pignatelli, General 67
Pitt, William, 99, 100
Poulet, Colonel Giuseppe, 171, 172
Pratese, Antonio, 124, 128, 130
Pratt-Barlow, Bobby, 215, 247
Pyramids, Battle of the (1798), 63

Quattrocchi, Girolamo, 242

Radice, Benedetto, 12, 17, 26, 56, 78
Rainieri, Brother, 22
Randazzo, 18, 19, 22, 26, 28, 46
   in the 15th century, 32
   conflict with the Abbey, 35–6
   rivalry with Bronte in 16th century, 39–43
   rising of 1647, 45–6
   see also John, Marquis of Randazzo
Reggio di Calabria, xxiii, 6
Revolution of 1848, 160–2
Revolution of 1860, 163, 167–72
Richard I, King of England, 13
Riso, Baron, 163
Risorgimento, 172, 173, 177
   see also Revolution of 1860
Rocca, Brother Alberto, 28
Roderigo, Gonzalvo, 32
Romans, xxiv–xxvi
Ruffo, Cardinal Fabrizio, 69, 70, 71–2

Saitta, Luigi, 167, 169, 171, 172
Salvo, Abbot, 27, 28
St George, Mrs Melesina, 82
San Blandano, (church), 37, 38

San Filippo, Gregory, (Prior), 38
San Filippo di Fragala, 7, 8, 10, 17, 33, 35, 37–8, 123
San Giorgio (church), 8
San Giorgio di Agrappida (wood), 13
Santa Maria di Gollia (granary), 17
Santa Maria di Maniace (abbey church),
   foundation of, 5, 9, 10–15,
   in the 13th century, 17–23
   in the 14th century, 25–8
   in the 15th century, 29, 32–5
   joined with San Filippo di Fragala (monastery), 33
   final decline of, 36–8
   under Graeffer's stewardship, 79
   repairs under Alec Hood, 180
   after Second World War, 245, 253–4, 260, 261
Scoto, Abbot of Maniace, 14, 19
Scratchley, Major Alexander, 244
Second World War, 236–4
Sharp, William, xxi, 198, 208
Sherrill, Culver, 247
Sicans, xxi, xxiii
Sicels, xxi, xxiii
'Sicilian Vespers' uprising, 20
Sinisio, Angelo, (Prior) 27
Skurry, John, 119
Smith, James, 124, 127–8, 129, 134–6, 7
Smith, Captain Thomas, 149
Smyth, Dame Ethel, 215
Somerville, Edith, 195, 215
Spedalieri, Cecilia, 198
Spedalieri, Gioacchino, 131
Spedalieri, Giuseppe, 136
Spedalieri, Nicolo, 50, 199

Spedalieri, Nuzio Radice, 169
Spinola, Andava Lo, 27
Stephanos, 5, 6
Stephen du Perche, Chancellor of
    Sicily, 10, 11
Stuart, General Sir Charles, 70,
    111
Syracuse, xxiii, xxv, xxvi, 4, 18
    uprising of 1837, 159

Tancred of Lecce, King of Sicily,
    13
Taormina, xvi, xxv, 201–6,
    214–15, 241, 247
    La Falconara at, 205, 237, 246
    in Second World War, 239, 243
Teck, Duchess of (Princess Mary
    Adelaide), 196
Teck, Princess May of, see Mary,
    Queen
Tedesco, Nicolo, 32
Theobald, Bishop of Monreale,
    11
Theocritus, xxiv
Theokles, xxiii
Thompson, Jane, 179, 183, 188
Thovez, Frank, 168
Thovez, Henry, 140, 141, 142, 159
Thovez, Philip, 124, 127–9, 130,
    132–3, 134–7, 139–45, 158
Thovez, Rosaria, 159, 162
Thovez, Wiliam, 159, 160, 173,
    174, 175, 176,177, 178–9
Timeo, Hotel, 202, 203, 204
Timothy, Abbot of Maniace,
    11–12, 14
Tissa, xxiii
Toulon, surrender of (1793), 57,
    59
Trafalgar (battle 1805), 82
Transaction of 1861, 173–4, 176

Trevelyan, Florence, 203, 204
Trewhella, Gertrude, 215, 247
Trewhella, Gwennie, 237, 241
Trewhella, Percy, 215, 247
Triggs, Inigo, 203
Troina, 6, 239, 240
Troubridge, Admiral Sir
    Thomas, 62, 70, 81

Ulloa, Pietro, 159
Urban II, Pope, 7

Valguarnera, Corrado, 163
Vanguard, HMS, 62, 64, 66, 67
Ventimiglia, Giovanni, 28
Victoria, Queen, 175, 176, 183,
    184, 185, 195, 196, 197, 198,
    217–18
Villeneuve, Vice Admiral Pierre
    Charles, 90,
van Meurs, Sheila (later Lady
    Bridport), 244, 236
von Glöden, Wilhelm, 202–3, 209,
    237

Walter of the Mill, 10
Ward, Nelson, 106
Ward, Philip, 105–6
Whitaker, Tina, 199, 205
'White Terror', 74
White, Maude Valérie, 198, 199,
    215
William, Abbot, 20, 21
William I, 'the Bad', King of
    Sicily, 9
William II, 'the Good', King of
    Sicily, 10, 13
William III, King of Sicily, 14
William of Blois, 11, 21
Williams, Charles, 215
Williams, Leader, 214

Williams, Lilyan, 214
Wood, Charles 'King Carlo', 205,
    214, 236–7, 239
Wood, George, 121
Woodhouse, John, 134, 146,
    220
Woods, George Dubois, 220, 223,
    224, 225, 226, 227, 228, 229,
    230, 235, 239, 243

Xarech, Domenico, 33

Youssoupov, Prince Felix, 215

Zuccaro, Filomena, 202
Zuccaro, Gregorio, 131